T0078010

THE **A B C** OF

COUNSELING

Biblical Counseling Simplified

PASTOR STEPHEN KYEYUNE

authorHOUSE®

AuthorHouse™
1663 Liberty Drive
Bloomington, IN 47403
www.authorhouse.com
Phone: 833-262-8899

Published by AuthorHouse 11/08/2021

ISBN: 978-1-6655-4255-5 (sc)
ISBN: 978-1-6655-4256-2 (e)

CONTENTS

This book is dedicated to my son Ivan Ssenyonga (September 26th, 1983 – January,19th 2021)

ABOUT THE AUTHOR

Pastor Stephen Kyeyune is currently the senior pastor of the Multicultural Family Fellowship Church at South Bend IN U S A. He is the author of several books including The New Generation of Worshipers; The Spirit is the Crown of the Heart; The Acts of the Holy Spirit; When God Calls a Man; The Legacy of the Hero; A miracle at Prairie Avenue; Devotional Journal Living; Imparted Wisdom in Troubled Times, Making a sense of the senseless situation; Today's Prayers – Praying through the Scriptures; Securing the Never Ending Peace in Times of Trouble; A series of books > Shaping the Society – Culture vs Christianity. You can order now at AuthorHouse 833.262.8899. Or contact me @ stephkyeyu@hotmail. Com. Telephone – 574- 8851014.

FROM MY DESK

I am privileged to put this book into your hands. I am positioned to teach biblical counseling due to the following factors: Apart from my academic credentials, my illuminating years in ministry have been punctuated with series of counselings which is compulsory for effective pastoring. Experience is the best teacher. "The better you look, the more you see." Much more, hope you would be exposed to the ideas that inspiration generates to simulate your minds rather than to emotionally excite you. We live in the age of massive knowledge but that is also saturated with deception and uncertainty. Your mind can go ahead and imagine what it wants to imagine, and believe what you want to believe but the Bible warns us against having a wandering mind that is unstable. "The spirit of a man is the lamp of the LORD, searching out his inmost being." (Proverbs 20:27). The spirit of man, breathed into him at first by the Creator (Genesis 2:7), and afterward quickened and illumined by the Divine Spirit, is the "candle of the Lord," given to man as an inward light and guide. In other words, God uses our spirit as a candle to show us what He wants to show us. His Spirit walks hand in hand with our spirit to lead and speak to us. And He does it gently. These are inspired words of wisdom associated with true virtue. The Scriptures tip us how to discern the Spirit of Christ from the spirit of this age (1 John 4:2-3).

A ministry is deeper than being able to preach a good sermon. You need to teach the whole counsel of God and you need to get out and get involved in nurturing it to growth in individual members of the congregation. The ministry of counseling does not stop at the pulpit. That is why it is important for the pastor to get acquainted with the individual families that make up the congregation. It is the role of the Church leadership to

1

help the pastor to get involved in all of the family activities. When the pastor has to visit every sick person, do every wedding and funeral and make regular house calls, attend every meeting, and lead every bible study or group, he or she becomes incapable of doing almost anything else. Inevitably, pastoral leaders with larger churches can't keep up and end up disappointing people when they can't get to every event anymore.

There are some pastors out there who want to keep their churches small, or who don't care about church growth out of fear that the church will grow into a big congregation, at which point the pastoral care expectations become crushing. The solution is in the division of labor. Jethro's advice to Moses about delegation is applicable in a situation like this one (Exodus 18:17-18). Jethro does not say that Moses is doing a bad job. Jethro's advice looks to Moses' personal care and for the wellbeing of his congregation (Israel). If pastors could figure out how to better tackle the issue of pastoral care, I'm convinced that everything will be fine. "In some respect, pastoral care establishes classic co-dependency. The congregation relies on the pastor for all of its care needs, and the pastor relies on the congregation to provide their sense of worth and fulfillment: the pastor needs to be needed."

Normally, when a person tells me that they think they are ready to step into a pastoral ministry, the first thing I ask them is "Are you equipped with the right resources for the counseling ministry." When they admit, I give them the following scripture: "How can you say to your brother, 'Let me take the speck out of your eye,' while there is still a beam in your own eye?" (Matthew 7:5). It gives a new motive to the work of self-scrutiny and self-reformation. Before you counsel others you must be counseled by the Holy Spirit. Before you become a counselor, you are a human being living in the real world like everybody. It is important to unburden yourself by surrendering your will to Christ before stepping up to unburden others. A physician that can't heal himself dents his professional and is doomed to fail.

A pastor is the first responder whereby self-awareness is an essential ingredient in the very fabric of every first responder. A pastor's integrity matters. People must be able to see what a preacher preaches in his or her lifestyle. The message and the vessel carrying the message must not be in contradiction. A preacher's humility matters. People want to see a preacher

2

identifying with their misery, and not just only telling them what to do but helping them to do what he tells them to do.

God calls you as a person. He doesn't call the person you pretend to be. He calls the real you. It is important to know yourself. You are a child of one true God. God is your Father. He knows you better than you know yourself. The more you engage God in your life the more He will reveal to you who you are. "The only bond worth anything between human beings is their humanness." You are a human being living in the real world. Know your personality so that you use it to bless others instead of hurting them unknowingly. God has a unique purpose for all of us. knowing to handle your affairs is the key to knowing your purpose. Do you have questions about your purpose in life? All you have to do is look to God. Look upward to your God for direction! Look inward into yourself and discover your talents! "Time determines the occurrence of possibilities and impossibilities, but God determines the time for the occurrence of possibilities and impossibilities."

Counseling is a broad subject covering the totality of your life and how you relate to others. In the real world, people are not what you think they are, even when they tell you or prove you otherwise. The only atmosphere of certainty is the atmosphere of the Kingdom of God. The only way the kingdom of God is going to be manifested in this world before Christ comes is if we manifest it by the way we live as citizens of heaven and subjects of the King of heaven and earth. There can be no Kingdom of God in the world without the Kingdom of God in our hearts. It means that as of now, the kingdom would not be inaugurated with spectacle or splendor; there would be no great and magnificent leader who staked out a geographical claim and routed the Romans as the Jewish religious leaders expected. God is ruling in the hearts of the true believers, and the King Himself is standing among them. You have to make a U-turn from the kingdom of this world in order to access the kingdom of God. "Don't ever rule out the option of U-turn in your life, because one day you will need it! The moment you realize that you are going in the wrong direction, turn to the right direction instantly, with a beautiful U-turn!"

We live in this small world as a community. "Everyone is here because he or she has a place to fill, and every piece must fit itself into the big jigsaw puzzle." Life is not what it is but what you make it to be. "The art of simplicity is a puzzle of complexity." There are principles of life that can't be manipulated. No speculation. No probabilities. No possibilities. Life is not managed by a concoction of some foggy ideas. "To float an idea means to suggest something unusual or unexpected, with the objective of determining whether people like the idea or not. When you float an idea, you want to see what happens to it." The Word of God is the Divine power that works in us and for us when we constantly get engulfed in impeccable devotions.

You have a key to make this world a better place. Your personality, talents, and gifts are all pieces of the puzzle that make you effective wherever you are positioned to be. If you pick the Bible and use it as your compass to navigate life, everything will fit exactly where it is supposed to be. I used the Bible as a book of reference to write this book. By reading my book, there is a good chance you will find some important pieces of the puzzle that you have been missing. Life without the guidance of God is complected. The world is a hostile environment. "In the end, it's not the obviousness or the complexity of the matters that's deluding mankind. It's man himself." It takes Divine interference to move in the opposite direction.

The Bible instructs us to seek knowledge. It is an instruction to readjust our thinking in a manner honoring God. Acquired knowledge is a recipe for success. I can't promise you a trouble-free world. But I can assure you that the acquired knowledge will boost your confidence to sail peacefully through the tribulations of life. The positives and negatives of life are partners of life. The purpose of the negatives of life is to help us understand we are the ones who cause it. The negatives are contradictory ideas to civility and morality, and they are the major causes of our downfall. When you allow God to replace negative thoughts with positive ones, you'll start having positive results. Remember that falling is part of life. But we don't fall to stay down. We fall and get up. "Never forget that there is beauty in how we fall, strength in how we continue to breathe, courage in how we decide to keep fighting, and fierceness in how we rise." You could jump so much higher when you had somewhere safe to fall. Make eternity your landing place by falling into the hands of the Lord.

True learning involves understanding. In the kingdom of God learning begins with a revelation, continues in inspiration, and ends in empowering.

During the earthly ministry of Jesus, the Apostles spend about three and half years being taught by Jesus but they did not graduate with a degree because they didn't grasp anything. After Jesus rose from death He breathed over them and instructed them to receive the Holy Spirit (John 20:22). They entered the spiritual realm of revelation, followed by forty days of waiting to be filled and empowered by the Holy Spirit on Pentecost. They were inspired as they went to reach out to the lost world. Now they were qualified and ready to go and turn the world upside down.

The gospel is the power of God to change a soul. The gospel involves the life, death, and resurrection of Jesus Christ. Resurrection is not just consolation — it is restoration. The resurrected life of Christ is the glory of the Church. The resurrected life of Christ is the only spot on earth that reflects the glory of heaven. Apart from the glory, everything is the vanity of vanities. God is most glorified when you are most sanctified in Him. God is going to mold even your hardships to be for His glory. "Do not be afraid to enter the cloud that is settling down on your life. God is in it. The other side is radiant with His glory."

Biblical counseling engages godly wisdom in solving human predicaments. True fulfillment comes from God and it is accessed in Christ. The only time we become dissatisfied is when we take our focus away from Christ. "When everything has gone down, God wants you to look up". The Psalmists said that my help comes from the Lord (Psalm 121:2). Never surrender your hopes and dreams to fate. Any counselor who suffers the lack of abundance, joy, love, fulfillment, and prosperity in their own lives really has no business imposing his or her self-limiting beliefs on others. You can't give what you don't have.

The secular world opts for temporary happiness but God opts for eternal things by depositing His joy deep inside your heart. It means that only eternal is important. Life has no meaning, the moment you lose the conviction of being eternal. When you are connected to God through Christ, you are never alone. You are eternally connected with each and every believer with shared values. We have the same need and answers to our problems. That is why other believers will understand you even before you open your mouth to speak because the same Spirit dwelling in you dwells in them. The same God created a new heart in you and in them.

We are people of clean conscience because we are people of the book

(Bible). Confused people are confused regarding where to get the truth. The source of the truth validates the truth. The Bible says that God is pleased by our faith. Faith is embracing the truth. The truth is absolute. But the truth cannot be found in us unless it is revealed to us by the only One that is true.

Philosophy teaches that there is no absolute truth. They say that truth depends on the beholder. "The idea of finding any truth or meaning to life has escaped modern man. This statement reflects the inability to conceive of something outside of one's self: There are no rules by means of which we would discover a purpose or a meaning of the universe" (Hans Reichenbach, The Rise of Scientific Philosophy, p. 301). The idea behind such a statement is that there is no absolute truth to believe in, and thus the act of believing is all there is. I want to say that it doesn't matter how sincere you are in your beliefs, as long as as the object of your belief is wrong, you are lost like sheep that get lost nibbling away at the grass because they never look up, we often focus so much on ourselves and our problems that we get lost. That is why it is tough to win the so-called elites to Christ because they focus absolutely on their intellect while ignoring the possibility of a revelation.

Faith begins with the revelation of Jesus Christ. According to Josh McDowell, belief is only as good as the object in which we put our trust. Someone may come to me and say, "Hey, let's go for a ride in my new plane!" If I come to find out that his plane hardly runs at all and he does not even have a pilot's license, then my faith, no matter how much I have, is not well-founded. God requires man to put his faith in Jesus Christ; nothing less will satisfy either them or Him.

Psychology is the major threat to biblical counseling. Psychology is not necessarily evil but neither is it pure. Psychology deals with a nonphysical world. Psychology is considered to be science simply because it follows the empirical method – It is this emphasis on the empirically observable that made it necessary for psychology to change its definition from the study of the mind (because the mind itself could not be directly observed) to the science of behavior. The bottom line is that Psychology is not science because science deals with tangible experimental facts. Psychology has turned out with self-love as its principle doctrine contrary to the Christian doctrine of self-denial. According to psychology, self-love is the seed from which inner peace, fulfillment blossoms. Christianity teaches that fulfillment comes from beyond us, from loving God and your neighbor. We are new creatures in Christ. "Every living organism is fulfilled when it follows the right path for its own nature." Our new nature is spirit. Spiritual Psychology is founded on the principle that we are each spiritual beings having a human experience. We are not human beings striving to be spiritual; we are already spiritual beings.

The influence of psychology on Christian counseling cannot be ignored. Yet, the source of information used in psychology is disturbing. For example, psychologists use animal behaviors to determine human behaviors. Ironically, where you get your philosophy determines how you value people. I appeal to you not to embrace any secular views including psychology without checking them out to see if they are in line with the scriptures. Every ideology whether it be from psychology, Greek Philosophy, New age movement, needs theology to make it moral and legal. It is wise to listen to all of these ideologies and resist implementing any of them unless they are biblical. Never compromise your personal principles in order to accommodate others or to please people. Remember that knowledge without character destroys absolutely.

Psychology cannot go inside you and transform your nature and character. Psychology deals with the symptoms from the outside without finding a cure from inside the heart. Psychology embraces the spirit of the age. The spirit of the age is against the Spirit of Christ. The spirit of the age refuses us to own our wrongs; it always points to somebody other than you as the reason for your misery. Psychology says that your problems are outside you, and your solution is inside you. Whereas the Bible says that your greatest problem is inside you, and your solution is outside you. We are victims of our corrupt nature. And we are doomed until God comes to our rescue. "Depression, suppression, compression, and repression from all dimensions of life are indeed too unbearable without God, for it's Him to save us from such mess." It makes a difference when you have God. Remember that the trials of life do not make you who you are; they reveal who you are. In the same way when you shake the bottle and empty it. What comes out of the bottle is what was there originally. In other words, what comes out of the bucket is what is in the well.

"The heart of the human problem is the problem of the human heart."

The first and most important step in seeking a cure is an accurate diagnosis of the problem. In Matthew 15, Jesus teaches a vital lesson in spiritual diagnosis. What He says is fundamental to living the Christian life. It is not what goes into a person that defiles him. It is what comes out of him — the corrupted streams that flow from a corrupted heart. "For out of the heart come evil thoughts, murder, adultery, sexual immorality, theft, false witness, slander. These are what defile a person. But to eat with unwashed hands does not defile anyone" (vv. 19–20).

The human heart is the seat of your personality, and it is deceitful. Jesus teaches us that there is something far more fundamental to our sinfulness than the actual sins we commit. Our sins do not make us sinful. Rather, we commit sins because, at the very center of our lives, we are sinful. "The sinful nature is the stubborn, self-centered attitude that says, "My way or the highway." The sinful nature is all about self: pleasing self, promoting self, preserving self. I have a sinful nature! So do you. Under the right circumstances, you will do the wrong thing. You'll try not to, but you will. You have a sinful nature. You were born with it."

The doctrine of total depravity asserts that people are, as a result of the fall, not inclined or even able to love God wholly with heart, mind, and strength, but rather are inclined by nature to serve their own will and desires and reject His rule. The corruption of the human race after the Fall was radical and universal: "God saw that the wickedness of man was great in the earth, and that every imagination of the thoughts of his heart was only evil continually" (Gen 6:5). Jesus reached out to us when all that we could offer to God is rebellion. Whenever you hear the gospel and see no need to be saved remember that, like any other unsaved person, you are naturally walking in rebellion, the end result of which is condemnation. Jesus was not sent to condemn the world; He was sent to the already condemned world to save it from condemnation (John 3:16-18).

God redeems and pours into us His love in anticipation of His love to come out of us. God's love is something every believer can celebrate today and every day even when there is nothing in us worthy for God to love. How consoling to a soul bowed down under a sense of guilt are the following promises: "When I passed by you and saw you polluted in your own blood, I said unto you...Live; yes, I said unto you when you waste in your blood, Live" (Ezekiel 16:6). Then comes the source of mercy: "I have loved you with an everlasting love: therefore with lovingkindness have I drawn you" (Jeremiah 31:3).

Everyone is entitled to celebrate God's love and pass it on. Freely we are given and freely we are required to dispense it except in this one area where God is overprotective: The Bible restricts us to give affection to false teachers. "If anyone comes to you and does not bring this teaching, do not receive him into your house, and do not give him a greeting; for the one who gives him a greeting participates in his evil deeds" (2 John 1:10-11). Any false teaching is intended to deprive you of your freedom in Christ.

Faith, hope, and love – the greatest of these is love (1 Corinthians 13:13). But the truth is greater than love! The truth will liberate you today or judge you later. Jesus is the truth (John 14:6). The Word of God is the truth (John 17:17). The greatest psychology book you will ever read is the Bible. I encourage you to read, understand and implement. Failure to execute what you learn yields to nothingness. The Bible says "Be doers of the word, and not hearers only. Otherwise, you are deceiving yourselves" (James 1:22). Those who deceive themselves may not altogether be hypocrites; there is a subtler danger of being blind, and nevertheless exclaiming "We see."

The Christian life is a spiritual life of faith that is void of human frailty. That is when we put our faith in Christ to work on our behalf. Faith involves manifested good deeds. Naturally, you have to keep on practicing in order to produce good results consistently. We practice faith by studying the Word and heeding. Belief precedes behavior. People's behaviors are influenced by their beliefs. Given the fact, our behaviors can be a good tutor because some people learn from experience. When they see the results of their actions, they determine that it is the right thing to do. In this case, they believe after seeing. The perfect submission of faith involves believing without seeing.

"God woos us with a whisper. And His whisper is the breath of life." The breath of God is the wind of life. The breath of life (Holy Spirit) is the divine grace of God that initiates change in us and through us. Real change begins with the transformation of the heart and then the renewing of the mind. In a natural man, the mind is biological in its nature. But in a regenerated person, the mind is both spiritual and biological in its nature. The renewed mind of a born-again person becomes the sight of the soul.

God entrusts us with the power of His grace in order for us to be what the renewed mind projects us to be, in accordance with the written Word. Therefore, best place to be is to take refuge in the Word of God.

By the grace of God, everything is subject to change – the physical to the spiritual, the natural to the supernatural. A new heaven and a new earth. We believe that the supernatural works naturally in us to change us from glory to glory. C.S. Lewis insinuated that "Nothing is yet in its true form because things are subject to change. You're in this constant state of flux and transition." The winds of God are always blowing, but you must set the sails. Remember that nothing is interesting if you're not interested. "The wheel of change moves on, and those who were lagging behind go in front, those who were looked down go up, and those who considered themselves to be up – go down." God is ready to give rest to the problems weighing you down. Give Him a chance.

Faith is not a work; it is a gift from God. But true faith must produce a lifestyle of obedience to God. Paul said, "For to me, to live is Christ, and to die is gain." (Philippians 1:21). This, of course, means "Christ is my life," yet not just in the sense that He is the source and principle of life in us, but that the whole concrete state of life is lived in Him such that it becomes a simple manifestation of His presence. The moment we put our trust in God the new begging ushers in. YHWH begins something new in us that has no end. The kingdom of God is always advancing and is never-ending. Faith is when we focus on intimacy, and our relational connection with YHWH and our union with Him, it would undo a lot of the fear of the uncertainty of the future, because God is our future! In Him we live, move and have our being.

The opposite of faith is unbelief. I am going to use the example of the Agnostic. It means a person who views the existence of ultimate truth as unknowable, particularly when it comes to the existence of God. "A person who believes that nothing is known or can be known of the existence or nature of God or of anything beyond material phenomena; a person who claims neither faith nor disbelief in God."

In the real world where we dwell, it is impossible for somebody to make something of great value and fail to put on it a trademark and a logo marking the ownership. There are some teams and logos you see, no matter where you are in the world, and you know exactly who they are and what they mean. It's common, noticing labels, logos, on even simple things like clothes and shoes. The point I am trying to make is that Our God could not create this magnificent and massive universe without putting on a mark of ownership.

Our God reveals Himself in two main ways: God reveals Himself in nature to be known that He is the creator. Creation as a part of God's general revelation, affirms certain facts about God. Nature testifies to God's existence as Paul wrote to the church at Rome: "What may be known of God is manifest in them for God has shown it to them. For since the creation of the world His invisible attributes are clearly seen, being understood by the things that are made, even His eternal power and Godhead, so that they are without excuse" (Romans 1:19-20). The vastness of the universe gives testimony to God as Creator. The psalmist wrote: "When I look at your heavens, the work of your fingers, the moon and the stars that you have established; what are human beings that you are mindful of them, mortals that you care for them" (Psalms 8:3-4). "Natural revelation is more than sufficient to make humanity responsible and to show them they are "without excuse." Consequently, humans should attempt to find out who this Creator is and what He requires of them. Unfortunately, many people have corrupted the revelation of God in nature and have chosen to worship and serve the creation rather than the Creator."

The second way whereby God reveals Himself is called the special revelation. Special revelation is a Christian theological term that refers to the belief that knowledge of God and of spiritual matters can be discovered through supernatural means, such as miracles or the scriptures—a disclosure of God's truth through means other than through reason. "Humanity needs to be able to correctly interpret the truths that God has revealed by means of general revelation. In addition, these truths are limited. Therefore, humanity desperately needs God's special or supernatural revelation." The special revelation reveals the truth and gives us the capacity to walk in it.

Jesus said "All things are delivered unto me of my Father: and no man knows the Son, but the Father; neither knows any man the Father, save the Son, and he to whomsoever the Son will reveal him. ... No one knows the Son except the Father, and no one knows the Father except the

Son and those to whom the Son chooses to reveal him." (Luke 10:23). Humility is embracing God as the Son says He is. The transfiguration was intended to reveal the glory of God during the earthly ministry of Jesus Christ. The word 'transfiguration' also means metamorphosis. The transfiguration is compared to the change of form of the caterpillar to the beauty of the butterfly without losing its DNA. Jesus briefly revealed His divinity without ceasing to be mankind. He is very God and very man. There appeared with Jesus, Moses (representing the Law), and Elijah (representing the prophets). And the voice from heaven said that "This is my beloved Son, with whom I am well pleased. Hear you him." (Luke 9:35; Matthew 17:5). It means that all of the prophets and laws of God received their glory from the Son of God.

The Bible says "For in Him all things were created, things in heaven and on earth, visible and invisible, whether thrones or dominions or rulers or authorities. All things were created through Him and for Him. He is before all things, and in Him, all things hold together." (Colossians 1:16-17). By Him, all things consist.--That is, hold together in unity, obeying the primeval law of their being. This clause is attributed to our Lord, not only the creative act but also the constant sustaining power, in which all lives move and have their being. We must see everything in the eyes of the Creator. We believe in the non-created God that created the world and everything within it. According to the Scriptures, before the world was in existence, there was the creator to create it. Therefore, the Creator must be self-existence, self-sustenance, and *Self*-sufficient - He is without any need beyond Himself but He sustains all things in existence as the Bible claims our God to be. Christianity is the only religion that believes in the non-created or self-existence God.

Christianity is a monotheist. We believe in one God who has revealed Himself to us in three persons (Father, Son, and Holy Spirit). Through Christ, God entered humanity, and eternity entered time and space. The Son gives us access to God. The Father and the Son indwell us through the Holy Spirit. We cannot know God without knowing Jesus intimately. This fact separates Christianity from the rest of religions. We don't worship the same God that the other religions worship because our God can only be known through Jesus Christ alone. Jesus said that "I am the way and the truth and the life. No one comes to the Father except through me." (John

14:6). He did not say that He is one of the ways but that He is the only way to know God. Not every person can worship our God. Jesus said that true worshipers worship in spirit and truth (John 4:23).

"The Word became flesh and made His dwelling among us. We have seen His glory, the glory of the one and only Son from the Father, full of grace and truth." (John 1:14). Dwelt among us – The Greek word means "tabernacled." "sojourned" among us. Mankind became a son of God because the Son of God became man. It was amazing condescension for God to put on the human nature to tabernacle with men on earth. In Christ was the fullness of the glory of the Godhead on display (John 2:19). The same Godhead indwells us by His Spirit (John 14:15). Worshiping is whenever the divine glory from within darts through the veil of flesh (body) for others to behold. True worshiping comes from God (from the Spirit seated on the throne of the heart) and goes to God seated at the heavenly throne. Jesus is exalted at the right hand of the Father to be worshiped. The Bible says that "So that at the name of Jesus every knee should bow, in heaven and on earth and under the earth, and every tongue confess that Jesus Christ is Lord, to the glory of God the Father" (Philippians 2:10-11). The Spirit of God puts us in the state of spiritual exaltation and ecstasy. The Bible says "Therefore I inform you that no one who is speaking by the Spirit of God says, "Jesus be cursed," and no one can say, "Jesus is Lord," except by the Holy Spirit." (1 Corinthians 12:3).

We were created to worship God. Psalm 27:4 - "One thing I ask from the LORD, this only do I seek: that I may dwell in the house of the LORD all the days of my life, to gaze on the beauty of the LORD and to seek him in his temple". The Psalmist yearned to be in a place of divine worship all the times where the Lord guaranteed His presence. The grace made it possible for us to be in God's presence forever. We are God's dwelling place (temple). His presence follows us wherever we go. He made it possible for whosoever is willing to worship Him wherever they are. Whosoever means people from all races, tribes, and gender. The book of Revelation says "After this, I looked, and there before me was a great multitude that no one could count, from every nation, tribe, people and language, standing before the throne and before the Lamb. They were wearing white robes and were holding palm branches in their hands. 10 And they cried out in a loud voice: "Salvation belongs to our God, who sits on the throne, and to the Lamb" (Revelation 7:9). Jesus is worshiped wherever He is. He is worshiped in heaven and on earth. Heaven is not about a place, it is about who is there, (God/the Lamb). God's dwelling place is called the temple. The Bible says that heaven and earth cannot contain God (1 Kings 8:27).

Christ the King is a title of Jesus in Christianity referring to the idea of the Kingdom of God where Christ is described as seated at the right hand of God (as opposed to the secular title of King of the Jews mockingly given at the crucifixion). Jesus is seated on the highest throne in heaven but rules in the hearts of every believer where the Holy Spirit presides. Jesus is the King of the domain of His kingdom. Those who partake of His nature are adopted in the royal family. They are called princes and princesses. They get their titles from the King of kings. The blessings of the King are relational. Real eternal blessings are reserved for those who are intimately related to the King. They are the ones who participate in the eternal kingdom of God. They are the ones who are sanctified by the Holy Spirit. They obey the Word of the King. By the way, the Word of the King is final. When the King says that "Thou shall not touch this tree" it must be fully obeyed. There is a dire consequence in case of disobedience. When a King says "No" and you respond by reversing His "No" to "Yes", you are in deep trouble. In the secular world, it is considered to be treason because overriding the word of the king is akin to overthrowing the king from His throne.

The Bible says that "This is good and pleasing in the sight of God our Savior, who wants everyone to be saved and to come to the knowledge of the truth." (1 Timothy 2:3-3). Salvation begins with repentance; it is the changing of the mind from your will to God's will. "And be not conformed to this world: but be ye transformed by the renewing of your mind, that ye may prove what is that good, and acceptable, and perfect, will of God." (Romans 12:2). Regeneration is a gift of God's grace to mankind. A regenerated soul is instructed to renew the minds and to do the perfect will of God. The Word of God projects the perfect will of God. The perfect will of God is God's plan for your life and your destiny. It is the upper calling of God in Christ Jesus. When we embrace the perfect will of God, we let God plan what we want to do, and guide our steps all the way to the end – No human resources or input is involved. I want to add that we should seek the perfect will of God not just in spiritual matters but even in the decisions and plans we make daily – For example, the man or woman to marry, the career or ministry to pursue, and so on. It will require you to be very patient and trust God because He wants to give His best, which has His full blessings, not the second-best.

The permissive will of God is when we plan and ask God to bless our plans regardless of His perfect will. God's permissible will does not have His full blessings. In 1 Samuel 8, God wanted to be the king of the Israelites but the people saw how other nations had a king and desired one for themselves. They cried and complained to Samuel who went to God in prayer. God permitted them to have a king but then problems started; they experienced war after war. The permissible will always have consequences because God gave you what you wanted because you were crying day and night over the issue and you would not be patient enough to wait for His alternative offer at His timing. "We must be ready to allow ourselves to be interrupted by God. We must not assume that our schedule is our own to manage, but allow it to be arranged by God."

God's intention is to replenish the earth with His morality. God gave Moses a set of Ten Commandments (Moral Law) to enforce His morality. Jesus summarized the Ten Commandments into one law of loving God and loving your neighbor. In the kingdom of God, there is one law of love. How you love your neighbor tells how you love God. Somebody said that "The measure of your love for God is determined by the measure of your love for the person you love least."

God sent us to preach the gospel of the kingdom of God in love. God does not ask us to preach the gospel out of contempt. We are not instructed to enforce the morality of God but to proclaim it and demonstrate it. The Bible says concerning Paul, "And having entered into the synagogue, he was speaking boldly for three months, reasoning and persuading them concerning the kingdom of God." (Acts 19:8). Paul convinced them to receive the gospel of the kingdom of God. In this case, the use of the phrase "the kingdom of God" is a compendious description of Christian doctrine.

Morality is determined by God because He alone is moral. We are naturally attracted to morality. That is why the constitutions of most governments have a Judeo-Christian background. For example, American moral and ethical ideals have their antecedent in the Judeo-Christian tradition. "Our Constitution was made only for a moral and religious people. It is wholly inadequate to the government of any other." John Adams (Federer, p. 10). "It is impossible to rightly govern the world without God and the Bible" George Washington (Federer, p.660). "Of all the dispositions and habits which lead to political prosperity, religion and morality are indispensable supports....And let us with caution indulge the supposition that morality can be maintained without religion.....Reason and experience both forbid us to expect that national morality can prevail to the exclusion of religious principle." George Washington's Farewell Address.

The most stable governments in the world weaved the Moral Law in their constitutions. They respect and enforce the Moral Law as provided in their constitutions. For example, it is a crime to steal, kill, lie, take somebody's wife, and etc. Here are more quotations from our early leaders: "Suppose a nation in some distant region should take the Bible for their only law book, and every member should regulate his conduct by the precepts there exhibited! Every member would be obliged in conscience, to temperance, frugality, and industry; to justice, kindness, and charity towards his fellow men; and to piety, love, and reverence toward Almighty God ... What a Eutopia, what a Paradise would this region be." John Adams, February 22, 1756 (Federer, William J., America's God and Country Encyclopedia Of Quotations, FAME Publishing, Coppell, Texas, 1994, p.5) "These laws laid down by God are the eternal immutable laws of good and evil .... This law of nature dictated by God Himself, is of course superior in obligation to any other. It is binding over all the globe, in all countries, and at all times: no human laws are of any validity if contrary to this... "The doctrines thus delivered we call the revealed or divine law, and they are to be found only in the holy scriptures ... [and] are found upon comparison to be really part of the original law of nature. Upon these two foundations, the law of nature and the law of revelation, depend all human laws; that is to say, no human laws should be suffered to contradict these. William Blackstone (Federer, p.52)

The Bible says that "The law of the LORD is perfect, converting the soul: the testimony of the LORD is sure, making wise the simple. The statutes of the LORD are right, rejoicing the heart: the commandment of the LORD is pure, enlightening the eyes. (Psalms 19:7 – 8).

"Proclaim liberty throughout all the land unto all the inhabitants thereof." (Leviticus 25:10) "Ye have not hearkened unto me, in proclaiming liberty, everyone to his brother, and every man to his neighbor: behold, I proclaim a liberty for you, saith the Lord" (Jeremiah 34:17).

"If my people, which are called by my name, shall humble themselves, and pray, and seek my face, and turn from their wicked ways; then will I hear from heaven, and will forgive their sin, and will heal their land" (2 Chronicles 7:14). Also, "And ye shall know the truth, and the truth shall make you free." (John 8:32)

Biblical counseling is intended to spread the wings of morality over the hierarchy of life beginning from the grassroots to the highest office. The common view is that morality is relative because it depends on what is acceptable to the people in a particular geographical religion. The biblical view is that there cannot be morality without the moral entity that is holy. He alone has the integrity to prescribe morality to rest the fallen world. The death of Jesus Christ on the cross implies that there is no morality outside Jesus Christ that can save mankind. According to the Bible, Jesus, going a little farther, fell with His face to the ground and prayed, "My Father, if it is possible, may this cup be taken from me. Yet not as I will, but as you will." (Matthew 22:39). He was asking for an alternate route to redemption, and there was found none but the cross.

BIBLICAL COUNSELING SIMPLIFIED

God is the author of wisdom because wisdom resides in God alone. True wisdom, the wisdom which is a "tree of life," does not come from below, from man; it comes from above, from God. God protects wisdom as the "tree of life" (Genesis 3:34). After Adam sinned, the return to Paradise was closed forever. Jesus gave mankind a second chance to access to the tree of life. God wants us to desire His wisdom as a "tree of life," and to look for it in His Word and pursue it by keeping His commands. Let us not persist in the very thing which brought about the fall of Adam who disobeyed the only commandment given to him by God by touching the forbidden tree (Genesis 2:17).

Our Father is the greatest counselor. The Bible says regarding the wisdom of God: "The counsel of the Lord stands forever, The plans of His heart from generation to generation" (Psalm 33:11). The wisdom of God is unimaginable. "For God has consigned everyone to disobedience so that He may have mercy on everyone. O the depth of the riches both of the wisdom and the knowledge of God! how unsearchable are his judgments, and his ways past tracing out! "Who has known the mind of the Lord? Or who has been His counselor?" (Romans 11:32-34). "How unsearchable are His judgments, and His ways past finding (rather, tracing) out! (cf. Psalm 26:6; Job 9:10; Job 11:7). For who hath known the mind of the Lord? or who hath been His counselor? (Isaiah 40:13, quoted accurately from the LXX.). Or who hath first given to him, and it shall be recompensed unto him again? (cf. Job 41:11, where the Hebrew has (Revised Version), "Who hath first given unto me, that I should repay him?" The LXX. (Job 41:2)." (Pulpit Bible Commentary).

The Bible says that as far as the heavens higher than the earth so is God's wisdom higher than our wisdom. "For as the heavens are higher than the earth, so My ways are higher than your ways and My thoughts than your thoughts" (Isaiah 55:9). God's wisdom is for our guidance. We can petition for it whenever there is a need. "With Your counsel, You will guide me, And afterward, receive me to glory" (Psalm 73:24). The wisdom of God is the greatest answer to each and every prayer request we present before God because we need God's guidance in everything we do. "Give me the mind of Christ" is an appropriate prayer to pray when we recognize we're having an unloving attitude or we lack wisdom. By faith, we welcome His thoughts, emotions, and affections as though they are our own. Because we have access to the mind of Christ, we don't need to respond out of our human weakness.

Jesus is the greatest counselor. "For a child will be born to us, a son will be given to us; And the government will rest on His shoulders; And His name will be called Wonderful Counselor, Mighty God, Eternal Father, Prince of Peace. (Isaiah 9:6). Wonderful Counselor is the first title referring to the Messiah, found once throughout the Bible, in Isaiah's prophecy(Isaiah 9:6). The Hebrew word for "wonderful counselor" is *pele-yoez*. The first term (*pele*) means "a miracle, a marvel, a wonder" which indicates "something extraordinary, incomprehensible, inexplicable." The second term (*yoez*) means "to advise, counsel, devise, purpose." Both definitions combined reveal that the child will be miraculously born to become an amazing adviser who marvelously works in all things for God's purpose (Romans 8:28) because the Holy Spirit dwells in Him with all wisdom, understanding, counsel, strength, knowledge, and honor to God (Isaiah 11:2).

The Holy Spirit is our teacher and counselor. "But the Counselor, the Holy Spirit, whom the Father will send in my name, he will teach you all things, and bring to your remembrance all that I have said to you." (John 14:26). The Holy Spirit stands in place of our Lord as our counselor. "I will ask the Father, and He will give you another Helper, that He may be with you forever; that is the Spirit of truth, whom the world cannot receive, because it does not see Him or know Him, but you know Him because He abides with you and will be in you. "I will not leave you as orphans; I will come to you." (John 4:16-18). The Holy Spirit unites the believer with

Christ and places him in the body of Christ, the church. He also unites the believer with Christ in His death, enabling him to live victoriously over sin. The Holy Spirit controls the believer who yields to God and submits himself to God's Word. When these conditions are met, the believer lives in the power of the Spirit and produces the fruit of the Spirit.

The Word is the source of wisdom for counseling. If the Lord is the Counselor, we expect Him to counsel us by what He says to us – His Word. That's how counsel is given and expected to be received. Whenever we abide in Christ, and His Word abides in us, we are grounded in the wisdom and faithfulness of God. The Bible says that "Your testimonies also are my delight; They are my counselors." (Psalm 119:24). Also, "The entrance of Your words gives light; it gives understanding to the simple." Those who will admit that they are naive, not wise, simpletons needing wisdom, God's Word will give it. The understanding comes by the light of the Word shining in. "The entrance of Your words gives light." (Psalms 119:130).

Faith comes from one place – The Word. God placed wisdom in the same place where He placed our faith. We are informed; we don't have blind faith. That is why God is pleased by our faith (Hebrews 11:6). Wisdom focuses on the Word. The Word of God is "the whole counsel of God" or "the will of God" or "the whole purpose of God." The disciples of Jesus are sent to counsel the world: "Also we have obtained an inheritance, having been predestined according to His purpose who works all things after the counsel of His will" (Ephesians 1:11). Paul preached the whole counsel of God. "-----for I did not shrink from declaring to you the whole counsel of God." (Acts 20:26). The Christian who seeks a deeper experience of God by ignoring the hard sayings of Scripture gets nowhere. The full nourishment of the soul requires feeding on the whole counsel of God. "The Preachers commission is to preach the whole counsel of God, but the cross is the center of that counsel."

The disciples of Jesus are sent to counsel the world: "Also we have obtained an inheritance, having been predestined according to His purpose who works all things after the counsel of His will" (Ephesians 1:11). Paul preached the whole counsel of God. "-----for I did not shrink from declaring to you the whole counsel of God." (Acts 20:26). The Christian who seeks a deeper experience of God by ignoring the hard sayings of

Scripture gets nowhere. The full nourishment of the soul requires feeding on the whole counsel of God. "The Preachers commission is to preach the whole counsel of God, but the cross is the center of that counsel."

Doctrine precedes duty. Christian learning precedes serving. Biblical counseling is an approach to counseling that uses the Bible to address the issues in the lives of individuals, couples, and families. The Bible teaches that our thoughts, motives, attitudes, words, and actions flow from the sinful selfishness of our hearts. Without God's wisdom, a man's teaching is merely a clanging cymbal. Biblical counseling addresses the heart using the wisdom and approaches revealed in the Bible.

The Bible is rescuing you from thinking that you can live the life you were meant to live while relying on the inadequate resources of your wisdom, experience, righteousness, and strength. God is pleased by our faith. Faith comes by hearing the Word. The Christian life is a spiritual life of faith that is void of human frailty. Faith in Christ is manifesting His life in us and through us. It is trusting in what Christ can do on our behalf. God delights us with His goodness to enjoy.

On a deeper note, it's easy to acknowledge Jesus as Lord in our theology, but how much do we invest our energy into following Him? Do we actually seek out His counsel and leadership in our lives, or are we "modeling Christianity" without having a real relationship or obedience to the One we claim to serve? Are we a headless mannequin, or a living son or daughter of God serving Him out of love?

Wisdom begins with God. "The fool says in his heart, "There is no God." They are corrupt; their acts are vile. There is no one who does good." (Psalm 14:1). The word "fool" means immoral. Rejecting God is therefore not an intellectual issue but a moral issue. Atheism is accompanied by deep moral corruption. In fact, it takes more faith to believe that God does not exist than to believe that He exists. Wisdom is acknowledging His existence and guidance.

The counsel of God's imperishable truth is found in this treasure house, the Bible. God's Word gives us the wisdom to make wise choices. Wisdom is basically putting knowledge to proper use. Being armed with knowledge without wisdom can be fatal because it is possible to hurt others with your knowledge instead of helping them.

Biblical counseling begins with the gospel. The gospel is the good news. But before you know the good news you have to know the bad news. The bad news is that you are dead in your sins (Colossians 2:13). You are alienated from God (Ephesians 4:18). You are utterly lost without a possibility of being found unless God intervenes. "When I look at myself I don't see how I can be saved but when I look at Jesus I don't see how I can be lost. Indeed, Jesus saves."

Salvation has God as its author. He must take the glory for our salvation and for all of our accomplishments after we are saved. "In every view of salvation, the place given in it to the glory of God provides the ultimate test. The proof that it is truly scriptural is that it gives all the glory to God. None must be reserved for ourselves or for anyone else. The Apostle Paul keeps on repeating it—'to the glory of God', 'the glory of his grace', 'to his glory.' Elsewhere he writes, 'But of him are ye in Christ Jesus, who of God is made unto us wisdom and righteousness and sanctification and redemption; that, according as it is written, He that glorieth, let him glory in the Lord'" (1 Corinthians 1:30–31).

Salvation brings to us wisdom. The new nature acquired involves the renewed minds of Christ. Salvation avails to us the character of Christ. Wisdom is revealed in holy conduct and godliness. The Bible specifically instructs us to pray for wisdom. "Now if any of you lacks wisdom, he should ask God, who gives generously to all without finding fault, and it will be given to him." (James 1:5). We don't have to ask God for intellect. God created us with intellect; we just need to sharpen it. We can naturally become intellectuals through education and experiential knowledge but the Bible specifically instructs us to ask God for wisdom. Acquired wisdom brings proper understanding in accordance with the Divine perspective. Heavenly wisdom results in the knowledge of the deep things of God, which is able to make us wise all the way to the end or eternally. Heeding is the evidence of understanding.

Salvation brings truthfulness. Truthfulness counters hypocrisy. It is impossible to be a witness to the gospel of Christ when you are living a double life or while you are sharing the worldly lifestyle with the people of the world whom you are supposed to minister to the saving grace. Truthfulness eradicates hypocrisy by seeking to manifest the righteousness of Christ.

Those of us who are redeemed have the responsibility to tell others about the goodness of God, His saving grace, and the godly wisdom that comes with salvation. The Church has a mission and the commission of outreach. The church herself is the mission drawing the attention of the people to Christ. The mission of the Church is the proclamation of the gospel. Also, the Church has the responsibility to confront injustice and alleviate suffering, to express God's love for the world without losing its primary calling to the Great Commission. Whatever you do, and wherever you go, your priority is to preach the gospel in deeds and words. I like this quotation: "The mission of the church is the task given by God for the people of God to accomplish in the world. In simplest terms, the mission of the church is the Great Commission—what Philip Ryken calls "a clear, unambiguous statement of [the church's] mission to the world." Our task as the gathered body of Christ is to make disciples, by bearing witness to Jesus Christ the Son in the power of the Holy Spirit to the glory of God the Father."

The prophetic message says "The Lord GOD has given Me the tongue of discipleship, to sustain the weary with a word. He awakens Me morning by morning; He awakens My ear to listen as a disciple." (Isaiah 50:4). The Lord God hath given me the tongue of the learned; literally, the tongue of disciples; i.e. a trained tongue, a well-taught tongue. A true scholar of the Bible is a disciple of Christ. We are taught by Jesus, as He was taught by the Father: "So Jesus said, "When you have lifted up the Son of Man, then you will know that I am He, and that I do nothing on My own, but speak exactly what the Father has taught Me" (John 8:28). The Crucifixion and Ascension are implied here as the means by which Jesus will return to His Father's throne. Then He will send the Holy Spirit to be our tutor. "And I will ask the Father, and He will give you another Helper, that He may be with you to the age" (John 14:16). The Holy Spirit is God's promise of wisdom to us. He guides us into the fullness of truth. "However, when the Spirit of truth comes, He will guide you into all truth." (John 16:13). Our Lord delivered to His disciples nothing but the truth; the truth liberates you now or condemns you later.

The Spirit of the Father and the Son indwells you. This is your uttermost security. Jesus was like a white background that exposed the dirty of the world. No wonder He made the religious leaders nervous and uncomfortable. Never be surprised if the world rejects you; after all, they rejected Jesus! Remember that the glory repels the natural. When Simon Peter saw the glory of God in Jesus, he fell at Jesus' feet. "Go away from me, Lord," he said, "for I am a sinful man." (Luke 5:8). When heaven opened and Isaiah saw the glory of God, he cried, "Woe is me, for I am a man of unclean lips" (Isaiah 6:5). Never be afraid to be rejected due to your faith.

Faith does not restrict or erode the intellect or the potential for the use of intellect. The Spirit of Christ engages our renewed minds. Therefore, being spiritual does not mean dropping your thinking hat. Generally speaking, people choose good counselors. People don't care whether you are a theologian, scientific, or intellectual. People simply want the virtuous, thinking and compassionate counselors who have some nuggets of truth that are indisputable, and impeccable character that they can live on.

Value your clients. Customers are the most important asset that any business has. Without enough good customers, no company can survive, and to survive, a firm must not only attract new customers but, perhaps more importantly, also hold on to its current customers. Ironically, every person is a potential client.

A client is privileged to have you as a real model. Give yourself as a model. Preach what you practice. A counselor is like a visible standard before his or her clients. A counselor is like a parent. Parents want their children to succeed. In this case, success means becoming like them; they want to reproduce themselves. Pray that your values make bed in the hearts of your clients and produce fruit. The Bible has a profound and overwhelming impact on the character of a person. Stick to the principles of the Bible. Don't move the fence.

Help realign the priorities of those you love including your clients so that they remain relevant to the biblical moral values. Expose them to profitable wisdom and skills side by side the moral education. "Do not forget to mention the centrality of character. Character is integrity plus honesty. Without character, we are just different characters."

A healthy relationship is a life whereby we counsel each other. We are supposed to learn from each other. Every person needs a mentor, and a person they are mentoring. Learn from those who you agree with and those who disagree with you. People have a right to doubt everything you say. Doubting is a form of thinking. Tell them something and show them its validity – no hallucination from your minds, no illusions but facts.

Dig deep and do some research in the areas of your influence in order to be more effective. Spiritually, consult God in prayers. Seek His counsel in the Bible. Introduce to your audience the Holy Spirit who can bring a revelation.

Biblical counseling is intended to produce profound results. It is not intended to give your client temporary soothing, making them feel like they have exerted some sort of control on a situation that is out of their hands. Any good counseling aims at fundamental change. It erodes believing into a false sense of peace. An application of simple logic shows that any counseling that targets appeasing emotions without impacting the heart is pointless and useless. Emotions steps in the moment you put God aside and get absorbed in your own thinking without the help of God.

Your client has the valuable information that you need in order to help them better. Be investigative but whenever it is necessary show them that you identify with them and you trust them. "In order to emphasize with someone's experience, you must be willing to believe them as they see it but not as you imagine their experience to be." ~ Brene Brown

Types of clients or people whom we are supposed to counsel: 1) Those who admit that they have a problem, know the solution and are willing to be counseled to confirm that they know. 2) Those who don't admit that they have a problem and see no need to be counseled 3) Those who admit that they have a problem and know the solution but they are not willing to accept the solution. 4) Those who admit that they have a problem but don't know a solution and are searching for a solution from us.

Diligence is required in the work of faith. According to Doctor John Piper, every serious Christian should receive six habits of mind and heart: (1) careful observation, (2) accurate understanding, (3) fair evaluation, (4) proportionate feeling, (5) wise application, and (6) compelling expression. Without these habits of mind and heart, you will be of little use to anyone in any situation. Without careful observation, you will be run over by a truck. Without careful accurate understanding, you will always miss the point. Without fair evaluation, you will drink sweet poison. Without proportionate feeling, you will take your jackhammer to a broken heart. Without wise application, you will be sidelined as useless. And without compelling expression, your learning will be bottled up and serve no one.

Study your clients. Whether at the office or out with friends, the body language of the people around you speaks volumes. It has been suggested that body language constitutes more than 60% of what we communicate, so learning to read the nonverbal cues people send is a valuable skill. Study your clients well. It is important to know that the body has its own language that can express feelings before words are spoken. Examples of body language: handshake means thankful. A hug means being comfortable with each other. A kiss means affection. Holding hands means deep intimacy. On the negative side, foot-stomping is a sign of insubordination and defiance. Rolling eyes is a sign of disrespect. Eye contact and eye behavior can be very telling. When communicating with someone, pay attention to whether he or she makes direct eye contact or looks away. Inability to make direct eye contact can indicate boredom, disinterest, or even deceit – especially when someone looks away and to the side. If a person looks down, on the other hand, it often indicates nervousness or submissiveness. Often, the victims of abuse tend to feel ashamed and look down while trying to avoid any direct contact. Just to mention a few.

Although people are more likely to control their facial expressions, you can still pick up on important nonverbal cues if you pay close attention. Pay particular attention to the mouth when trying to decipher nonverbal behavior. A simple smile body language attraction technique can be a powerful gesture. Smiling is an important nonverbal cue to watch for. There are different types of smiles, including genuine smiles and fake smiles. A genuine smile engages the whole face, whereas a fake smile only uses the mouth. A genuine smile suggests that the person is happy and enjoying the company of the people around him or her. A fake smile, on the other hand, is meant to convey pleasure or approval but suggests that the person smiling (smiler) is actually feeling something else. A "half-smile" is another common facial behavior that only engages one side of the mouth and indicates sarcasm or uncertainty.

The body is just a vehicle used to communicate ideas but it does not own the ideas. The idea is rooted in the minds. Any manifested act begins as an idea in the mind. Behavior is a projection of your thoughts or the things you habitually think about. But the behaviors are regulated by our beliefs. Ironically, every person believes in something. Find the motive behind the behavior.

A good counselor takes a keen interest in the affairs of his or her clients without becoming nosy. Watch out for the general behaviors of your clients with prior interests of helping them. For example, if a married couple traditionally and religiously wears their wedding rings, and you happen to see one not wearing it, there might be a possibility of serious marital discord. If they normally walk in church while holding hands and sit next to each other as a couple, and all of a sudden they start acting individually, it is a sign that they are drifting apart. Early intervention can be a remedy to the deteriorating situation.

The victims of abuse behave differently. A child who's being abused may feel guilty, ashamed, or confused. He or she may be afraid to tell anyone about the abuse, especially if the abuser is a parent, another relative, or family friend. That's why it's vital to watch for red flags, such as withdrawing from friends or usual activities. Changes in behavior — such as aggression, anger, hostility, or hyperactivity — or changes in school performance. Depression, anxiety or unusual fears, or a sudden loss of self-confidence. Attempts at running away. Rebellious or defiant behavior. Self-harm or attempts at suicide. Specific signs and symptoms depend on the type of abuse and can vary. A Sexually abused child wants to sit on the lap of an adult face to face, with her open legs wrapped around the adult. Abused children normally have sexual behavior or knowledge that's inappropriate for the child's age. They tend to have inappropriate sexual contact with other children. Please keep in mind that warning signs are just that — warning signs. The presence of warning signs doesn't necessarily mean that a child is being abused. But it gives you a reason to investigate. Any intentional harm or mistreatment to a child under 18 years old is considered child abuse. Child abuse takes many forms, which often occur at the same time. In many cases, child abuse is done by someone the child knows and trusts — often a parent or other relative. Everyone including the clergy, teachers, people in the medical field, and councilors is required by the law to report any suspect child abuse, report abuse to the proper authorities. Sexual child abuse is any sexual activity with a child, such as fondling, oral-genital contact, intercourse, exploitation, or exposure to child pornography. It is estimated that 1 in 4 girls and 1 in 6 boys will be sexually abused before they turn 18 years old.

Emotional child abuse means injuring a child's self-esteem or emotional well-being. It includes verbal and emotional assault — such as continually belittling or berating a child — as well as isolating, ignoring, or rejecting a child. Medical child abuse occurs when someone gives false information about illness in a child that requires medical attention, putting the child at risk of injury and unnecessary medical care. Child neglect is failure to provide adequate food, shelter, affection, supervision, education, or dental or medical care.

Although abuse and neglect can negatively impact anyone at any age, it has a much bigger impact on children. This is because children rely on their parents or other family members that they trust for love and protection. If these parental figures are abusing that trust and are the source of trauma, the child then doesn't have the family support that they desperately need.

Physical child abuse occurs when a child is purposely physically injured or put at risk of harm by another person. I am going to discuss child abuse in the name of discipline. This kind of abuse is exercised by the parents to reproof and reprimand. The majority of children experience this kind of abuse. Most parents do it out of good intentions, but there is no excuse for any kind of abuse. No discipline should bruise the body of a child.

The opponents of regular spanking say it leads them to become violent kids, and hit other kids. There are a couple of scriptures recommending carpal punishment. "He who spares the rod hates his son, but he who loves him is careful to discipline him." (Proverbs 13:24). Also, "Do not withhold discipline from a child; if you punish him with the rod, he will not die." (Proverbs 23:13). The Lord uses discipline to reveal our sin to us. The phrase "spare the rod, spoil the child" is a modern-day proverb that means if a parent refuses to discipline an unruly child, that child will grow accustomed to getting his own way. He will become, in the common vernacular, a spoiled brat. The problem is not with the rod but with the attitude of the parent holding the rod. There is a recommended measure of prescribing the rod discipline. It is true that our children should grow up with a mindset of taking responsibility for their mistakes. They should know that there are consequences to their actions. But any kind of discipline should be intended to educate them rather than to hurt them. It works well to discipline a child at the moment he or she is caught in wrongdoing. However, a parent should never prescribe any discipline measure when he or she is angry. Sometimes it is good to back off from disciplining until you regain calmness. Physical discipline should always be done in love, never as a vent to the parent's frustration.

Yelling is another part of discipline used when the child shows defiance. It can be used as a tool, one that lets parents release a little steam and, sometimes, gets kids to listen. Yelling can become an abuse in case a parent overreacts. Research shows that verbal abuse can, in extreme situations, be as psychologically damaging as physical abuse. There is a possibility of your yelling to recycle in the brain of your children during their youthful age all the way to adulthood. They can experience nightmares while sleeping when you are yelling at them. This is something they might have to deal with for the rest of their lives. Additionally, children's brains are still developing. Creating a foundation of toxic stress and trauma basically wires the foundations of the brain to continue to build that way, making it much more deep-seated and harder to change than trauma experienced in adulthood.

I want to say that the words of your mouth are the biggest stick in the corner of your house, that you can pull out and use effectively. Value it, and know when to use it. Avoid yelling at your children all the time. Once they get used to your yelling it will no longer be effective. Save your yelling for the right moment so that it can attract their attention. Enforce your 'No' – Never let your children override your 'No'. They should know that when Dad or Mum says 'No' it will always be a no.

Children absorb pain and release it by crying their lungs out. If a child were to experience large amounts of pain, it makes sense for them to experience anxiety, shame, and sorrow in their adulthood. These victims of childhood trauma often need comfort, and that source of comfort can sometimes be drugs or alcohol. After all, they've already learned that comfort can't be found in the adults around them.

Childhood experiences play a significant role in determining issues that occur later on in life. If a child is neglected or abused in some way, the frequent and extremely high levels of stress can impede normal brain development. Multiple studies have proven that these stress levels cause childhood victims of Trauma to be more vulnerable to substance abuse in adulthood.

"Speak out on behalf of the voiceless, and for the rights of all who are vulnerable" (Proverbs 31:8). A good counselor steps in as an advocate for the children. He or she pleads for them in case they are oppressed and pleads with them in case they are wrong. According to a respected family counselor, there is a less harmful measure of disciple out there that can produce the required results.

Time out is very common today. Time outs have been a popular tool since psychological behaviorist Arthur Staats coined the term and proved its effectiveness in the 1950s. Time out involves isolating a kid briefly from family interaction, with instruction to think about what they have done wrong. After the timeout is over, they are asked why they were sent to time out and what they could have done to avoid time out.

Some counselors suggest that taking away privileges can be an extremely effective discipline strategy when your child misbehaves. Whether you decide to take away a fun event or you remove a favorite toy, there are some strategies that will make privilege removal an effective consequence that can encourage your child to make better choices in the future.

You can take away a cake or dessert from the plate of a disrespectful kid during the time of dinner. Don't take away things children need, like meals or their beds. Making a child go to bed hungry or sleep on the floor is not an effective use of discipline strategy. Instead, it is bordering on abuse. Target to take away the privileges that the kids enjoy casually but do not necessarily need, like riding a bike, using electronics, going to the movies, playing with their friends, and playing with toys.

In summary, discipline is positive training toward a better future. Like touching a hot stove, we learn from the consequences of our actions. Discipline in childhood helps children avoid "learning the hard way" later in life. Light spanking can be prescribed to strong-willed children. Children need a clear answer to the question "Who is the boss?" Mom and Dad embody the security and limits that come from submitting ourselves to a loving heavenly Father. God has delegated oversight of your child's welfare and development to you, placing you in a position of authority over them. But avoid using unnecessary excessive force that will make you regret your actions soon or later. As I said, punishment is negative; we don't make our kids pay for what they have done; we discipline them in form of educating them to do right.

VERBAL COMMUNICATION

I have discussed how the body has a language of its own. Now I am going to briefly discuss verbal communication. It is important to note that before a person listens to you, they first look at you. Present yourself in a respectable manner. The outside appearance of the vessel carrying the message matters; it gives the message weight. Some people determine if you are worth their time just by looking at you. Some people are in an indecisive mood till their first glance at you. Your face value can actually influence your audience to listen to you or to lend their ears to you. "Fashion is anything which is you and reflects your personality, and if you are comfortable with what you wearing, you'll look trendy and fashionable for sure."

Confidence is a suit you need to wear nonstop. Always be confident. Speak from your heart direct to their hearts. Be prepared, rehearsed, and confident about the material you will be presenting. There are many "techniques" or "skills" that a professional speaker can incorporate into a presentation to add interest. Be yourself, don't pretend to be somebody. They say that 38 percent of your charisma comes from the way you talk. The more appealing your voice is to people, the more trust they will put in you, but the opposite is also true. Stuttering, talking too fast, not breathing properly, can ruin your charisma and make people unable to enjoy your company. Don't let your speech be anesthesia putting your audience to sleep.

Speak nothing but the truth. But speak the truth in love. "The truth only hurts when you want to believe a lie." The truth, as they say, hurts. But they also say it sets you free. The truth will set you free now or condemn you later. Public Speakers have been ridiculed, abused, and even killed for expressing contrary views to generally held beliefs. Christians are not exceptional. All of the twelve apostles apart from John were murdered. Paul was beheaded too. Martyrdom comes from the Greek word μαρτυρια, meaning "witness". The Apostles accepted death instead of forsaking the truth. The willingness of the apostles to suffer and die as martyrs for their faith is one of the most commonly cited arguments for the resurrection. No body would willingly choose to submit to a painful death for a lie.

Communication involves two parties – the person doing the talking, and the audience listening to the person talking. The effectiveness of the spoken words depends on the listeners. I am going to focus on a one-to-one conversation involving a counselor and a client. "Often in contemporary pastoral training, there can be such an emphasis on training to preach that there is insufficient time to train preachers to be effective shepherds. This is why, in my experience, most pastors are more comfortable with the pulpit or public ministry of the Word than they are with the private ministry of the Word. (By "pulpit or public ministry of the Word," I mean preaching and teaching classes. By "private ministry of the Word," I mean one-on-one conversations with people about personal questions, trials, or sins.)"

The people who are called in ministry need to be trained for one-to-one ministry (whether it's considered counseling, comforting, or advising). Counseling involves pursuing peace by building up others. Counseling is not a one-sided conversation. A skilled counselor must be a good listener. The more you listen to your client, the more you know what to say. Listening to your client carefully gives you a clue even to the unspoken words. Take time to listen and speak to be heard probably. Be proud of that moment of silence you didn't miss.

The attitude that underpins effective communications skills is recognizing that, as the speaker, we must take responsibility for our listeners. Take responsibility to ensure that they understand. It is not enough simply to speak and then pass the buck to them. The fact that we are speaking means that we have a vested interest in them to understanding. It's us that lose out if they don't understand.

Make your presentation great – one that is informative, motivating, and inspiring. But slow down the speed of your words in your presentation so that your listener doesn't have to rush listening to you. The digital commercial advertisements on radio and television speed up words so that they can register extra time for more advertisement. The challenge the digital marketers face is capturing the attention of the viewers and at the same time hammering home the intended message in a very limited time. They have to repeatedly play the same advertisement in order for them to archive their objectives. A counselor does not need speed in their presentation but to slow down. Repeat yourself whenever it is necessary to hammer home a point.

During the first meeting, a counselor is likely to come without prepared notes or speech since he or she is not acquainted with the details of the case. But it is important to write down the main points you want to discuss. Go through them over and over before presenting them for discussion. Writing it down will improve your recall of the really important information. Writing things down doesn't just help you remember, it makes your mind more efficient by helping you focus on the truly important stuff. And your goals absolutely should qualify as truly important stuff. Also, take your note and write down some important nuggets during the discussion. It will help you to be orderly during the discussion. People are likely to take you more seriously when they see you writing down what they say. Much more is to refresh your minds later on when you sit down alone getting ready to take the next step.

Think twice before you speak. Don't be that person who opens their mouth before their minds kick up. Never rush to give an answer unless you are sure it is the right answer that your client needs. Take a break if it is necessary in order to pray and to consult God, and do some research if necessary. A delayed right response is better than a rushed premature judgment. My dad was considered to be one of the admired counselors. The secret behind his success is that he was always in control. He never allowed his client to rush him to respond prematurely. Even when he had the right answer, he would ask his clients to give him time to pray and to think about the right answer. He would carefully listen, and then ask them to come back the next day for an answer. And most times he gave them the right answer.

Always get the details of the story before coming to a conclusive decision. Never take people at face value. People are likely to come up with appealing information in order to win your sympathy. In case a conflict involves two people, get information from all parties involved before coming to conclusion. A one-sided story is a one-way street headed in one direction..while avoiding the other direction. There's always another side to the story, requiring your investigation. Have awareness of the possible limitations of facts: there could be contrary facts, the facts could be only partially or tentatively known, the facts may need to be related to other information in order to get a complete picture. Dig deep for full openness to knowledge, including facts that might go against your own view.

Whenever you are listening to the story of your client, know that there is the possibility of not telling it all. A good counselor analyzes what is said in order to figure out what is not said. Analysis in the realm of thought leads to great discoveries and solutions. If you analyze properly you'll eventually fit the pieces of information provided in their right places.

First and foremost, you must start by understanding your client rather than exaggerating their motives. Evaluate the information provided. Make sure that your client is in a stable mind. Watch out for some unconscious thoughts and beliefs that may be creating suffering and oppressive behaviors. It takes the gift of discerning and experience to study your clients. A good counselor is capable of discerning the uprightness and the truth behind appearances.

Expect disagreement whenever you are going to counsel somebody. You are going to counsel some people whom you don't agree with. Again, use your skills to avoid any possible confrontation. Remember that you are not there to win an argument but to prove a point to somebody that is not willing to accept it. "Never wrestle with pigs. You both get dirty, and the pig likes it." Your primary mission is the welfare of the soul of the client. Avoid the possibility of winning an argument and losing the soul.

Avoid a biased attitude. "Biases and blind spots exist in big data as much as they do in individual perceptions and experiences." Naturally, we are biased creatures. Bias can happen unintentionally. It can happen unconsciously. It can happen effortlessly. The reason is that we are naturally biased. Bias can be meditated on and intentional. "People will sometimes put each other in boxes and have biases toward one another because of what they look like or where they come from or who they are. But ultimately, it's up to us to decide who we are." Bias can be a result of being self-opinionated. Being opinionated means to be "conceitedly assertive and dogmatic in one's opinion". Synonymous of opinionated:

dogmatic, of fixed views, dictatorial, pontifical, domineering, pompous, self-importance, arrogant." (Dictionary.com)

According to a psychologist "We are all in favor of emotional intelligence. Intelligence can take emotion as a privileged counseling partner. However, it does not allow emotion to take possession of us, besiege our minds, and subjugate our thinking. Our emotions must regulate our thoughts, not manipulate nor substitute them. Our perception is only a biased picture of reality, and emotions are individual or provisional. Therefore, critical thinking and emotional thinking must go hand in hand.."

I want to say that our emotions are corrupt and dominant. Even some of our decisions that we consider to be logical decisions, the very point of such a choice is arguably always based on emotion. Emotions can be bypassed when we let the Spirit of God takes control of our hearts and guide us. We should never allow our emotions to dictate to us what to do. I believe that the only place where our emotions die is the renewed minds (Romans 12:2). That is a place where godly wisdom grows. The more you grow in wisdom, the more you discover that you don't know. And the more you want to know more. Always strive to find yourself in places where you keep learning. The noun disciple comes from the Latin word *discipulus,* which means "student, learner, or follower." One of the earliest places "disciple" showed up was in the Bible, where it means "a follower of Jesus," sometimes specifically one of the twelve Apostles. According to Judaism, a Rabbi often walked on the streets while teaching and had his disciples following him and listening to his teaching. We are followers of Christ because we follow the guidance of the Holy Spirit through the scriptures.

Emotions are highly expressed in feelings. Avoid embracing something just because you feel good about it. Feelings must be checked by beliefs. Our emotions are corrupt and biased. Avoid being emotionally motivated. Faith does not originate in our emotions, or our feelings, or our senses. Faith is God's free gift to us. That is when we decide to perceive in our hearts something as real fact even when it is not yet revealed to our minds and senses. If God said it and inspired it to be written down as scripture, it must be true. The basis of faith is the love and trust of God. The basis of emotions is the love and trust of self.

Avoid using your personal experience as a standard of living. However positive your personal experience might be, regardless of the good results experienced, your personal experience should be validated by the Word (truth). I know somebody that was supernaturally healed of cancer when he was living a very promiscuous lifestyle. A friend of mine got saved while he was a Jehovah Witness follower, and left the cult later after he was convicted. God can reach you wherever you are; it does not mean God's approval of what you are doing. We should be careful of occultism that has penetrated the church. Again, never use your personal experience to determine the truth, unless it is biblical. At times God rewards our prayers even when He doesn't approve of the motivations of our petitions. Use scriptures alone. *Sola scriptura* is a theological doctrine held by some Protestant Christian denominations that posits the Christian scriptures as the sole infallible source ..

There is one way of determining whether God is involved in what you say and do. There must be biblical proof and God should receive the ultimate glory of everything you say and do. God gives us brains for thinking and planning. But true wisdom begins with God. The Word of God is the indisputable standard at our fingertips to determine what is glorifying to God. The Bible is the inspired Word of God containing God's commandments and promises. Most of the promises of God are conditional. This means that God is not obligated to keep those promises if we don't meet the conditions first. For example, Romans 10:9 tells us that if we confess with our mouths that Jesus is Lord and we believe that God raised Him from the dead, then we will be saved. The understanding here is that if we don't confess or believe then we will not receive salvation. In Matthew 6:14-15, we are told that if we refuse to forgive others their sins against us, then our Father will not forgive our sins – again, conditional.

Our spiritual warfare primarily involves fighting ideologies that exalt themselves above the true knowledge of God. We are fighting against the brainwashing brought about by the lies of the devil. Spiritual warfare takes place in the minds. The demonic propaganda is out there selling like 'hot cakes' to our youth who call evil good.

The Ten Commandments are known as the ten rules defining morality. In order for anything to be considered moral, it must not contradict the Ten Moral Laws. Jesus quoted Deuteronomy 6:5 and summarized the Ten Commandments into two commandments of loving God with all your heart, and with all your soul, and with all your mind and loving neighbor as you love yourself. He said, "On these two commandments hang the whole Law and the Prophets." (Matthew 22:34-40). Everything you say and do must be wrapped in the love of God in order for it to be glorying to God. Faith is the essence of Christianity. And faith is revealed in love. Faith is love in action.

Biblical counseling involves passing on morality and knowledge to others. It's an opportunity to take your leadership and life to the next level through coaching others. Morality is absolute; it cannot be redefined. Jesus said that heaven and earth shall pass away but not a single jot, not a stroke of a pen, will disappear from the Law (Matthew 5:18). If the almighty God who wrote the Moral Law could not change even a comma from it, we can't change morality to fit our tastes.

Good councilors don't hide good news from their clients. As long as they discover knowledge, they share knowledge. But you must know the doctrine of the Word of God in order to acquire knowledge and in order to pass it on to others. The word "doctrine" means teachings. The Holy Spirit (the greatest teacher) puts ideas into the heart of a believer through the Scriptures. It means being immersed in the teaching of the scriptures and being a living example of the gospel. The Word of God must become the way of your thinking in order for you to line up with the will of God. Wherever you go and whatever you say and do, your lives should be the praises (doxology) of Christ.

Treat every client as a new baby born to you. "It is not that you give birth to a child that matters most. Rather, it is what you birth into them." Show your clients that you are not there for business but to leave great footprints on whosoever you meet and to be remembered for the change you initiated. Knowing how to solve problems and helping people move forward is a job well done and is extremely fulfilling. Always remember that God's primary concern is to change the hearts of people in order to change their behaviors. Be the instrument that God uses to archive His mission.

People come to you for counseling because they trust you. They trust your capability to deliver. Much more they trust in God whom you represent. The first thing to do when you meet your client for the first time is to let them know that you are a born-again believer. It gives you accountability to protect the integrity of the name of Jesus whom you represent. People are going to respect you and trust you on the basis of the character of Christ. The more they trust you, the more they are going to open up for you to have access to their deep secrets. Remember that effective counseling depends on the quality and quantity of information you gather from your client. Therefore "trust" is the knob that opens or seals the springs of knowledge. Trust is earned not bestowed because of a position. Trust involves the capability to keep secrets. When your client trusts you with their personal secrets, they reserve the rights to that information; they don't give you the right to share it with others. A loose tongue is a habit of talking too much about things that are private, secret, etc. The tongue reveals every corner of a shallow mind. "The best time for you to hold your tongue is the time you feel you must say something or bust."

I like this quotation: "Words can be medicines; they can also be poisons. Words can heal; they can also kill... It all depends on how, when, and where they are used and against whom! Let us not abuse our words. It's a misuse of the tongue!" The Psalmist prayer is "Set a guard, O Lord, over my mouth; keep watch over the door of my lips!" (Psalm 141:3). Paul instructed us that "Let no corrupting talk come out of your mouths, but only such as is good for building up, as fits the occasion, that it may give grace to those who hear." (Ephesians 4:29). Wisdom gives you control over your tongue. And controlling your tongue brings wisdom to you.

Martin Luther King, Jr. said that "Occasionally in life there are those moments of unutterable fulfillment which cannot be completely explained by those symbols called words. Their meanings can only be articulated by the inaudible language of the heart."

Again, the moment people can't trust you to keep the information they share with you; the moment they give you their private information and it ends up leaking to other people, your carrier as a counselor is over.

The times when a therapist has to break confidentiality are generally set forth in state laws:

1) When the client poses an imminent danger to themselves or others, and breaking confidentiality is necessary to resolve the danger.
2) When the therapist suspects child, elder, or dependent adult abuse.

3) When the client has directed the therapist to share information about their case.

4) When the therapist receives a qualifying court order.

Watch out for who you talk to and what you say. Satan can use other people to bring you down. Some of our confrontations are spiritual in nature. The devil uses human beings to operate in the physical world. The Bible says that "Submit yourselves, then, to God. Resist the devil, and he will flee from you." (James 4:7). The hardest advice of all, to a man reliant on himself, is submission to any, more especially to the Unknown. We are called to shut the mouth of the devil, not by screaming or rebuking him but by speaking the wisdom of God from His Word.

Skillful speakers know how to use words skillfully. They stitch the words together in order to deliver an appealing message verbally. The quality of everything matters even in communication. We need quality brains for quality performance. It is important to know what to say, when to say it, and how to say it.

What you deliver matters. Do your research carefully. Don't let people question your integrity because of what you say. Avoid saying things out of presumption. I mean a presumption that is not supported by all the facts. Say the truth in love rather than saying what people want to hear. Stay focused and positive. "It is important to stay positive in times when things press you to think negative."

When you deliver matters. Know the right time to deliver. The intention of delivering is what you delivered to be received effectively. Study the recipient whether they are in good mood to receive your delivery. It is useless to ship when what you ship is not going to be received. In the case of communication, you are delivering a message with prior intention to be received. Know when and how to say something to somebody. Study their mood. Deliver your message when the person to whom you are delivering is in good mood, is not busy, is not distracted, has no company and etc. Your target is not just to deliver a message but your message to be received and to produce the intended results.

How you deliver matters. Your message when wrapped differently or when flavored can be more appealing and effective. The language you use matters. It works better to ask somebody to do something than to instruct them to do something. For example, if you want the door to be closed, you have an option to say it in several ways in order for somebody to comply. You may say to him authoritatively: "Keep that door closed." You may say to him in a request manner: "Can you please keep that door closed". You may say it to him tactically: "Don't you think that it is better to keep that door closed". The last two requests have a flavor of politeness, and they are more appealing than the first one.

Polish your language when dealing with people whom you don't agree with. Show them that you respect their opinions. If you show them that you are listening to them and that you understand them, they will be more willing to listen to you and accept your opinion. Don't just say "I disagree", show them that you are listening and that you understand them before you explain your opinion. You can do this by using statements like - "Yes, but... I see what you mean, but...... I agree up to a point, but......." For example: instead of saying "I think we should wait until a better opportunity comes along." You can say that: "Yes, but we might not get another opportunity like this for a while." or instead of "I think we should ask for a 20% discount because it will show them that we are serious." You can say that: "I see what you mean, but I think 20% might be a bit too much. It might put them off."

The two small words used most in our conservation are "Yes" & "No". The most commonly used word has three letters..... Yes, I agree. Yes, I agree ... It's omnipresent in language usage; we can't imagine English without it. "Yes Means Yes": Affirmative Consent · Yet, most people use it casually. Ironically, it is used in a manner that is not worth its salt. The two-letter word "No" means solid "No". Yet, quite often we are afraid to say "No". We are afraid of saying no because our biggest fear is rejection. We are afraid that every time we do this, we would disappoint someone, make them angry, hurt their feelings, or appear unkind or rude. We have in our mind that having people think negatively of ourselves is the ultimate rejection. The reality is that the more we delay saying "No" the more we disappoint others. If it is "No" say it in good faith, and allow the other person to move on.

Get used to saying the magic word: "Sorry". This word can be used in many ways: to interrupt, to apologize, to show you don't understand, to disagree. It diffuses tension and allows you to start a statement more comfortably. For example: "Sorry, but can I just say something here; Sorry, but I don't really agree", And etc.

Rudeness turns off communication. Use little words to soften your statements. Break down negative sentences with some softeners. Don't say: "I don't like it." Say: "I don't really like it I'm afraid." Don't say: "Can I say something?" Say: "Can I just say something here?" Don't say "I can't" Say: "I am afraid, I cannot"

Avoid 'finger pointing' statements with the word 'you'. This is aggressive and too direct. Try to avoid saying 'you' and put the focus on 'I' or 'we'. Don't say: "You don't understand me." Say: "Perhaps I'm not making myself clear." Don't say: "You didn't explain this point". Say: "I didn't understand this point." Don't say "You are causing us to lose". Say: "We are positioned to lose".

Watch your language. The Bible forbids swearing: "But above all, my brothers, do not swear, either by heaven or by earth or by any other oath, but let your "yes" be yes and your "no" be no, so that you may not fall under condemnation." (James 5:12). We might think of saying to someone, "I swear on a stack of Bibles that I'm not lying," or "I swear on my mother's grave that I'll pay you next Thursday." Jesus forbid Christians from doing this, and James confirmed that teaching. The issue appears to be about honesty. Truthfulness should be the absolute norm for those who trust in Christ. Our simple yes or no should be completely binding since deception is never an option for us. If an oath is required to convince someone of our honesty or intent to be faithful, it suggests we may not be known for telling the truth in other circumstances.

As I said, an oath is the worldly means to enforce honesty. Likewise, a covenant is required in a situation where there is no trust between the two parties involved in making an agreement. Covenants are often put in place by lenders to protect themselves from borrowers defaulting on their obligations due to financial actions detrimental to themselves or the business. Our yes or no should be able to override all the above restrictions.

Avoid using slang words. Take away any curse words from your vocabulary. Due to the corrupt nature of man, it is right to presume that there are no languages that have no swear words. Such words are like gray hair to be picked from the head because they tarnish the natural beauty. Intriguingly, some of these words are acceptable by society depending on when you use them. For example in the Liberal cancel-culture, the F-word is widely acceptable depending on when you use it. "Courts have held, for example, that if an employee accidentally bangs into something sharp and shouts, 'Oh f---!' that would be understandable. On the other hand, if an employee glares angrily at a supervisor and shouts, 'F--- you' and [uses] other offensive languages, then it's more likely to constitute harassment when taken together with other inappropriate behavior." I want to say that just because the culture & society approve something it does not make it moral. Morality is neither determined by people nor by governments nor by courts but by God.

There is a place for professionalism even in the era of communication. Act like a professional. Dress professionally. Use your language professionally. It's the use of the language that attracts your clients to you. Always use plain and clear language to communicate with your clients. The more you use plain and clean language, the more your audience will want to listen to you. Remember that respect does not automatically come to you; it is earned. What comes out of your mouth determines the respect you get. When you respect yourself people are going to respect you. It is consistent with the ethical principle of respecting "the inherent dignity and worth of the person."

THE PERSONALITY FACTOR

Now I am going to elaborate on the personality issue. Personality is when conduct, attitude, thinking, character, and sentiments are consolidated. Everybody loves a decent personality and each individual likewise needs one. A great personality is significant in the event that you need others to like you. Having a superior personality is significant for everybody. I believe that God created us with a variety of personalities in order to complement each other. But there is a godly personality that is common to all of us. "I believe in doing the right things; that is my character and personality."

Personality defines us and how we interact with the world. Though there are different theories about what personality really is and how our basic personality traits are first formed, the general consensus is that personality is shaped by early life experiences and tends to stay stable over time. According to the most widely accepted model of personality, there are five basic personality dimensions that can define us as individuals.

The Big Five personalities traits is a suggested taxonomy, or grouping, for personality traits, developed from the 1980s onward in psychological trait theory. Some words used to describe aspects of personality are often applied to the same person. It is possible for somebody to have more than one personality. The theory identifies five factors:

1) Extroversion (outgoing/energetic vs. solitary/reserved) - Extraversion includes traits such as talkative, energetic, assertive, and outgoing. Social interaction is the key here. Extraverts often take on positions of leadership; first to offer their opinion and suggestions.

2) Agreeableness (friendly/compassionate vs. critical/rational) - They are willing to put aside their interests for other people. These individuals are helpful, friendly, considerate, and generous. Their basic belief is that people are usually decent, honest, and trustworthy.

3) Openness to experience (inventive/curious vs. consistent/cautious) - A person with a high level of openness to experience in a personality test enjoys trying new things. They are imaginative, curious, and open-minded. Individuals who are low in openness to experience would rather not try new things. They are close-minded, literal, and enjoy having a routine.

4) Conscientiousness (efficient/organized vs. extravagant/careless) - Conscientiousness is the personality trait of being careful, or diligent. Conscientiousness implies a desire to do a task well, and to take obligations to others seriously. Conscientious people tend to be efficient and organized as opposed to easy-going and disorderly.

5) Neuroticism (sensitive/nervous vs. resilient/confident) - Neuroticism is a trait characterized by sadness, moodiness, and emotional instability. Individuals who are high in this trait tend to experience mood swings, anxiety, irritability, and sadness. Those low in this trait tend to be more stable and emotionally resilient.

According to https//www.hiresuccess.com, each person is a unique combination of four personality types. We refer to those personality types as A, B, C, and D, respectively. Learning how to identify people by personality type can bring a higher level of understanding to interpersonal relationships and team building, especially for employers looking for ways to improve employee hiring and retention.

A Type A personality likes to be in charge and be in control of their environment and their lives. They're normally not very detail-oriented, choosing to delegate details to others. They're usually very goal-oriented and practical in their solutions. And arriving at their solutions and goals will entail a no-nonsense, bottom-line approach. People with Type A personalities can typically be identified by the following traits: Goal-oriented, Risk-taking, and Good under stress.

The Type B personality is a very outgoing, energetic, and fast-paced individual who likes to be around people and enjoys being the center of attention. They're good relationship builders, and most people like them right away. Their driving need is for approval, so they try to like everyone in hopes everyone will like them too. Compliments, acknowledgment of their achievements, words of admiration, and even applause from groups will be the most important thing you can do for them. Type B personalities love to talk about themselves. Some may view that as self-centered, but a Type B's real motivation is to be liked. For an extreme (and funny) example, think of the character played by Bette Midler in the movie Beaches, when she invited an old friend up to see her lavish apartment and told her about her great success. Then she said to the friend: "Enough about me. Let's talk about you. So, what do you think of me?"

The Type B personality's biggest fear is being humiliated in public, since that might make many people disapprove of them, and the thought of that would be devastating. The B personality doesn't want to appear unattractive or unsuccessful either, so they'll make sure their appearance is impeccable and will always give the impression of being very successful at whatever they do, whether they are or not. Some of the strengths you can count on from the Type B personality are their enthusiasm, outgoing behavior, friendliness toward others, and their ability to persuade even the most skeptical of people. They tend to be dreamers and can often turn those dreams into very practical ideas in the workplace. Type B personalities are normally spontaneous and use their quick wit and humor to make people like them. They aren't very good about hiding their own feelings either, so if they're hurt or disappointed, you'll probably be able to read it in their mannerisms and overall disposition.

The Type C personality is a very detail-oriented individual who likes to be involved in things that are controlled and stable. They're interested in accuracy, rationality, and logic. People who can't seem to control their emotions will bother them because Type C personalities believe being emotional makes objectivity difficult or perhaps impossible. They also dislike being around people who are full of hype, since they desire facts, accuracy, and logic. Other people's emotions may not be a priority for them, as they tend to strive for the facts and let the chips fall where they may.

Type C personalities tend to be quite controlling, both of themselves and others. They don't like things to get out of hand and may not appear very expressive at times because they don't really want themselves to display a lot of emotion. They're very outcome-driven and will be sticklers for following procedures and protocol in getting the job done. They're careful, resourceful, and, above all, excellent thinkers who will look at all aspects of an issue before taking a stand. Once they take a stand on an issue, though, they'll have the facts to back it up, so anyone who challenges them better be prepared. They like their jobs to be clearly defined and want to know exactly what's expected of them. Knowing those facts, they will be able to prioritize their tasks and see them through to completion. When in decision-making roles, they're cautious and logical, requiring many details and facts before they make a decision. People who try to sell them something by trying to get them emotionally involved usually fail; the Type C personality would consider such an effort to be hype and would wonder what facts the other person is trying to hide. In more public roles, the Type C personality will strive for originality, cleverness, and uniqueness in all things. Because of their detailed orientation, they're meticulously prepared to defend their decisions against any possible objections. Many accountants and lawyers, for example, are Type C personalities. They're excellent for any job that requires creative thinking based on patience, facts, and accuracy.

A Type D personality takes a slower, easier pace toward their work and life in general. They seek security and longevity on the job and are very happy doing a repetitive task, day in and day out. The repetition allows them to become very skilled in what they do. Likewise, they won't like it if the rules change a lot, as that's contrary to their desire to minimize change and stick with what they know works. For the Type D personality, even though the current way may be unpleasant, they worry that the unknown may be even worse. They seek the respect, sincere admiration, and acceptance of others. The Type D personality will gladly work hard to please the people they work for as long as they feel appreciated and receive plenty of reassurance that they're needed. They need that sense of security. Type D personalities often think the Type A personality is crazy for taking so many risks and not showing much concern for security and longevity.

Type D personalities are usually very organized; being around a messy environment or disorganization will bother them. They're also good at playing a very supportive role with others and are normally very caring, thoughtful, and compassionate. They are patient, tend to be good listeners, and will persevere when all others have given up. They especially like working in a group or on a team and will be a stabilizing force in these scenarios. Although they may not be as fast as others, they're accurate and thorough. They'll usually keep their feelings to themselves and are reluctant to express themselves, even if a more assertive type seems to be taking advantage of them. They tend to go along to get along. To attract the Type D personality, be sure to talk about the company benefits package and the long-term growth potential within the company. Having a secure, stable environment will be very important to the Type D personality.

Whenever two or more personality types are equal in strength within a person, that person is considered a Type X personality. For example, if an individual's two highest-strength personality types were A and B, they might be identified as AX and BX. In the extremely rare event that all four personality types were identical, that person would be considered simply as a Type X personality.

a good counselor acknowledges the personality of his or her client. "The best counselors in the field aren't necessarily those who are most well known but rather those who are always reaching toward greatness and flat out working harder than everyone else, Kottler says. "[These counselors] are constantly questioning what they do and why, being brutally honest with themselves about their work and its outcomes," he says. "They are always soliciting feedback from their clients and colleagues, begging for the most frank assessments about what is working and what is not. Most of all, they are often so humble that they don't seek attention or the limelight but just quietly go about their extraordinary commitment to helping others."

A counselor is trained to question, doubt, scrutinize, test, and get to the bottom of things. "A truly great counselor integrates all aspects [of] effective counseling practice by masterfully developing the therapeutic alliance, instilling hope, quickly centering on achievable objectives, judiciously selecting evidence-based practices, maximizing out-of-session change opportunities, and facilitating treatment adherence and follow-up to make sure treatment gains are maintained long after termination."

A counselor's personality matters. A counselor is a voracious entrepreneur who wears many hats – He is a leader, a servant, and a mediator. Leaders are referred to as bosses. Being bossy is not a good personality for counseling. Being bossy is pretty obvious with some people. They are straightforward in demanding that things be done, planned, and accommodated their way. They radiate a sense of unease, limit general conversations to what can be salvaged during coffee, and ride on you with their titles slapped on your back for saddles. They have their own — and often harsh — ways of setting the company culture, drafting strategies and deadlines, and principles to be nurtured. They breathe down your neck. They strong-arm you. They go to ends to have you unsettled and concerned—so much until you get the paper done, complete your work, and subsequently don't lack in your performance any time after.

If you want to be a good counselor stop being bossy, then you have to learn to give up some control and to have faith in God. The more you get closer to God, the less opinion of yourself you have. That is when everything about God matters and nothing about you matters. Learn to trust the people around you, and to dedicate responsibilities.

Personality changes can still occur depending on new life experiences. As our lives change, so do our personalities. The desire to alter personality is not uncommon. Shy people might wish they were more outgoing and talkative. Hot-tempered individuals might wish they could keep their cool in emotionally charged situations. They don't just wish, they try to change to a personality that draws people towards them instead of away from them. The question is, do you really want to change your personality?

Any personality can be discarded or improved on. If you can discard anything, you are in control of it. Something that you can't get rid of is obviously in control of you. If you can't get rid of the weak personality, it controls you. As I said, you can improve on a healthy personality. Learning more about (and understanding) your personality type is extremely beneficial for you, your many relationships, and even your career! You can never develop your personality when you quit learning.

You alone can change your personality. In my book "Growing in the Spirit" I said that if a carnal Christian and a hard personality Christian applied for the same job in my ministry, I would readily choose to hire a carnal Christian. The reason is that I am anointed to change him or her. But a person with a hard personality can only change himself or herself.

I can't change him or her. I am anointed to break the yoke of the enemy that is holding people in bondage. Personality is a natural issue rather than a spiritual bondage. "The anointing is what enables us to labor, without having to apply any special effort. The anointing is what overcomes every difficulty that would beset us, that we in our own strength and with our own abilities would normally not be able to cope with." But a person with a hard personality can only change himself or herself. I can't change him or her. I can teach them and show them how to improve on their personality but it is up to them to comply.

I want to end by saying that the grace of God can use your personality for the glory of God. Never be afraid to offer the little you have. God uses us in our inadequacies because that is when He gets the glory. When people see you doing impossible things they acknowledge the hand of God working through you. The story of Gideon, in the book of Judges, is about God, and how He operates in the lives of His children. God's interactions with Gideon are gentle, loving, forbearing, and intimately personal. Gideon was threshing secretly or hiding for fear of the Midianites. The angel of the Lord found him and called him a mighty man of valor (Judges 6:11-13). God didn't call Gideon a mighty man of valor because He saw that character trait in him from the beginning. Gideon was called a mighty man of valor because of who God is. God had plans to make Gideon a mighty man of valor because God is the Mighty Warrior of valor. Over and over the Lord assured Gideon what His mighty power would accomplish through him. The bottom line is that God sees what we are becoming instead of what we are.

YOU CAN BE THE ANSWER
TO YOUR PROBLEMS

Success is defined differently depending on whom you ask. Growth is not necessarily development and development is not necessarily growth. The growth we proclaim today does not involve everything or everybody. It is always exclusionary, not inclusive. In economic terms, it emphasizes things or services and targets a few people, a few targets, and building a money economy, not a people economy. Therefore, it is anti-people, anti-community. Success is not monetary. Money can be used to fund temporary development or to fund human adjustment to a higher level. Just celebrating money cannot be a success.

The Bible defines ultimate success. Biblical success does not depend on individual merits. It is embracing God's plan for your life. Success is to effectively put to use what God has invested in you (eternity, fruit of the Spirit, gifts of the Spirit, talents) to impact others. Transformation of our inner lives is God's goal for us. No amount of money can transform the heart of a person. God transforms and abundantly provides good physical gifts to His children (food, clothing, houses, etc.), and He loves to do it.

Every person is looking for success. In real life, overnight success does not exist. It takes patience and perseverance in order to succeed. you must have a purpose and a goal. Passion is created by purpose. Passion is finding something to live for and to die for. Passion takes you all the way to the finish line. The recommended passion should be void of selfish motives.

The challenges of life are real. The first place to look for the trouble causer is in your mirror. Examine yourself sincerely to know your strength and weaknesses. A true genius admits that he/she knows nothing, and craves for more knowledge. Be open to knowledge, whatever anguish of spirit it may cost, and be ready to fix it. "For the wise have always known that no one can make much of his life until self-searching has become a regular habit until he is able to admit and accept what he finds, and until he patiently and persistently tries to correct what is wrong." — Bill W.

It is important to know who you are and your value. Your identity is in Christ. This is a place of permanence in the Spirit. It is the spirit that quickens life (John 6:63). God created you as an original. Never substitute your identity or place your identity in something you can lose, place it firmly in Christ because you are one with Him in the Spirit forever. The price tag on the commodity determines its value. The cost of a thing is the amount of what is required to be exchanged for it. You are the most precious thing on the face of the earth because God valued you by His blood. In the economy of the world, some people say that value is more expensive than price because people spend money to purchase (buy) what they want more than the money they spend on it. It makes sense but the shocking truth regarding our redemption is that when God redeemed us He redeemed His lost image and nature in us. To turn to the Lord, who is Spirit, is to turn to the Spirit which is His, which dwelt in Him, and which He gives to us as our new nature. Therefore, the redeemer and the redeemed are of the same value.

The Bible projects that we are one body of Christ of which Christ is the head. The Bible clearly says that God is a personal God dealing with the individual member of the body on personal basis. That is why we have the personal Lord and Savior. "But God has put the body together, giving greater honor to the parts that lacked it, so that there should be no division in the body, but that its parts should have equal concern for each other." Your soul is desperately in search of the real you. Without finding it, life is essentially nothing but a mystery. We were created in God's image to manifest God's life. Such life is restored to us by Jesus and is explicitly revealed in His sacrificial selflessness love. Agape love is, therefore, more than emotional compatibility; it is spiritual and supernatural. It is the kind of love that puts God and neighbor above 'self', and can only be afforded by a regenerated soul. Our new nature is the nature of Christ. It is supernaturally revealed to us, and evidently manifested by the way we live, in particular how we relate to others. Your new nature is automatically attracted to the new nature in others. We are one body of Christ (church), and we are intuitively connected. The new nature makes us compatible and helps us to deal with incompatibility. Discover yourself by being other-centered. Your life cannot be lived in secrecy. Naturally, we have multiple gifts, talents and personalities to share with others. Your life cannot be separated from the mundane lives you are living.

You are separated from the rest of the world because you are the very dwelling place of God – You are the temple of God. just as God said, "I will dwell in them and walk among them; And I will be their God, and they shall be My people. Ezekiel (36:27). God refused to dwell in temples made by mankind but decided to dwell in the temple made by His own hands. "This is what the LORD says: "Heaven is My throne, and earth is My footstool. What kind of house will you build for Me? Or where will My place of repose be?" "Who is able to build him a house, seeing the heaven and heaven of heavens cannot contain him? Who am I then, that I should build him a house, save only to burn sacrifice before Him?" But who is able to build a temple for him, since the heavens, even the highest heavens, cannot contain him? Who then am I to build a temple for Him, except as a place to burn sacrifices before Him? (2 Chronicles 2:6). God needs no "house;" and we cannot build Him a house that could be in any way worthy of Him. We, moreover, are unworthy to build him any house, which is the real ground of the refusal. "Who is able to build him a house, seeing the heaven and heaven of heavens cannot contain him?" The Bible has the answer: "Now we have this treasure in jars of clay to show that this surpassingly great power is from God and not from us. God is the treasure in us." (2 Corinthians 4:7). The treasure in us is God, and the goodness out of us is of God. The excellence of the power which we exercise comes from God, and not from ourselves. The moment you become born again, God's Spirit (Holy Spirit) moves in to indwell your heart. "---do you not know that your body is a temple of the Holy Spirit who is in you, whom you have from God, and that you are not your own?" (1 Corinthians 6:19).

The gospel is the testimony or story of what God has done for those who were alienated from God on account of our sins, and God alienated from us because of His wrath against our sins. God saves and sends us out as vessels of reconciliation. He saves by occupying the heart of a repented sinner. The Holy Spirit turns the written Word of God into the truth of the heart. "Your word I have hidden in my heart, that I might not sin against You." (Psalm 119:11). Psalm 119 exalts the Word of the Lord like no other passage in Scripture. The Word is referred to in every verse and is referred to by many different names: the Law, commandments, testimonies, statutes, precepts, judgments, ordinance, Word, and way. The benefits of the Word are numerous. "Those who keep His testimonies … do no iniquity" (vv. 2, 3). His statutes prevent shame (v. 6), and sin (v. 11), and can be our song (v. 54). His testimonies bring delight (v. 24). His Word revives (v. 25), strengthens (v. 28), and cleanses (v. 9); brings salvation (v. 41) and mercy (v. 58); gives life (v. 50) and hope (v. 74); and keeps us from straying (v. 67). His commandments give understanding (v. 73). And that is only the beginning!

In Christ, we are fulfilled because we have everything we need spiritually. Therefore, in this world, losing for the sake of Christ is gaining. A Christian has no reason to despair. We are trekkers on an expedition built on faith and hope. We encounter trials in course of our cosmic journey but despair is not for us. Faith is looking beyond this world and beholding the coming glory of our destiny. We may lose everything this world has to offer but we retain our reason for living. The good news is that we are not indebted to this world. We are all debtors to our Savior's infinite grace—a debt we can never repay. In fact, He died for us because we couldn't pay our debt. At the cross, He said "It is finished" - It is paid in full. "The borrower is a slave to the lender." This world owes us nothing. In Jesus Christ, we are debt-free, and in Him, we find an antidote for emptiness.

The Christian life is a spiritual life of faith. Our faith has the person of Jesus Christ as an object. He is our provision and protection. We are partakers of His resurrected eternal life. We communicate with Him through His Word in order to increase our faith in Him. We are in spiritual warfare. Satan is the greatest adversary and challenge to your faith. He has allies of your corrupt nature and the corrupt world. No wonder the Bible says that "Whoever chooses to be a friend of the world renders himself an enemy of God" (James 4:4). Satan establishes strongholds in our minds to hold us captives. These are cages not made of iron bars but of thoughts. A stronghold is an area where we're stuck in bondage—any part of our lives in which Satan imprisons us. He does this by causing us to think a certain way—a way based on deception. We are called to take captive every thought that exalts itself against the knowledge of God. (2 Corinthians 10:5). *Faith is the shield that* extinguishes the flaming missiles of the evil one (Ephesians 6:16). It is the faith of patience and endurance, trusting in God's protection and submissive to His will, on which the darts of temptation, whether from fear, or from lust, or from doubt, fall harmless.

God allows Satan to tempt you in order to test you and to grow your faith. God allows the tests (trials of life) not to torment you but to prove that you won't fall to the schemes of the adversary. Satan is our accuser —he accuses us day and night before our God. (Revelation 12:10). God counters Satan's accusations by allowing him to tests our loyalty to God. "Then the LORD said to Satan, "Have you considered My servant Job? For there is no one on earth like him, a man who is blameless and upright, who fears God and shuns evil." (Job 1:8). Every believer should strive to be that perfect and upright man, the one whom God brags about as that fears God, and eschews evil.

Wisdom begins with knowing God intimately through Jesus Christ. There is a massive ignorance of God among people of all classes; elites and illiterates. Ignoring ignorance is ignoring sin, and the repercussion of ignoring sin goes beyond this life. See yourself as God sees you. The problem with people is to do as they feel reasonable to do. You hear them say "This is what I believe". Pause and ask yourself "What does God want me to believe?" God has a plan for you. Embrace God's time of intervention and step into the redemptive plan for your life!

God created you and even gave you the power to accept Him or to reject Him; to serve Him or not to serve Him. God did not create us as Robots that can do His will whenever He wills. Robots have to do what they're told to do. God could have made us like robots where we had to always do what He says. But God created us with "free will". We all get to make choices. "Free-will" means being able to make choices. God wanted to have a meaningful relationship with us whereby we choose to have affection for Him and fellowship with Him. When we choose not to obey God, that is called sin. The Bible testifies to the need to acquire freedom because no one actually clearly sees the need to obey God unless they are freed from the bondage of sin. All of the choices and ways of the unredeemed person are crooked. It is after repenting and accepting Jesus

Christ as their Lord and Savior that the choice to obey or disobey God is made clear to them. People possess natural freedom but their "voluntary choices" serve 'sin' until they acquire freedom from "sin's dominion." God created you for His purposes. God has before the foundation of the world, by sheer grace, according to the free good pleasure of his will, God chose us in Christ to salvation. (Ephesians 1:4). Walk worthily your calling. Know the grace in truth.

God cares for the big and little things in your life. He cares for your salvation and the day-to-day affairs of your life. God saves you and uses you to draw others to Him. Every believer is called to serve. The moment God calls you in the ministry, He sees you in what you are becoming as opposed to what you are. Your good works are evidence and reward of your salvation. Put your priorities right. Physical, and financial prosperity is not salvation but fruits and benefits of salvation. "Happiness is not a goal...it's a by-product of a life well-lived." Serve God joyfully. "A new song for a new day rises up in me every time I think about what He did for me. Ecstatic praise pours out of my mouth until everyone hears about the goodness of God – How God has set me free. Many will see hear His praises; they'll stand in awe of God and fall in love with Him! (Psalms 40:3). I'll boldly declare who He is and what He has done in my life all of the day of my life."

Self-esteem, as defined by the world is your overall sense of personal value and self-worth or confidence in one's own worth or abilities; self-respect. Basically, according to psychology, self-esteem is a positive or negative orientation toward oneself; an overall evaluation of one's worth or value. Self-esteem is to have a high opinion of yourself. This kind of self-esteem can lead a person to feel independent and prideful and to indulge in self-worship, which dulls their desire for God. In one sense, low self-esteem is the opposite of pride. Some people have low self-esteem because they want people to feel sorry for them, to pay attention to them, to comfort them. Low self-esteem can be a declaration of "look at me" just as much as pride. It simply takes a different route to get to the same destination, that is, self-absorption, self-obsession, and selfishness. Instead, we are supposed to be selfless, to die to self, and to deflect any attention given to us to the great God who created and sustains us. James 4:6 tells us that "God opposes the proud but gives grace to the humble."

Paul says we are to esteem others as better than ourselves (Philippians 2:3). This does not mean that Christians should have low self-esteem. It only means that we should love as Christ loved us. Our sense of being a good person should not depend on what we do, but rather on who we are in Christ. According to the biblical interpretation, self-esteem begins with dying to self. God does not instruct us to pull ourselves up by our bootstraps. The reason is that we lack such capability. In fact, if you had the capability to pull yourself out of your mess, you would have done it long ago. God asks you to surrender to Him so that He can pull you out of your predicaments. Jesus looked at people who had broken hearts, and out of compassion, He cried out that "Come to Me, all those toiling and being burdened, and I will give you rest." (Matthew 11:28). It is an open invitation to all who need Him, and an unconditioned promise of welcome. We come to Him by surrendering to Him. He gives us rest by coming to dwell (tabernacle) in us by His Spirit. Christ in us is the hope of all glory (Colossians 1:27). Christ's presence in us, and His truth are full of "glorious riches." Our once dead, darkened spirits are made alive. Christ is in our hearts, and we know that there is life beyond this earthly existence—a life that will be glorious beyond all imagination. That is our blessed hope in which we take pride.

Biblical self-esteem is not to be what you want to be but to be what God wants you to be. Biblical self-esteem is when God reveals who we are, where we are, and where He wants us to be. We are spiritual beings made in the very nature of God for His purposes. Our citizenship is in heaven but we are temporarily dwelling in a sick world. "For our citizenship exists in the heavens, from whence also we are awaiting a Savior, the Lord Jesus Christ, who, by the power that enables Him to subject all things to Himself, will transform our lowly bodies to be like His glorious body" (Philippians 3:20-21).

Now I am going to discuss another predicament called self-entitlement. We need each other. But avoid a self-entitlement mentality. The entitlement mentality is defined as a sense of deservingness or being owed a favor when little or nothing has been done to deserve special treatment. It's the "you owe me" attitude. Such people think that other people have to do things for them regardless. It's not known exactly how this mentality develops. It may be due to social factors like the way people were brought up by their parents; The environment they grew up in; The policies of the government and etc. People with a sense of entitlement act autonomously – They think the rules don't apply to them. They always think they deserve better treatment than they have already received.

The spiritual solution to self-esteem and the self-entitlement mentality is to crucify the old nature or the old you. Dying to self is one of the major themes taught in the Bible. The Bible teaches us to die to ourselves. Simply put, it means we must "deny" ourselves – our sinful, worldly, and fleshly desires, thoughts, lusts, and longings (see Colossians 3:5-10). It's a very strong command, one that came from the very mouth of the Lord Jesus Christ: "Then Jesus said to His disciples, "If anyone will come after Me, let him deny himself, and take up his cross, and follow Me. For whoever would save his life will lose it, and whoever loses his life for My sake will find it." (Matthew 16:24-25). In the fallen world we dwell in, the pronouns 'I', "Me" & "Myself" are central to humanity. But in the kingdom of heaven where "self" is crucified, loving God and neighbor is paramount or is the priority. It is a bitter pill to swallow but the only one you need in order to get better.

Jesus reconciles us to God. He restores peace first with God, then peace within you and your neighbor. Given the fact, it is important that you really treasure yourself, love yourself, and have a sense of self-worth. It all begins with God transforming you and revealing to you the real you. The peace of mind begins when we know that we belong to God, and acknowledge that regardless of the situation, He is in charge and in control of everything going on around us. Life is already tough and it is getting tougher. God shows us that He is in control by putting us in a situation that we cannot control to show us that He is in control. It is better to go through hardship and grow than to take an easy path without the possibility of growth. The safest place to be is in the storm when Jesus is in it.

It is important to be reminded that God created you for His own purposes as opposed to your own purposes. You were planned for God's own pleasure (Ephesians 2:1-10). Acknowledging this fact will revolutionize your thinking. Mankind was created in the perfect image of God. But we are born after the corrupted image of Adam. We can find the original perfect image that we lost in Adam in Christ. I love this analogy: "When

God wanted to create fish, He spoke to the sea. When God wanted to create trees, He spoke to the earth. But when God wanted to create man, He turned to Himself. Thus God said: "Let us make man in our own image and likeness". Note: If you catch a fish out of the water, it will die; and when you remove a tree from the ground, it also dies. Similarly, when man disconnects from God, he dies. God is our natural environment. We were created to live in HIS presence. We must be connected with Him because only with Him does life exist. Let's stay in touch with God. Let us remember that water without fish is still water, but fish without water is nothing. The soil without the tree is still soil, but the tree without soil is nothing. God without man is still God, but man without God is nothing."

We have many wants but Jesus is everything we need. The name Jesus means "Jehovah the Savior" and "the salvation of Jehovah"(Matthew 1:21). He is the great I am; as the I AM, Christ is everything to us for our experience and enjoyment, for His being, I AM means - "I am whatever you need". He is all-sufficient to us. But we cannot discover His sufficiency unless we discover our emptiness. The closer we draw to Jesus the more we see the magnitude of our nothingness.

We were created to serve God and our neighbors. We serve God in everything we do. This is the essence of our daily worshiping. We worship God by serving others in the biblical recommended ways. We serve God by allowing His perfect works to be manifested in and through us. It means we cannot serve God unless we surrender to Him. The Christian life is a lifestyle of dependence on God. That is when the radiance of His glory shines through us. The Bible says that He reigns in us, and we shall reign with Him. "If we endure, we will also reign with Him; if we deny Him, He will also deny us" (2 Timothy 2:12). While to the faithful and the believer He will grant to sit down with Him on His throne, the faithless and unbeliever will have no share in the glories of the life to come. Jesus promised that "And behold, I am coming quickly, and My reward is with Me, to give to everyone according to his work." (Revelation 12:22). His reward upon His return is to make those who have His imputed righteousness to be righteous forever and ever. And those who have rejected His righteousness to be wicked forever and ever. It means that the believers who have the deposits of eternity within themselves move to eternity with eternity.

True fulfillment does not come from tangible material gain or any physical relationship with other people. It isn't what you have or who you are or where you are or what you are doing that brings true joy. It is what you believe in. True fulfillment begins with your relationship with Jesus Christ. After that, the Bible says that "Rejoice always, pray without ceasing, give thanks in all circumstances; for this is the will of God in Christ Jesus for you." (1 Thessalonians 5:16-18). This verse appeals to our mental attitude toward conduct in life and relationships. The term "for this is the will of God in Christ Jesus for you" is in reference to praying, praising, and rejoicing in the Lord. You don't know the will of God for your life? This is it.

We live in a consumer & materialistic culture whereby success is measured by what you have, where you live, what you drive, and the size of your bank account and etc. I am not against having material things. I am against your heart being consumed by material gains. We should pray and work hard to get the wanted material things but we should not manipulate or look for shortcuts to become rich. A little bit of wealth earned by a fraudulent scheme will fault all of your resources including the clean-hard-earned money. Remember that just a little bit of salt will spoil the entire pot of milk. When you can't have what you want, start wanting what you have instead of manipulating others to get what you don't have. The more principle-centered and faithful you become, the more unselfish you will be, and hence, caring for the good fortune of other people as you care for yourself.

The Bible warns that "He that hastes to be rich hath an evil eye, and considers not that poverty shall come upon him."(Proverbs 28:22). It is a warning to pursue virtue before you pursue wealth. Paul warned that "But if we have food and clothing, we will be content with these. Those who want to be rich by hook or crook, however, fall into temptation and become ensnared by many foolish and harmful desires that plunge them into ruin and destruction. For the love of money is the root of all kinds of evil. By craving it, some have wandered away from the faith and pierced themselves with many sorrows." (1 Timothy 6:8-10). The lust for riches leads to destruction and perdition. "Destruction" refers rather to wreck and ruin of the body, whilst "perdition" belongs rather to that more awful ruin of the eternal soul.

Your labor is the industry of your well-being and a reflection of your image. The harder you work, the better the impression you set on the people around you. A good impression should have an influence on you and should have an impact on others. We work hard to have nice things, however, real blessings come to us by giving. We should be like a river that receives water and flows to water other gardens. The water in the river that does not flow stinks. Excessive accumulation of stuff can become a vehicle of our destruction instead of a blessing. The Bible says that "One person gives freely, yet gains even more; another withholds unduly, but comes to poverty" (Proverbs 11:24). This scripture applies to the material gains and the spiritual gifts consecutively. He that generously uses the spiritual gifts, and disperses and dispenses the word of God, and spreads the truths of the Gospel, and freely and fully preaches them, increases himself in spiritual knowledge and understanding. Faith increases in the abundance of knowledge. "It is more blessed to give than to receive" (Acts 20:35). Thus liberality, by God's blessing, secures increase, while penuriousness, instead of expected gain, procures poverty. The spirit of deception searches for abundance life in the accumulated abundance stuff. Ironically, the same things we yearn for are the same things that the miserable people of the world possess in excess, and they are not fulfilled! 'Abundance life' does not come from the things we do or possess but from the things we let God do for us.

Unfortunately, worldliness has become the order of the day!, The get-rich-quick spirit is holding sway among believers who have forgotten Paul's counsel to be content with what they have (1 Timothy 6:6-11). "The end justifies the means" philosophy that is growing in the Church today is contrary to the virtue of the Christian discipline. The Word of God says everyone shall give account for his or her actions (Romans 14:12).

Contentment begins by acknowledging that Jesus Christ is all you need. When you have Jesus Christ, your prayers should be dominated by thanksgiving for what He has already done instead of a list of things that you want to be done. Contentment is the key to happiness and is the antidote to greed, stress, and depression. "Be thankful for what you have; you'll end up having more. If you concentrate on what you don't have, you will never, ever have enough." Have confidence that the blessings of God will follow you. You don't have to force them to come your way. "Anything that comes your way by force was not meant for you. Everything that locates you on its own was yours and will be yours forever."

To live successful lives, we must have a firm belief. In the economy of the world, success is defined by material gains. And it is challenging to our faith. Don't go outside of obeying God to get something because you will have to stay outside God to keep it. Materialism is the recipe for unrestrained greed. Unrestrained greed in an individual can lead to callousness, arrogance, and even megalomania. A person dominated by greed will often ignore the harm their actions can cause others. A simple life of contentment and sharing will clothe us with perpetual happiness, good health, and long life.

I want to warn you that contentment does not mean settling for less than what God called you to have or to do. The Israelites were poised to enter Canaan. Before they crossed the Jordan River and moved west, God spoke to Joshua some words of encouragement. Included was a promise of even more land later (Joshua 1:4). For the time being, though, the land they would inherit would be west of the Jordan (Joshua 1:2). Yet, even before the Israelites entered the Promised Land, the tribes of Reuben, Gad, and the half-tribe of Manasseh had already staked out their claim—they chose to settle east of the Jordan. Never settle for less than what God has commissioned you to possess spiritually and materially. Morality is desiring to have the exact measure that God wants you to have in whatever you do. Lust is desiring to have in excess of what God commissioned you to have. Lust is a psychological force producing an intense desire for an object, or circumstance while already having a significant amount of the desired object.

Jesus is life. Jesus does not just give you life, He wants to be part of every second of every day of your life. This gives you a reason to be confident in spite of the circumstances. Jesus used the figure of speech of 'moving the mountain' in order to describe the valid faith. "Truly I tell you that if anyone says to this mountain, 'Be lifted up and thrown into the sea,' and has no doubt in his heart but believes that it will happen, it will be done for him." (Mark 11:13). The promise is specific rather than general in its form, in such a way that the only one who can move the mountain is the One that made the mountain. You can put your trust (faith) in Him to move your mountains.

"There are going to be painful moments in your life that will change your entire world in a matter of minutes. These moments will change you. Let them make you stronger, smarter, kinder. But do not go and become someone you are not. Cry. Scream if you have to. Then straighten out that crown and keep it moving. At the end of the day, everything will be alright because God seated on the highest throne is ever in control." Never give up because of hardship. Remember that the toughest journey to travel is the one heading to hell where there is torment forever and ever. And you are not taking that direction because of the finished works of Jesus Christ at the cross. The cross became God's pulpit of love for you. You have a destiny and a future in the presence of God forever and ever.

How you respond to adversity speaks volumes about your character. The Times of London magazine reported the results of the survey regarding how people responded to quarantine life during the global epidemic catastrophe. The survey was carried out on 2000 British adults. The study assessed the reaction of the people tying it to the personal traits they were associated with. They divided people into five categories: Firstly – the largest group of people groups are pragmatic realists, secondly – nervous dependents, thirdly – resentful pessimists, fourthly – diluted optimists, fifthly – skeptical trouble makers. Regardless of the validity of the research, we (Christians) aren't called to introduce people to a philosophy that challenges us, but to a person (Jesus Christ) who changes us.

We choose to respond in certain ways but our choice is not absolute. The choices we make are often influenced by some internal and external factors. I mean internal factors like personalities and what we believe in. External factors like the circumstances surrounding us. For example, when people walk into my church, they choose where they want to seat. Sometimes I see them changing places. Their choice of places is not independent. There are various reasons why they choose to sit where they sit. Some go for front seats in order to see well. Some want to sit next to their families or friends. Somebody might choose to sit next to the door in anticipation to walk out of the church early before the church ends so that he doesn't cause a commotion. The list goes on and on..... You see, our choices are not independent of other influences.

Dr. Alistair Begg says that when he is teaching his congregation, people respond differently. Part of the audience is either listening and questioning, or listening and complaining, or listening and thinking or impatiently looking at their watches ready to walk out. Each sector has a motivation that influences the behavior. For example, the impatient people in the church are typical of our impatient culture. "We live in a fast-food culture, in which we are led to believe that we need to have everything now; it is a culture that causes people to lose a sense of a future worth waiting for." The reality is that much of the world's moral compass is broken. Life should be a gift but has quickly become an unsolvable mystery. And the world is just a mega-prison with so many prisoners struggling to be free. Indeed, life without Christ is like a poem without a rhyme.

The culture is utterly corrupt. Yet we embrace it with both hands and bow down to societal norms. We do things just because that is how they have been done without questioning their validity. We grow up into certain traditions and we naturally yield to them even when they are oppressive. Sometimes such traditions provide temporary solutions to our problems, and we end up embracing them for our comfort. Also, we do it in order to impress others or avoid pressure for the people around us. We accommodate the devastating traditions of life and shrink back to the bully of culture with dire consequences. "Everything about Jesus Christ was counterculture." God calls us to come out of all ungodliness. "See to it that no one takes you captive by philosophy and empty deceit, according to human tradition, according to the elemental spirits of the world, and not according to Christ" (Colossians 2:8)

God has called us to look and act differently. We are called to be kingdom-minded regardless of the circumstances. The children of God have a moral compass that is just unshakable, they can have ethics that run to the core. "God is building a stronghold of love that is void of fear in our lives – large, solid, and immovable. He is deconstructing puny structures of our human failings, spawn-built lies, witchcraft, demon-induced perversity, and faulty carnal thinking." There is nothing stable in the world. Thank God that we are not permanent residents of this world; we are in this world but not of this world. Whereas there is panic in this world, there is no need to panic because in heaven there is no panic.

Naturally, we are pragmatists. We don't stick to any ideology. We try an idea and when we error, we toss it out and try another one. If it works, fine, we continue with it. We are not enamored with any ideology unless it serves our interests. The Bible instructs differently. "Trust in the LORD with all your heart, and lean not on your own understanding" (Proverbs 3:5). The admonition does not mean that we are not to use our own understanding, and employ legitimate means in the pursuit of our ends; but that, when we use it, we are to depend upon God and His directing and overruling providence. The word 'trust' implies confidence. The Holy Spirit, through the scriptures, indicates the direction that we are supposed to take with confidence. Faith demands absolute trust in what God can do in us and through us. Faith has no coincidences and probabilities but absolute certainty. That is why God is pleased by our faith only (Hebrews 11:6).

Faith involves embracing the beauty and strength of the grace to work in you and for you. "Our worst days are never so bad that you are beyond the reach of God's grace. And your best days are never so good that you are beyond the need of God's grace." Grace allows God to work directly through us. Those of you who believe in the gifts of the Holy Spirit also called the gifts of the grace, read them in 1 Corinthians chapter 12, 13 & 14. Chapter 12 has the gifts of the Holy Spirit. Chapter 13 has the spirit of the gifts of the Holy Spirit, which is love. Chapter 14 has the governance and benefits of the gifts of the Holy Spirit. (Regarding the gifts of the Holy Spirit, please read my book called "Growing in the Spirit").

Faith allows us to operate in the spiritual dimension. Faith leaves no room for unbelief. The opposite of faith is not doubt but unbelief. Doubt might have some good intention of believing. For example, at the end of the day, when Thomas (the greatest doubter) saw the scars of Jesus, he believed, and he gave to us the model of our confession when we believe: "My Lord and my God!" (John 20:27-28). But unbelief is utterly refusing to believe.

We naturally make emotional choices because we are emotional animals. Our enemy targets our emotions because they are corrupted. "When the woman saw that the fruit of the tree was good for food and pleasing to the eye, and also desirable for gaining wisdom, she took some and ate it. She also gave some to her husband, who was with her, and he ate it". (Genesis 3:6). It wasn't the evil side of the tree of the knowledge of good and evil that Eva was attracted to but the good side of the tree. We are vulnerable because sin polluted our emotions. Learning to recognize the signs of damaged emotions allows you to identify problems sooner and alter the behaviors that perpetuate them. On the contrary, making choices out of emotions leads to deception. Most times the things appealing to our emotions are not necessarily good as they appear to be. Everything which glitters like gold is not necessarily precious. There are utterly valueless things that look like gold and taking them at their face value is unwise. Goodness and perfection do not go with gaudiness.

As I said, no one is exempted from emotions. Everyone struggles at some point in their lives. Don't let this struggle define you. Never react emotionally. You can manage your emotions by pausing in a simple prayer before reacting. This is true in particular when you feel annoyed — or maybe downright angry, when you feel disappointed, when you feel pressured or stressed about the circumstances. Pause or withdraw and say a simple prayer. Postpone your reaction for the right moment after you calm down. "You will continue to suffer if you have an emotional reaction to everything said to you. True power is sitting back and observing things with logic. True power is restraint. If words control you that means everyone else can control you. Breathe and allow things to pass."

A born-again person is supposed to have the renewed minds of Christ. A mind that resists negativity to enter the soul through what they see and hear. A mind that trains the tongue to confess positive words of faith. The renewed mind has biblical thinking because it feeds from the Bible – It is an ongoing process or lifestyle. "Be careful about what you think and what you say during your times of trial and tribulation. The attitude you have while in the wilderness determines how long you stay there."

It is unfortunate that many believers are now living lives of deadly compromise. Integrity is now considered to be old school. God calls us to obey Him absolutely rather than selectively. Partial obedience is basically disobedience. We can't pick and choose what we ourselves will keep or get rid of, or do & not do. If the Bible says it, just do it. If God is tagging your heart to do something, you must obey.

The Bible says "Whatsoever things are good, pure, perfect and of good report, think on these things." (Philippians 4:8). "Pure" is righteous in essence, in the thought, which cannot be thwarted by the traditions of men. Do not fall into the snare of filling your thoughts or your mind with the negativity and the darkness of the world. Guard your heart with the truth, by doing so, you are ensuring God's guidance, provision, and protection.

True believers are single-minded as opposed to double-minded. Commitment eradicates doubt. A consecrated Christian rests absolutely in Christ. They don't have one foot in the kingdom of glory, and the other foot in the corruption of the world. They don't publicly embrace the gospel and then secretly implements the vices of life like fornication, witchcraft, and other demonic activities.

I want to say that a double-minded person is the most miserable person; he is even more miserable than a nonbeliever. The reason is that he misses enjoying the fullness of what the world could offer, and at the same time, he misses the benevolences (benefits) of heaven on earth. The Bible says that "........he who doubts is like a wave of the sea, blown and tossed by the wind. That man should not expect to receive anything from the Lord. He is a double-minded man, unstable in all his ways." (James 1:6-8). A double-minded person is like a wave of the sea, blown and tossed by the wind because neither Jesus nor Satan trusts him or her. At least Jesus gives us chances to repent but Satan would rather see a double-minded person die before they make up their minds to commit their lives to Jesus Christ because only then do they belong to him permanently in hell. Isn't it is scaring!

Have you ever wondered why a backslider is more proud of his depravity than a person that has never been born again? "And when people escape from the wickedness of the world by knowing our Lord and Savior Jesus Christ and then get tangled up and enslaved by sin again, they are worse off than before. It would be better if they had never known the way to righteousness than to know it and then reject the command they were given to live a holy life. They prove the truth of this proverb: "A dog returns to its vomit" (Proverbs 26:11). And another says, "A washed pig returns to the mud" (2 Peter 2:8-22). This scripture is really speaking to you right now: "For if we sin willfully after that we have received the knowledge of the truth, there remains no more sacrifice for sins" (Heb 10:26-27). The moment you reject the grace you willfully volunteer to be a candidate for the coming judgment and fiery indignation, which shall devour the adversaries of God. God does not send you to hell; you choose to go there by rejecting God's grace.

Those who perpetually live a carnal, sensual life, must expect no other fruit from such a course than misery and ruin: "For to be carnally minded is death, but to be spiritually minded is life and peace" (Romans 8:6-11). It is self-deception to do things endeavored to satisfy your lustful minds, at the expense of the divine will, hoping that God understands your weaknesses. Certainly, God forgives all the times when we repent but at times He does not undo the done things. He lets things play out (naturally evolve) or happen the way we planned them by our poor judgments and decisions so that we learn from our mistakes. Sometimes you must experience a low point in life in order to learn a lesson you wouldn't have learned any other way. "Never let an old flame burn you twice".

The Bible says that "Now, therefore, fear the LORD and serve Him in sincerity and truth; cast aside the gods your fathers served beyond the Euphrates and in Egypt, and serve the LORD. But if it is unpleasing in your sight to serve the LORD, then choose for yourselves this day whom you will serve, whether the gods your fathers served beyond the Euphrates, or the gods of the Amorites in whose land you are living. As for me and my house, we will serve the LORD!" (Joshua 24:14-15). Stay on the course, don't sway to the left or to the right. "Blessed is the man who remains steadfast under trial, for when he has stood the test he will receive the crown of life, which God has promised to those who love him." (James 1:12). This wording closely matches Jesus' statement in Matthew 24:13 where we are told that only those who endure to the end will be saved. This is not to say that in the final analysis salvation rests on our ability. The Bible clearly shows that we cannot save ourselves and that only the sovereign electing and preserving grace of God will bring us into His presence (Psalm 69:13-15; Romans 8:29-30; Philippians 1:6). Nevertheless, the presence of God's electing grace in our lives is demonstrated by the fact that we cling to Him even in times of our trials. We know that we have true faith only as we work out our salvation in fear and trembling, resting our hope of salvation on Christ alone (Philippians 2:12-13). True believing is to make your belief real in your life. Faith is a gift from God. Faith by itself is not a work but faith cannot stand alone. Faith without works is dead (James 2:17). Faith makes the already sanctioned, existing things by God, which are invisible to be visible (to manifest). The works of faith do not make nonexistent things exist. Faith makes the invisible character of

Christ visible in our lives. Our invisible faith should be manifested by the visible love for God and neighbor. It means that everything we do is empty without the works of love as Christ teaches us in the Word. I mean loving God and loving neighbor as projected in the Gospels.

Jesus gave to us only one commandment of love: "A new commandment I give unto you, That you love one another; as I have loved you, that you also love one another." (John 13:34). "Love others as I have loved you." Jesus loved us unconditionally regardless of our flaws. He calls us to love others unconditionally. Jesus loved us all the way to the cross. We must love others all the way – sacrificially. We are called to love even when we don't fully understand why we love. Love has called your name so that you might live the life of Christ for others. "We do not live for ourselves only, and we do not die for ourselves only. If we live, it is for the Lord that we live, and if we die, it is for the Lord that we die. So whether we live or die, we belong to the Lord." (Romans 14:7-8).

We are called to love. And we should love up to the standard of the One that called us to love. God wants to fellowship with His people. You can't be pro-God and anti-people at the same time. The word Antichrist means against or instead of Christ. The Bible says that the spirit of the Antichrist is already alive and active in the church. Since Christ is pro-people, the spirit of Antichrist is anti-people. The Spirit of Christ attracts people to you whereas the spirit of Antichrist repels people away from you. The Bible instructs us to treat every person around us as a neighbor – Love the neighbor as you love yourselves. In the economy of God, caring for yourself is equally important as caring for your neighbor. God's plan is that you learn to love yourself by loving others. In the real world where we dwell, some people are irritating such that it is tough to love them all as we are supposed to. Learn how to accommodate all people in their weaknesses without compromising on your basic values. "The way you alchemize a soulless world into a sacred world is by treating everyone as if they are sacred until the sacred in them remembers."

The neighbor is everyone you meet. Show them that you care. Caring makes us better people & makes the world a better place. Let's take time to care! Never believe that a few caring people can't change the world. Don't look around to see how many people approve of what you are doing. Jesus is the majority you need to have an impact on the world. The shocking truth is that the minority plus Jesus becomes the majority. Jesus is the undisputed world-changer.

To love others is to serve others. In the eyes of God, every believer is a leader in some sense to help other people to go where God intended them to go and to be what God intended them to be. God wants to make Himself real to you by revealing Himself to you so that He may touch others through you. It will change your attitude to see people the way God sees them. I mean seeing the people in the eyes of Jesus. He did everything including saving the lost, raising the dead, delivering the oppressed, healing the sick, feeding the hungry, and etc, out of compassion. "If you see the world and yourself through a lens smudged by negativity then you'll find much misery.......If you want to see a better world, change the lens through which you see it and do the work to make it better......If we could see through the lens of eternity, we'd weep with joy."

We embrace peace by loving others according to God's way. The evidence of the transformed heart is ever shedding light and comfort and peace. The peace that Jesus gives begins in the heart and the mind. The peace of the mind which the world cannot give is acquired when the minds are totally under the control of God or subdued by the minds of Christ through the Word. We need to be armed with the peace of God in our spiritual warfare against Satan. Ironically, this is the only war where peace is used as a conventional weapon. No wonder the most important thing Satan wants to steal from you is peace. Whenever you are confronted with the uncertainty of the world, trust in the God that you know, and who knows you well. "God provides for every dark cloud, an abiding joy and for every uncertainty, a calm assurance." ~ Liesel Kippen

Satan has access to you through the people around you. They might be your family members, relatives, or closest friend. Satan is going to use their mouths or actions to discourage you and to offend you. Always know that the people around you are not your enemies but Satan is. The Bible says that "For our struggle is not against flesh and blood, but against the rulers, against the authorities, against the powers of this world's darkness, and against the spiritual forces of evil in the heavenly realms." (Ephesians 6:12). In our spiritual warfare, we are fighting from victory to victory whereby there is no option of losing. But if you are fighting people you are fighting the wrong enemy, and you will never win because there will be always a person next to you. 'Our conflict is not with men, here denoted by "flesh and blood," which is usually a symbol of weakness, therefore denoting that our opponents are not weak mortals, but powers of a far more formidable order – against the principalities, against the powers in high places.' The Bible says in the epistles that Jesus declared His victory above all rule and dominion, and He is seated in the highest places, far above all principalities and powers. And we are seated there with Him.

Our peace is not the absence of conflicts but the presence of Christ. Christ neutralizes the tense situation brought about by Satan to divide, steal and kill. Jesus redeems us by His blood. He sanctifies us by His Word. The Bible says concerning the Church "…...to sanctify her, cleansing her by the washing with water through the word" (Ephesians 5:26). The cleaning up is of God by the Spirit of God through the Word of God but God respects your free will. Unless redeemed, the fallen man's will is programmed to choose temporary pleasure. A redeemed person chooses temporary painful measures in order to experience lasting peace. Remember that there can't be sacrificing without pain. Whenever a sacrifice was presented at the brazen, or bronze altar of the tabernacle in the wilderness, a place where the ancient Israelites sacrificed animals to atone for their sins, there was a knife, blood, and fire – All symbolic of pain. But the bronze laver, also called the "bronze basin" and the "laver of brass" stood between the temple and the altar, and it held water for washing, symbolic of the Word or promises of God that wipes away the mess or the pain resulting in the everlasting joy of the Lord.

Our sacrifices to God are our burden placed at the feet of Jesus. God loves us so much that He wants us to do exactly that. He sacrificed His Son so that we could live in freedom from sin. Jesus is our ultimate burden bearer. Only Jesus could bear the burden of our sin. He took the weight for our sin at Calvary. He absorbed in His body the sting of death that was reserved for us. He sacrificed His life for my life in Him. Beloved we are saved by His amazing grace. God's face was hidden from Christ when He carried our sins on Himself at the cross so that God's face is not hidden from us. God saw in Christ our brokenheartedness and teardrops. Therefore, cast your burdens on Him, and He shall sustain you (Psalms 55:22).

Your willingness to unlearn unhealthy cycles now is helping you to build a healthy relationship with God. Healing is a necessary moment in your process of overcoming. Use the scriptures to talk to yourself. Own the scripture by inserting your name in it. Your personalized scripture – Replacing personal pronouns like "I" and "my" with your name instead, it deeply personalizes the Word of God for you! Also, you can insert your spouse's name or the names of other people whom you are interceding for into relevant scriptures. Experience familiar Scriptures come alive again as your name is personalized into the text, e.g., God's provision / Psalm 23:1, "The Lord is Jennifer's shepherd. Jenifer should not want...". Fear/2 Timothy 1:7, For God, has not given Jennifer a spirit of fear, but of power and of love and of sound mind. Healing/Malachi 4:2, But for Lopez who reveres my name, the sun of righteousness will rise with healing in its wings. Lopez shall go out leaping like a calf from the stall. Discouragement/Psalm 90:14, Satisfy Jennifer in the morning with your steadfast love, that she may rejoice and be glad all her days. etc.

Talk to yourself in the scriptures and pray the scriptures out loud back to God. Write the Bible verses with names on a note-card, sticky note, in a journal, or type out and save where you will see them. It serves as a reminder to pray and also builds our faith. It worked for me, and it will work for you!

I want to say that our greatest security is our testimony. Satan wants you to be ashamed of your testimony because he knows if it is shared, it'll set the captives free. As long as you are born again you have the testimony regarding how God saved you. You have a history with God. History is His story of your deliverance. In the past, there are those who claimed to have had the Holy Ghost baptism but they did not have the Spirit without measure. The testimony of Jesus is the baptism of the Holy Spirit without measure (John 3:34). Jesus came with the Spirit without measure, and He gives the Spirit without measure. Look at the power of God that raised Jesus from death. The same power is available to transform you. Remind yourself over and over again about the great miracles that Jesus did in your life before. He did it before, He can do it again. It may be challenging to deal with your circumstances and failures but know that God knows everything about you. He will give you the strength and favor you need to overcome. Be thankful for your struggles, for without them, you wouldn't have stumbled across your strength in order to become the best possible version of you. You are like a diamond in the rough – The phrase is a metaphor clearly referring to the original unpolished state of diamond gemstones, especially those that have the potential to become high-quality jewels. There will be challenges, resistance, and above all pressure! These experiences enable us to grow, develop resilience & enhance our character, and ability to endure in order to be the vessels of honor that God intended us to be. God calls us not just to believe in Him but to trust Him. "He is looking for relationship with those who dare to trust him against all other odds."

Good memories can be inspiring but bad memories can be annihilating. Somebody made the following statement regarding the impact of memories: "While walking down the memory lane, we may discover in the remains of our early days, surprising little details that have been eclipsed under the mantle of forgetfulness or inattention. Those loose shreds in our remembrance can highlight the importance of the fundamentals that steer our daily lives. But they may also entice us to crack the particular value that we impart to trivial matters or quirky actions. Then, we are capable of discerning the uprightness and the truth behind the appearances."

Some may say, now wait a minute, God may be able to change the future, but no one can change the past, because what is done is done, the dye is cast and it cannot be changed. But we are talking about God, our great and mighty God, we must realize that the Bible says in Luke 1:37, "For nothing is impossible for God." He can heal our bodies, our minds and even change the events of our life, for nothing is impossible for Him. There are so many places in the Bible where God actually changed the past. Consider all those whom He raised from the dead, the most famous and well-known was Jesus Christ Himself, in the glorious resurrection. Jesus says "Behold, I make all things new." (Revelation 21:5). The change brought about by Jesus is genuine because it begins from inside to outside. Jesus does not just give you a makeover, He replaces the old relationship with the new relationship, the old life with the new life, and the old desires with the new desires. The characteristic of a new creature is that the old and the past are gone forever and ever. (Revelation 21:1-8). Jesus is saying to you "Behold, I am making everything new." Everything new without an iota of embarrassment to you – No shame; No guilt. It all begins now, in the present time with you.

Again, it is biblical to believe in yourself if you acknowledge that yourself is the new nature (life of Christ) in you. "Definitely, some will doubt you, but don't doubt yourself. Surely, some will hate your mission, but don't hate your vision. Truly, some will envy your vision, but don't change your vision. Surely, some will mock at your direction, but don't neglect your focus. Surely, you shall meet obstacles, but learn to overcome all obstacles with wit-----There is no great journey without issues, but learn to overcome all issues, and get to the end of the journey with distinctive footprints and a good sense of fulfillment. You were born for a purpose! Live it; achieve it! God is waiting for you at the finishing line; get there with a pleasant story for a glory!". You are destined to win. You are more than a conqueror because Jesus conquered on your behalf.

The Christian life is when the Spirit of God creates a new life in a believer. God is going to make us spiritually and morally new and glorious. The greatest frustration of this age is that we still sin. We don't aim at sinning but it happens. I believe Romans 7 describes this painful truth. For example verses 23–24: "I delight in the law of God in my inmost self, but I see in my members another law at war with the law of my mind." Elsewhere, Paul said "We know that the law is spiritual; but I am nonspiritual, sold as a slave to sin. I do not understand what I do. For what I want to do, I do not do. But what I hate, I do. And if I do what I do not want to do, I admit that the law is good" (Romans 7:14-16). This war is the most frustrating thing about living in this age—at least it is for the children of God. We want to be holy and we fall short of the holiness we long for. We want to love and we say hurtful things. We want to worship and we feel cold. We want to walk in peace and we feel anxiety. We want to be pure in thought and impurity bombards our minds. We need to be reminded that sanctification is a process of renewing our minds. There is progressive redemption as the Spirit helps us in our weakness. We might fall in sin but we don't contemplate or plan on sinning because our desire is to be holy. We are walking in the right direction towards holiness. As long as we are sincere, the grace of God takes care of our failures and victory. By faith we are spiritually and morally new—not just partially as now, but wholly. And it is our faith that pleases God. The world might see some dark spots in our lives but God sees purity alone because the only résumé of the believer He has at His fingertips is that of Christ. The marking highlight of the grace never drops below 100% of purity, in spite of our failures.

Certainly, God forgives all of our sins the moment we repent. In fact, God is willing to forgive you as many times as you are willing to sincerely repent in order to restore you by His grace. Unfortunately, most Christians have a hard time believing that they were forgiven all the bad things they ever did. Forgiving yourself is tough. But remember that when you don't forgive yourself you are using a higher standard of judgment than God who is our highest judge. You are like trying to override the "Not guilty sentence" pronounced by God who is the Highest, Supreme Judge seated on the highest throne in heaven. It might as well be called unseating God from His throne.

Satan uses our past failures to discourage us. Learn from your past but do not dwell in the past. "The only time you should ever look back is to see how far you have come". Concentrate your mind on the present in anticipation of the blessed hope. Close the door on the past. Don't let it have any of your energy, or any of your time, or any of your space. Don't beat yourself up, grace has brought you from far, and grace will carry you all the way to the end. Stand up and testify for the grace and the goodness of God.

Satan wants you to be a copy of your past tormenting life but God's Word brings hope. Wherever you see the word "God" or "Lord" in the Bible, you can substitute it with the word Love. Love created us – love breathed life into us – etc. Some people have personalities that block love or show signs that they were mistreated by an earthly parent, particularly a father, and they cannot receive the love of God. We need to pray that everyone has their eyes opened to the love of God and can experience that love firsthand. From the very first page through the very last, the Bible seems to demonstrate one relentless passion… that is, the Father's passion to see those whom He has created to walk in intimacy with Him. In Jeremiah 31:3 the Lord speaks to the people of Israel saying, "I have loved you with an everlasting love… and I have drawn you in loving-kindness." This verse is so beautiful not only because it reveals the depth of the Father's love toward us but also because it demonstrates God's passion to draw us into His presence.

Satan is our accuser. He will always remind you of your past sins.

Never allow your memories to recycle your bad past. According to the psalmist, God has removed our sin from us as far as the east is from the west (Psalm 103:12). God decided not to remember them, and you shouldn't. "When God takes out the trash, don't go digging back through it. Trust Him." Not only does God remove our past bad experiences, but He also saves our past good experiences by translating them into our current relationship with Christ. It means that if you don't have a relationship with God through Jesus Christ, every good thing you ever did or you will ever do is lost in thin air. They are like filthy rags before God (Isaiah 64:6). Every good thing we have ever done and we will ever do must be saved and preserved in the goodness of God through Christ. Christ is the beginning of reconciliation between man and God. Christ is the only way whereby we get back to God. Every good thing from a fallen man must be wrapped in grace in order for it to be touched by God. Grace is the only means whereby we can curb the spread of the corruption of sin by sanitation.

A conscience void of offense is a guiltless conscience. It is a clean conscience. Ignore the accusation of the devil by living according to your cleansed conscience and value discernment which is governed by Holy Spirit. A clean conscience is sprinkled by the blood of Jesus and is cleansed by His Word. "Your word is a lamp for my feet, a light on my path." (Psalm 119:105). The conscience of a believer is programmed in the Word of God. When you are defined by a clean conscience, you lose your vulnerability. Yes, at times we are vulnerable but our security depends on the conviction of our conscience rather than condemnation. That is when our vulnerability becomes the glue that holds us to our faith rather than a detour. Faith is the glue of our new life. In times of trials, nothing has stood between us and self-destruction but faith in the eternal Word of God. The revelation of the Word reveals to you what you want to be and the acknowledgment that you are not yet what you want to be but you are progressing to be what God wants you to be.

It is interesting to learn that, God loves us even when there is nothing worthy in us to love. God loves His image in us. I mean the lost image that He created us in, and the same image that He redeemed. Just know this, whichever method you choose: God is pursuing a love relationship with us that is real and personal. He is not going to give up. When you see a person who appears to be bent on destroying his life, then you are also seeing a person whom God is pursuing. And God is not going to give up. God is not going to stop caring. God is pursuing a love relationship that is real and personal. He will keep on sending to you people to remind you that you belong to Him. He is patient with you, not wanting anyone to perish, but everyone to come to repentance (2 Peter 3:9).

When God saves you, He gives you a vision. Satan's priority is to shoot down your vision. Satan is going to use the people around you to achieve his mission. Be brave enough to live the life of your dreams according to your vision and purpose instead of the expectations and opinions of others. When God gives you clarity to your vision don't mess up by associating with the wrong community. The vision involves keeping the knowledge, preserving that knowledge, and promoting that knowledge to the masses. The Bible says "My people are destroyed for lack of knowledge. Because you have rejected knowledge, I will also reject you as My priests. Since you have forgotten the law of your God, I will also forget your children" (Hosea 4:6).

Satan has this world in his grip and the majority of the people of this world are following him blindly. When you become born again, Satan parades his followers before you challenging the integrity of your decision to be born again. Satan will try to convince you that his way is right because everybody is doing it. Satan will try to convince you to do the very things you denounced when you became a born-again Christian. Don't listen to the devil. He is the father of all lairs. Don't follow the flow. Ask yourself that if everybody is jumping into the fire, will you follow them into the fire? The answer is No! Take a firm stand against Satan by standing for Christ. "When a brave man takes a stand, the spines of others are often stiffened" ~ Billy Graham

Don't embrace something just because everybody is embracing it. Ask yourself the spiritual benefits of embracing it. Professor Afunaduula says that "If you want your child to develop the trait of critical thinking, defeat fear and apply the virtue of reasoning in his or her life teach him or her that there are six important friends he or she should grow up valuing: Why, How, What, Who, Where, and when. But the most important friends are Why, How, and What. Why and How are superior friends to What. Anyone can ask what, who, when, and where without taxing someone's brain, but not many are courageous enough to ask why and how. They are very difficult friends but critical in developing critical thinking skills and critical reasoning skills. If you are quick to evoke those friends you have most likely conquered fear and docility. Everyone who cares to learn how to think critically and to reason critically must make Why and How close friends. Concurrently, one cultivates a high self-concept and values oneself highly. One won't mind if others undervalue one. One will keep taking oneself up as others endeavor to lower one's value. It is a good attitude to survive where the quality of life is falling meteorically. One remains floating."

Jesus is inclusive such that He calls whosoever is willing to join Him on the way to salvation (John 3:16). But He is exclusive such that He declares His way to be the only way to heaven. Jesus said, "I am the way, and the truth, and the life; no one comes to the Father, but through Me" (John 14:6) and, "For unless you believe that I am He, you shall die in your sins" (John 8:24). The apostle Peter echoed these words, "Neither is there salvation in any other: for there is none other name under heaven given among men, whereby we must be saved" (Acts 4:12). St. Paul concurred, "There is one God, and one mediator between God and men, the man Christ Jesus..." (I Timothy 2:5). It is therefore the united testimony of the New Testament that no one can know God the Father except through the person of Jesus Christ. "When it comes to eternal matters, we are going to ask the one who is alive the way out of the predicament. This is not Mohammad, not Confucius, not witchcraft, but Jesus Christ. Jesus is unique. He came back from the dead. This demonstrates He is the one whom He claimed to be (Romans 1:4), the unique Son of God and the only way by which a person can defeat the curse of sin (death) and have a personal relationship with the true and living God." (Josh McDowell).

Jesus calls us to walk a narrow path "Enter through the narrow gate. For wide is the gate and broad is the way that leads to destruction, and many enter through it. But small is the gate and narrow the way that leads to life, and only a few find it." (Mathew 7:13-14). Few there that find it.--The sad contrast between the many and the few runs through all our Lord's teaching. He comes to "save the world," and yet those whom He chooses out of the world are but as a "little flock." The Christian walk is reserved for a few of those whom God has opened the eyes to see the kingdom of God. Who have discovered the vanity or emptiness of this world with Christ. Jesus said that He handpicks His followers because He knows the hidden secrets of the hearts of men: "No one can come to me unless the Father who sent me draws them, and I will raise them up at the last day." (John 6:64). They are the ones who are called to walk with God day by day (to follow Him). It is not a sprint it is a walk with God.

Many people claim to have their lottery prayers answered after God blessed them with a Mega Millions jackpot or Powerball winning numbers. But consider it to be much more blessed than winning a Mega Million jackpot for you to be chosen by Christ out of over six billion people alive in the world today. Be ready to pay any price to secure God's favor bestowed over you. Don't mind about people rejecting you or abandoning you. "People who don't share the same horizons with you will stay in your life only for a while!" Those who leave are not good for your new life. It is normal for a healthy body to excrete unwanted (waste) products. Let nature takes its course. You are well off without them.

Don't look back. Don't hold on to what was when God is calling you into something new. The fear of the unknown will grip you and try to hold you back. The truth is that we usually don't understand that the finite details of things we're told will turn out for our good. But when we freefall into the deep waters of faith, we become stronger. The less we understand, the more we depend on God, who is our strength. It can be scary moving forward into the unknown. This doesn't mean we jump at every crazy idea. We pray. We submit ourselves to the Lord and invite His wisdom and counsel. Christ died so that those who live might no longer live for themselves but for Him. (2 Corinthians 5:15). "Follow Christ for His own sake, if you follow Him at all." It sounds selfish but it is the only formula that works for the salvation of your soul!

Everybody admits that nobody is perfect. Yet they ignore the consequence of not being perfect. "Not perfect" means separation from the perfect God forever and ever (spiritual death). The ideal perfectness is a fugitive that is never found in a physical realm. The reality is that we are all fugitives, with a death sentence hanging on our necks until the Love of God arrests us. The greatest of man's strength is the measure of his surrender. We should never be afraid to surrender because God has the best interests of our hearts. We are called to let go, and let God be. The first thing we do the very moment we are arrested by grace is to admit (confess) that we are sinners. The people of the world confess it causally while ignoring the consequences that come with it. The confession that "we are sinners" must be accompanied by denouncing our old ways and surrendering to Jesus or asking Jesus to fix our mess. When Jesus moves into our hearts, the peace that surpasses our understanding settles our souls; it may not make sense to our minds now; it will definitely be paradise inherited. No regret.

The benefits or benevolences of the redeemed life are staggering. The prominence of the providence of God is His security to the believers. Jesus at the cross stood as a net to catch every judgment that was supposed to come towards us. Most probably as a net placed over your bed catches mosquitoes preventing them from coming to you. In our darkest seasons, nothing has kept us from dispersion but the promises of the Lord.

Victory in Jesus is an exciting topic to explore! Victory in Jesus implies victory over death and the Challenges of life. The depth of the love of Jesus brought Him from the throne to become like one of us in order to save us. The heights of the love of Jesus make us seated at the right hand of the Father in Him. He came from heaven so that we could go to heaven.

Life is like music. It has high notes and low notes. No matter how high or low your notes may be, keep in tune with God and you'll never go out of tune in the music of life. Ask the Lord to make your heart His heart. "Always bear in mind that the primary narrative at the forefront of your thinking sets the preamble for what happens next in your life."

Being a Christian does not change what you deal with; it changes how you deal with it. I like this posting "You can't always choose the song but you can certainly choose your dance! You can't change the seasons but you can change yourself! Don't allow the misfortunes of life to break you! Use those moments for leverage to get stronger and better! Your purpose will always be paved with problems and pain! Because it's in those problems that you solve or the storms you withstand that build you to unbreakable! And as long as Jesus is first in your life, you will remain unconquerable! "I Never Lose, I Win or I Learn!" - Ronnie Hepperly

Life is not easy but you have been given everything you need to overcome. Refuse to be a victim but a victor. Look at the costs of being a victim, not only to you but also to all the lives you have to touch.

Determine that you're not going to let negative events become the defining moments of your life. Focus on what you still have, not on what you have lost and as you do, fresh enthusiasm and joy will spring forth from within you because there is something inside you that is greater than all the challenges in the world put together.

If you value life, you should value time. It is true time wasted is never recovered. Also, it is a mistake to think time is going. Time is not going anywhere. Time is here to stay until the world ends. It is you that is going. Basically, you don't waste time, you waste yourself. Given the fact, time is not eternal. Focus on the eternal things. Make better use of this time to acquire eternal life before you expire.

We started this topic by discussing success. Now you know what real success is. Success is synonymous with fulfillment. You can't experience success unless you are fulfilled. True fulfillment comes from God. It means that everything we need is in Him. We are thoroughly provided for through the finished work of Christ on the cross. You can tell from experience that the very worldly things we normally turn to for fulfillment bring temporary fulfillment and bring other side effects like hangovers. Looking for fulfillment from alcohol, sex, and other addictive beverages is another way of self-destruction. It is indeed drifting into the arena of the unwell.

The purpose of life is to know God and to seek God. I mean to know Him intimately most probably as you know every little thing about your spouse. You can't say that you believe in God without proof of actions indicating that you believe. God accepts from us the labor of love. It means that everything we do should be done out of our love for God rather than out of obligation. We don't have to memorize a list of things to do or not to do in order to please God. Our obedience to God is motivated by our love for Him. The labor of love involves passions to experience the presence of God. Such passions are healthy for our bodies – They do not make us weary. God made our bodies and He knows how our bodies work, and what works in the best interest of our bodies. Whenever God instructs you to do something, He is asking you to access His blessings. Whenever God says "you shall not do this" it is a warning to stay out of trouble. It doesn't matter whether you believe it or not, there are severe consequences whenever we do the things forbidden by the scriptures.

Now you know why, how, and what it means to be success-driven. I like this testimony: "Success used to look so different for me – starting with the model of car I drive, desired accolades, performance, and perfectionism. I used to find my worth in achieving, not in who I am, or Whose I am. No more. Now, God's pleasure is my passion. All else is wood, hay, and stubble. But getting to this place has taken most of my life, constant refining in the fire and fine-tuning by the Spirit of God. I am a slow learner, but He is faithful. I've learned that what qualifies as success in God's Kingdom far surpasses the acclaim of this world. I've learned His presence is more satisfying than anything this world has to offer. I've learned we can only fulfill God's plans through His power and strength, not our own. I've learned He holds me as a hidden gem in the folds of His garment, treasured, protected. And that is enough." ~ D J May Hejmanek

Success involves the prosperity of the total man (spirit, soul, and body). Prosperity begins with spiritual matters but it is extended to all areas of our lives—the soul and the body. Acknowledge your value by keeping your mind in check and your body in good shape. Most of the hurdles of life involve self-destructive tendencies like insecurity, pride, laziness, unchecked ambitions, integrity flaw and etc. Whatever you do, work heartily, as for the Lord and not for men, knowing that from the Lord you will receive the inheritance as your reward (Colossians 3:23-25). If Satan cannot use your old nature to destroy you, He will use the old nature in the people around you to destroy you. Watch out for destructive actions from people with defective minds. Not all people are well-wishers. "Never be distracted by naysayers, just remember God prepares a table for you in the presence of your enemies. Everyone doesn't want to see your growth or upgrades, but be certain that they will be cleaning up the table after you." Put God first in everything you do. Never give up even when you are teased and mocked. You are a witness to the gospel. And it is a moral obligation to do so.

Don't allow to be infected by the pollution of others. "One must be of a pure heart, to receive a polluted stream without becoming impure." Resist the strife in others to cause strife in you. Avoid bitterness. "Bitterness is like cancer. It eats upon the host." Avoid envy because it's so bad. Envy hinders one's success and destroys those that had already succeeded. Pray yourself into a position that is for the Kingdom of God, and not your own kingdom. Seek to serve rather than to be served. God put in you 'a seed' in form of talents and habits so that He can use you to serve others. Use everything at your fingertips to help all people regardless of their social status. Generosity is not about who wants our money. It's about Who wants our heart. Love the poor from whom you don't expect to get anything in return. "Don't tell me how you've stood with the great. Tell me how you sat with the broken, the down-trodden, the less fortunate, the forsaken, the excluded, the shunned & the poverty-stricken". Jesus said in His radical teaching that "Many will say to me in that day, Lord, Lord, did we not prophesy by your name, and by your name cast out demons, and by your name do many mighty works?" And then will I profess unto them, I never knew you: depart from me, you that work iniquity." (Matthew 7:22-23). The fruits of the works of inequity numb a man to the stench. Jesus is in search of the fruit of the Spirit. You must be open to the grace of God that is evidently visible among the people who are suffering – People who have various needs like being thirsty, hungry, poor, homeless, sick, and etc. Spotting the grace of God working among the unfortunate people increases our faith.

Self-control, in an athletic arena also may be called self-discipline, the ability to discipline yourself to achieve a goal. Self-discipline from the world's perspective will typically be for self-gain. Naturally, we try to will and work our way to self-control. Spiritually, we need Christ and the work of the Holy Spirit to develop consistent self-control in each of us. Remember, self-control is a fruit of the Spirit (Galatians 5:22-23). That means it is a product or result of the work of God's Spirit in your life. We play our part by cooperating with Him in His renewing work in us. The fruit of the Spirit is essential for the quality of your character and it will be used by God for the building up of others, and ultimately to bring God glory.

The word "control" sounds very negative. But it can be used positively. The greatest power at your fingertips is not controlling other people but controlling yourself. Controlling other people is what some people think power looks like. But trying to control other people is the first sign that you are out of control.

Work as a community of one while avoiding living after the world's opinion. Improve your relationships with others, and cope without overdoing it or getting addicted to it. Avoid the parasite mentality because it serves temporary relief. When you depend on someone else you suffer some setbacks including the capacity to think for yourself. Be independent-minded. Live your life rather than other people's lives. Gather courage and fight to be free from the shackles of relying on someone for your existence. Don't be people's imitator. God created you unique with unique capabilities. What works for others might not necessarily work for you. A cow eats grass and gets fat but if a dog eats grass, it will die. "To be nobody but yourself in a world that's doing its best to make you somebody else, is to fight the hardest battle you are ever going to fight." Never compare yourself with others. Run your race. "To find yourself, think for yourself." Look for your own potentiality, look for it and build on it. Remember that you are unique, with unique capabilities. Discover your uniqueness and peruse it to the uttermost.

Audit your fellowship. If you want success, find someone who has achieved the results you want and join hands with them, and do what they do. You'll eventually achieve the same results. Don't hang out with nonbelievers. Don't chat with them. The only private time you can give to a non-repented sinner is when you are ministering to them the gospel. My professor used to say that to fellowship with a nonbeliever is compared to a situation whereby you are standing on the table and a nonbeliever is standing on the ground, and each is trying to pull the other in his direction. The person standing on the ground (unbeliever) is most likely to pull you down instead you pulling him up because he has an advantage of gravity. Likewise, a nonbeliever is likely to bring you down to his level because he has an advantage of the corrupt world. The precaution you must take is to cut them off from any serious discussion. When they become demanding and aggressive, you are left with no option but to unfriend them.

Get rid of the past and forget it. Guilt by association is different from guilt conscience. Guilt by association involves moving around with the wrong characters. Letting go of the wrong people is the best choice you have done. You have to love yourself enough to not tolerate disrespect, disloyalty, and wish-washy feelings. If a person doesn't value you worthy of the blood of Jesus, move on. I like this lyric on the song: "Lord, I will sing of Your goodness because Your mercy never fails me. This is the story of the cross—"When I gave You my worst, You gave me Your best." I know

You as a Father; I know you as a Friend. You have been faithful to me all the time in spite of my unfaithfulness. Your goodness is just enough to me. I surrender all that I am and I have to You. I commit my will to You."

I have already discussed guilt conscience. I said that guilty conscience means dwelling in the past. Remember that every person is guilty of something. For example, every man is guilty of all the good he did not do. Just because you made a mistake, doesn't mean you are a mistake. But we don't deliberately do mistakes. We are not proud of our past, present, and future errors. And we don't make excuses for them either. We humbly repent, make it right with God in humility without arrogance, and move on with life. Don't get stuck at the point of your greatest mistake. By the way, we call them mistakes but God calls them sins. And God redeems the sinners by erasing their sins by His grace. No sin is greater than the grace of God. But we must repent sincerely.

Audit your time. God worked and rested. Not because He was tired but to give us the pattern (model) of life to follow. The rhythm of creation involves six days of creating (work) and one day of pausing (resting). "Thus the heavens and the earth were completed in all their vast array. And by the seventh day God had finished the work He had been doing; so on that day, He rested from all His work." (Genesis 2:2-3). God did not pick any other day but the seventh day after He finished creating. Seven is a divine number meaning complete. In this case, God ordained the number of seven as His number of resting. The Moral Law consists of the reminder to the Israelites to keep the Sabbath. God was not giving them a new commandment but He reminded them to keep the law that has been observed since creation. "Remember the Sabbath day, to keep it holy. Six days you shall labor and do all your work, but the seventh day is the Sabbath of the LORD your God. In it, you shall do no work: you, nor your son, nor your daughter, nor your male servant, nor your female servant, nor your cattle, nor your stranger who is within your gates. For in six days the LORD made the heavens and the earth, the sea, and all that is in them, and rested the seventh day. Therefore the LORD blessed the Sabbath day and hallowed it." (Exodus 20:8-11). The Ten Commandments are like ten segments on a chain whereby when you break off one segment the whole chain falls apart. It takes all of the ten commandments in order for us to have a set of one Moral Law in place. Keeping the Sabbath is the fourth commandment that must be equally observed as the rest of the commandments. Take time off from work and rest at the feet of Jesus, feeding on the Word and experiencing His presence in prayers. Jesus elaborated on what kind of work to do on the Sabbath: "Therefore it is lawful to do good on the Sabbath." (Matthew 12:12; Mark 3:4).

I have been discussing how you can be a dominant factor in determining the required successful life. Know yourself, and study yourself. Pray for yourself, and adjust where and when it is required. Change is inevitable, You are either backtracking on the basic principles of your values or matching forward (progressively) into your Divine destiny. Always stick to God. God is the potter, we are clay in His hands. Allow the hand of God to mold you. God is not yet done with you. "God created you with a purpose and for a purpose. Purpose to be who God purposed you to be."

Finish well. A good beginning is determined by good finishing. Paul said that "For I am already being poured out like a drink offering, and the time of my departure is at hand. I have fought the good fight, I have finished the race, I have kept the faith. From now on there is laid up for me the crown of righteousness, which the Lord, the righteous Judge, will award to me on that day—and not only to me, but to all who crave His appearing" (2 Timothy 4:6-8).

Today's prayer: "Lord, Life in this world is akin to traveling a dark journey. Every day is a journey that must be traveled no matter how dark it is. Be with me as I trek on this journey of life, for without you, I cannot see my path, and I can't know where it leads. At times, my wobble feet drag me into a speed wobble cruise and I crash. Then waves of guilt and condemnation come after me until you get hold of me. Lord, guide my steps with certainty, give me firmness with humility, love with passion, and steadfastness without dogmatism. In the name of Jesus, I pray."

The ironies of life:

It takes absence to value presence.

It takes commotion and noise to value silence.

It takes darkness to appreciate the light.

It takes sadness to appreciate happiness.

It takes hardships to value accomplishments.

It takes failure to value success.

It takes nastiness to value kindness.

It takes weakness to value strength.

It takes rudeness to value respect.

It takes inequality to value equality.

It takes favoritism to value fairness & integrity.

It takes fabrications to value honesty.

It takes insensitivity to value sensitivity.

It takes cruelty to value love & appreciation.

It takes fakeness to value genuineness/ authenticity.

It takes callousness to value courtesy & decency.

It takes coarseness/abruptness to value gentleness.

It takes a mighty strong individual to stand tall in the midst of adversity of diverse kinds and make a solitary stand.

Don't just learn, experience.

Don't just read, absorb.

Don't just change, transform.

Don't just relate, advocate.

Don't just promise, prove.

Don't just criticize, encourage.

Don't just think, ponder.

Don't just take, give.

Don't just see, feel.

Don't just dream, do.

Don't just hear, listen.

Don't just talk, act.

Don't just tell, show.

Dost thou love life? Then do not squander time, for that is the stuff life is made of.

"It is not that we have a short time to live but that we waste a lot of it."

"Waste, for example, is not a squandering of our resources. It is a poor use of His."

"Ever Tried. Ever Failed. No matter. Try again. Fail again. Fail better."

"I refuse to sacrifice for fear of what I will lose. But to not sacrifice is to ensure that I will lose."

"Our strength is not just in the size of our defense budget, but in the size of our hearts, in the size of our gratitude for their sacrifice. And that's not just measured in words or gestures."

"The greatest position in the kingdom of God is to be a slave of Christ. Servant-hood is an attitude. It is sharing your blessings that can never leave you empty inside."

Some run from the truth. But the brave run towards it. When God talks, listen completely. Most people hear God's voice but they never listen to His Word. Fanatic Christians are moved by the zeal of their own faithfulness and trustworthiness.

"Never be afraid to trust an unknown future to a known God."

"Whoever brings blessing will be enriched, and one who waters will himself be watered." (Proverbs 11:25).

"The Lord is my light and my salvation— whom shall I fear? The Lord is the stronghold of my life— of whom shall I be afraid?" (Psalms 27:1).

"He is my loving God and my fortress, my stronghold and my deliverer, my shield, in whom I take refuge, who subdues peoples under me." (Psalms 144:2).

"My God is my rock, in whom I take refuge, my shield and the horn of my salvation. He is my stronghold, my refuge, and my savior— from violent people you save me." (2 Samuel 22:3).

"My soul, wait for thou only upon the Lord; for my expectation is from him" (Psalm 62:5).

"A person may have many ideas concerning God's plan for his life, but only the designs of his purpose will succeed in the end." (Proverbs 19:21).

HOW TO COUNSEL A CLIENT OF THE OPPOSITE SEX

We are temporally situated in the chaotic earth to represent the interests of heaven on the earth. We are called to serve the interests of eternity within the limitation of time. The church is God's authorized location (embassy) in a foreign land. A counselor is a minister that represents Jesus Christ wherever he or she goes. Honor the name of the One whom you represent. Never live a question mark on your character. You can't minister to people beyond the respect they have for you. People are watching you because when you declared yourself to represent Jesus Christ, you did put your character on display for everybody to access and read. You are like an open book for every person to read. Be careful not to serve your critics with ammunition to shoot down your character. At the same time have thick skin to absorb any criticism.

"For it is time for judgment to begin with the family of God; and if it begins with us, what will the outcome be for those who disobey the gospel of God?" (1 Peter 4:17). If you are a true believer, you should not be concerned about the pending judgment that condemns a sinner to hell because you are already judged in Christ. The only concerns for a believer are the consequences of our actions that come to us at various times and in different measures as predetermined by God.

The Bible provides some precautions in order for us to be better representatives of Christ. We must be orderly. According to Orthodox Judaism, the Torah law forbids all physical contact between a man and a woman—or even for them to be alone in a room together—unless they are first-degree relatives or married to each other. This applies to any man and any woman, regardless of their ages or whether or not they are sexually attracted to each other. In Christianity, we don't have to go to that extremity but we are instructed to take certain precautions in order to eradicate unnecessary suspicions. I am going to outline the things you don't want to do when ministering to a person of the opposite sex.

1) Never close the door behind you when you are inside the office with your client of the opposite sex. In the case of the agency, invite a third party person to be there with you to witness everything going on. This is a precaution against false sexual harassment accusations.

2) Never pull aside a person of the opposite sex to talk to them in privacy. It might spark off fireworks of rumors. The public has a tendency of reading between the lines and come up with the conclusion that serves their best interests.

3) Never go to the house of a client of the opposite sex to counsel him or her unless you go with somebody

4) Never give a ride or go out to dinner with a person of the opposite sex unless you are accompanied by your spouse or somebody trusted – This is a step in the right direction for accountability purposes.

5) Always use your business cards as a means of providing contacts. Never ask a person of the opposite sex their phone numbers.

6) Watch your body language when communicating with a person of the opposite sex. My teacher told me a story concerning his friend who was fired from his job because he talked to his boss's wife while putting his small finger in his ear. According to Indian culture, that was a very seductive act.

7) Pray for a person of the opposite sex while avoiding touching them. Never lay hands on a person of the opposite sex unless they give you permission. The laying of the hands should be limited to the forehead.

It is important to look people straight in the eyes when counseling them. Eye gazing creates an opportunity for emotional connection. In a 2013 study of fifteen people, researchers found that direct gazing increased activity in the amygdala. This is the part of your brain involved in processing facial cues and people's emotions. There's a reason why people say that the eyes are the window to the soul. If you love somebody, there's some evidence that long eye contact can increase intimacy. According to a 2016 study Trusted Source, people are more likely to believe a person who's looking straight at them. This may be enhanced by continuously making eye contact. If you want to build trust with another person, try eye gazing. When you are counseling, looking straight in the eye of your client induces them into truthfulness and seriousness. On the contrary, an averted gaze can be mistaken for other intentions like lust.

Your personality determines your effectiveness in counseling. "Personality has power to uplift, power to depress, power to curse, and power to bless." People may not remember exactly what you did, or what you said but they will remember how you made them feel. Each of us has the work to do to address the stereotype threats in our ranks whether based on race, gender, learning difference, sexual orientation, or religion.

Avoid silly jokes. Be serious at work. Take advantage of every moment to deliver. You can do great things if you do small things the great way. "We're conditioned to think that our lives revolve around great moments. But great moments often catch us unaware-beautifully wrapped in what others may consider a small one."

ADDICTIVE BEHAVIORS

Addiction is defined by tolerance, withdrawal, and craving. We recognize addiction by a person's heightened and habituated need for a substance; by the intense control the desires have over him or her. These are some of the things to which people commonly get addicted to: Internet, alcohol, nicotine, drugs, pornography, gambling and etc. Some of these things have addictive chemicals in them. For example cigarettes, drugs, and alcohol. Drugs can cause mental sickness. According to the survey, most street people who are addicted to drugs end up having mental problems. The combination of the two is the major cause of suicide and domestic violence.

Other addictions involve embracing self-destructive behaviors like overnight partying, overeating, and etc. Addiction is possible when we embrace some vice behaviors. It's possible to develop a behavioral addiction. Some activities are so normal like sports and games that it's hard to believe people can become addicted to them. Yet the cycle of addiction can still take over, making everyday life a constant struggle. People may seek out more and more opportunities to engage in the behavior uncontrollably. The desire to experience a "high" from the behavior becomes so strong that the individual continues to engage in the activity despite negative consequences.

Dopamine is a chemical produced by our brains that plays a starring role in motivating behavior. It gets released when we take a bite of delicious food, when we have sex, after we exercise, and, importantly, when we have successful social interactions. In an evolutionary context, it rewards us for beneficial behaviors and motivates us to repeat them.

Drugs can alter important brain areas that are necessary for life-sustaining functions and can drive the compulsive drug use that marks

91

addiction. Brain areas affected by drug use include: The basal ganglia, which play an important role in positive forms of motivation, including the pleasurable effects of healthy activities like eating, socializing, and sex, and are also involved in the formation of habits and routines. These areas form a key node of what is sometimes called the brain's "reward circuit." Drugs over-activate this circuit, producing the euphoria of the drug high. But with repeated exposure, the circuit adapts to the presence of the drug, diminishing its sensitivity and making it hard to feel pleasure from anything besides the drug.

I want to clarify that addiction is not demonic. If you are fighting addiction you are not fighting demons but consequences of bad choices. Addiction may attract demonic forces but it is not caused by demons. Demons are fallen angels with personalities. Demons can plan against you, taking advantage of your weaknesses. A believer cannot be possessed by the demons because his house has a new occupant who cannot share it with the demons (Matthew 12:29; Luke 11:22). But a believer can be oppressed by the demons in case he or she puts the spiritual armor down. A believer can suffer from addiction if he or she is exposed to some addictive substances, and consequently be tormented by the evil spirit.

Some good behaviors can turn into addiction when we overdo them. For example, an addiction to social media is real. Platforms like Facebook, Snapchat, Whatsapp. and Instagram leverage the very same neural circuitry used by slot machines and cocaine to keep us using their products as much as possible. Some of the major causes of mental torment on social media are the illusion that others are more popular due to the number of "friends" or "followers" they have. Seeing pictures of a group of friends that you consider yourself to be close to but you weren't invited to join them. Seeing videos of some of your friends who are living such luxurious lives that you cannot afford, and you respond with envy.

Cell phones have become such powerful and versatile tools that, for many people, they feel literally indispensable. "Smartphone addiction, sometimes colloquially known as "nomophobia" (fear of being without a mobile phone), is often fueled by an Internet overuse problem or Internet addiction disorder.... Smartphone addiction can encompass a variety of impulse-control problems, including Virtual relationships." If you've ever misplaced your phone, you may have experienced a mild state of panic until it's been found. Most of us have become so intimately entwined with our digital lives that we sometimes feel our phones vibrating in our pockets when they aren't even there.

It's worth noting that there are some important similarities between cell phone overuse and behavioral addictions like compulsive gambling. The similarities include:

- loss of control over the behavior
- persistence, or having real difficulty limiting the behavior
- tolerance, the need to engage in the behavior more often to get the same feeling
- severe negative consequences stemming from the behavior
- withdrawal, or feelings of irritability and anxiety when the behavior isn't practiced
- relapse, or picking up the habit again after periods of avoidance

For many, addiction begins quietly. It may start with the recreational use of a drug. In the case of *opioids* and other painkillers, it may begin when a doctor prescribes a medication. Whatever the reason, once addicted, this disease affects a person's brain, and they will continue to use the drug despite repercussions. People addicted to pills, alcohol, tobacco, or illicit drugs, have an intense focus on using them to the point where the person's ability to function in day to day life becomes impaired. People keep using the substance even when they know it is causing or will cause problems.

When a person begins using addictive substances, he or she is in control but after addiction, the substances are in control of the user. The addictive substances dictates what, when, and how they could be used. Addiction overrides the will but there is still a thin exit involving the will of a person who is addicted. For example, I was counseling a friend who was addicted to nicotine. He told me that he is so addicted that he cannot afford to put down that cigarette. I asked him that "If I pointed a gun on your head and instructed you to put down that cigarette, or die, will you choose to die?" He answered that "No". I told him that you see, there is still a choice to override addiction even though it is a tough choice.

There is no excuse for using addictive substances. Some people say that they smoke, drink and use drugs in order to unburden themselves of problems. This is a shabby and unwise decision that produces a temporary solution. Addiction surges problems rather than solving them. Problems increase rather than solve addiction-related challenges. Addiction is a disease, but with support and treatment, there is hope.

Steps towards recovery:

1) Better understand the complex disease of addiction
2) Acknowledge that your addiction is a problem. Don't be one of those people who take pride in their addicted lifestyle.
3) Acknowledge that you need help beyond yourself.
4) Establish healthy boundaries by changing your environment. (Stay away from the people and the things that cause you to stumble).
5) Strengthen your own well-being (spiritually, mentally, and physically).
6) Acknowledge that it is going to take some tough decisions to be free. But with the help of God, it can be done.
7) Join support groups made up of people who are going through what you are going through or who have been delivered from what you are going through.
8) Establish direct contact with your counselor. Talk to them as much as they are willing to talk to you.
9) Get accountability from a person you trust and respect.
10) Start a journey of retreating. Decrease the use of addictive substances every day that comes.
11) Believe that everything will be fine. The walls of Jericho never collapsed instantly but they did collapse.
12) Pray daily and read your Bible daily. The Word of God is the cleansing agent that can delete the old version of you by renewing the minds. Allow the scriptures to be your daily dose of healing medicine. Use the scriptures as they direct you.
13) Fasting is a very good prescription for training the body not to yield to the corrupted thoughts that are intended to destroy you. You can fast by staying away from food, watching television, the internet, and all other addictive substances.
14) Honor God with your body by dedicating to Him all of your five senses (what you see, hear, taste, smell, and touch).

Everybody knows someone who struggles with addiction. Whether it is alcohol, drugs, cigarettes, gambling, pornography or something as seemingly harmless as shopping, television or food, an addiction is serious business. If nothing is done to stop it, an addiction has the power to ruin lives and destroy relationships. The indisputable deliverance from addiction begins with the relationship with the Savior and Deliverer. If you or someone you love is trapped in addiction the truth from God's Word can help anyone break free and stay free from addiction.

Spiritual deliverance begins with salvation. If you have tried to give up any addictive substance by your own efforts and failed, you need help from above. Acknowledge that you are a sinner. This is the beginning of the process of brokenness. Ask God to save you. Make Him your Lord. God is called "Lord" because He is a personal God. The word Adonai is simply the Hebrew word for "Lord." The sovereign LORD has always the grace available for everyone (whosoever) who comes to Him through faith in the Lord Jesus Christ. We respond to God by saying "Lord, I am available, all of me is yours. Do to me as You will. In the name of Jesus. Amen."

Jeremiah 17:9 - "The heart is deceitful above all things, and desperately wicked: who can know it?" Faith is a passionate intuition but we cannot make intuitive diagnoses of the human heart. God the omniscient, alone, knows the malice of the hearts of all men. He diagnosed the human heart as wicked. The word wicked also means sick and incurable by any natural means. The human heart is the darkroom where all kinds of negativity are developed. No matter how calmly you try to adjudicate there are those little things that will eventually produce bizarre behaviors. The human heart naturally inclines towards the fallen world. "The world is not dialectical – it is sworn to extremes, not to equilibrium, sworn to radical antagonism, not to reconciliation or synthesis. This is also the principle of evil." The heavenly virtues cannot be permanently implanted into a wicked heart unless God transforms our hearts by His Spirit and transplants his minds into us by His Word. "The nearer a man lives to God, the more intensely has he to mourn over his own evil heart."

True freedom of the body and the soul begins in the spirit. The Holy Spirit is God's refreshing breath over the broken soul. The Bible says that where the Spirit of God is there is liberty (2 Cor, 3:17). According to the scripture, Paul assumes, almost as an axiom of the spiritual life, that the presence of that Spirit gives freedom, as contrasted with the bondage of the letter — freedom from slavish fear, freedom from any bondage, guilt, and burden of sin, freedom from the tyranny of the Law (judgment).

Remember that you are more powerful than you know! Yet your power is not self-generated; rather, it emanates from the One who resides in you the One who is far greater than he who rules the dark realms of this world. (1 John 4:4.). When you have faith in Him there is no mountain that you cannot move. The ball is in your hands. If you believe it will happen, you will see opportunities to make it happen. If you believe it won't, you will see obstacles. But God is calling you not to wrestle climbing that mountain of addiction but to move it by faith; by His mighty and power as opposed to yours. Swing into action with the awareness that God is on your side. "For the eyes of the Lord run to and fro throughout the whole earth, to show Himself strong on behalf of those whose heart is loyal to Him." (2 Chronicle16:9).

I like this quotation: "Many of us are facing impossible situations where we need a breakthrough in our lives. Yet, most of us sit and wait for God to make it happen, and then we wonder why it is that we don't experience breakthroughs as often or as fast as we'd like. What we need to know is that breakthrough is not something we sit around and wait for. Breakthrough is God waiting on us to respond in obedience to what He has already commanded and already promised. Declare these things and watch that breakthrough begin to happen in your life. Amen." ~ Jecinta Normans

Justification is when God declares a sinner righteous by His grace. Sanctification is when God asks us to cooperate with His saving grace. I know some people who got saved and got supernaturally delivered immediately from addiction. But at times God wants to work with us through the process of deliverance. Jesus could have rained food from heaven but He asked for the lunch of young man and multiplied the bread and the fishes. Jesus could have rolled the stone away from the tomb of Lazarus by the word of His mouth but he asked the sisters of Lazarus to roll away the stone.

Embrace God's plan for your life. God had a plan for you before you were born. "Before I formed you in the womb I knew you, and before you were born I set you apart and appointed you as a prophet to the nations."

(Jeremiah 1:5). Have assurance that God conceived plans for you even before you were formed in the wombs of your mother. He has a blueprint for your life. His plans for you would not come to naught, and only His plans for you will triumph. We have good counsel from God Himself. We should not worry about tomorrow. Let's just leave everything to God, not fate. There's one thing I know wherever I go, Jesus' love has never failed me.

PORNOGRAPHY IS ADDICTIVE BEHAVIOR

The impact of pornography is enormous because lust is the number one problem of men. Sex is considered to be the greatest addiction among men. Pornography, as a term, refers to stimulating, visual materials that depict sexual acts with the primary intention to arouse the ones viewing them. The study researchers examined the impact of a family member's consumption of Internet pornography on the consumer's marital and family relationships. The study shows that the consumption of Internet pornography threatens the economic, emotional, and relational stability of marriages and families. Qualitative and quantitative research indicates that pornography consumption, including cybersex, is significantly associated with decreased marital sexual satisfaction and sexual intimacy. Men and women perceive the online sexual activity as threatening to marriage as offline infidelity.

Regarding the indirect impact on children living in a home where a parent uses pornography, there is evidence that it increases the child's risk of exposure to sexually explicit content and/or behavior. Children and youth who consume or encounter Internet pornography can have traumatic, distorting, abusive, and/or addictive effects. The consumption of Internet pornography and/or involvement in sexualized Internet chat can harm the social and sexual development of youth and undermine the likelihood of success in future intimate relationships.

The smartphone is the hub of new technology. The corona virus pandemic has increased our collective screen time, and that's particularly true on mobile devices. According to a new report from mobile data and analytic firm App Annie, global consumers are now spending an average of 4.2 hours per day using apps on their smartphones, an increase of 30% from just two years prior. In some markets, the average is even higher — more than five hours.

The impact of social media on marriage cannot be underrated. Pornography has made men insecure. The consumers of pornography ignore the fact that the characters involved in the nasty pornographic movies are actors. In real life, they do not practice most of the things they sell to their consumers. "Culture wants to destroy us by drowning us (men) with synthetic "happiness." It's not real. And it leads to addiction which will destroy your life and your capacity for real intimacy. Addiction to synthetic happiness – whether it be alcohol, narcotics, or porn – corrodes your soul and makes you unattractive and unable to perform the role God places you on earth to achieve. Men – you are created in the IMAGE OF GOD. Let's act like it and stop rotting our minds, bodies, and souls. Let us be real men".

Pornography like rape has been viewed as a male invention, designed to dehumanize women to reduce them to mere sexual objects to be exploited and manipulated sexually. Pornography is the undiluted essence of anti-women propaganda. Women are not exempted from pornography. Today, women are partners with men as consumers of pornography. Sociocultural and technological changes in the past few decades have made pornography more accessible and normalized to all people regardless of their gender. "Indeed, men and women consume pornography frequently, while some even share self-created sexually explicit photos and videos online; that is, 'amateur pornography'" (Hardy, 2009; Paasonen, 2011).

Think sexting and a lot of things come to mind… Fun. Racy. Sexy. Even romantic. However, it may not take long for the mind to wander to words like 'dangerous' – especially with reports of blackmail and revenge porn becoming all too common. But sexting and sharing nudes are not new. People have been creating and exchanging erotic imagery, photos and letters for centuries. What's different now is that the internet and instant messaging apps have made it really easy and quick to do so. At the click of the finger a young lady can download her nude photos and show them to you or to a group of people without fear and shame. That is how far we have fallen from the grace!

Study shows that there are some Christians out there who are struggling with the addiction to pornography. The mistake they made is to watch pornography hoping that they are too strong to be addicted to it. Some believed in the power of rebuking the demon of addiction while continuing to watch pornography and they ended up being victimized. The only escape route from pornography is to flee; run away from it as fast as possible. Never take the risk to look at it because it is very addictive. "Flee from sexual immorality. Every other sin a man can commit is outside his body, but he who sins sexually sins against his own body." (1 Corinthians 6:18). Run fast away because nothing is worth your relationship with Christ, absolutely nothing.

Satan hates virtues. He attacks us at our vulnerability and weakest point. The Bible says that "Be careful! Watch out for attacks from the Devil, your great enemy. He prowls around like a roaring lion, looking for some victim to devour (1 Peter 5:8). Without Christ, we are no match for Satan. We run from Satan by running to Christ.

God is willing to deliver you from any kind of sexual addiction which has enslaved you. But you must be prepared to fight. It is going to take the discipline of the minds to win. "No good Captain would want his troops to go into battle without good preparation. And the first stage of preparation is boot camp. Boot camp is where the soldier gets in shape, gets equipped, and learns the basics of fighting in battle. The early stages of boot camp get the soldier into fighting shape. This involves discipline, and the discipline you're going to need to battle the enemy on the porn field only happens when you develop your scriptural muscles. You desire to avoid sin, I assume?! Well, God's word is clear on this."

Decide to stay away from all places where you can be exposed to pornography. Get rid of all those nasty adult channels, websites, videos, and porno magazines. When I was in a Bible collage, I heard my roommate screaming and shouting at the television because they had a movie involving sexually explicit content and nude characters. What bothered me is that he screamed while at the same time he continued to watch. I asked him that if he is so mad why not change the channel or turn off the television?

Remember that your body is a temple of God. In 1 Corinthians 6:19-20, Paul asks, "Or do you not know that your body is a temple of the Holy Spirit within you, whom you have from God? ... You are not your own, for you were bought with a price." You are responsible for the sanctity of the body (temple). Temple maintenance involves the discipline of the physical body by controlling the five senses in particular the sense of what you see.

If you are serious to fight addiction, get accountability from trusted people. If you are married, get accountability from your spouse. Get accountability from a trusted person whom you respect. I mean a friend that can look in your face and tell you that you are wrong. Give them access to your computer. Give them a right to call you at midnight and check on you. It is going to take away part of your freedom but it is worth doing it.

GAMBLING IS ADDICTIVE BEHAVIOR

Approximately 10 million people in the United States live with a gambling addiction problem. A gambling addiction occurs when a person continues to gamble despite negative effects that may impact their finances, relationships, or well-being. Gambling addiction involves compulsions to seek out gambling, betting, and wagering, and the end result can be devastating for the gambler as well as his or her family.

Most people think of gambling as a quick money-making method but it is one of the addictive behaviors affecting millions of people. In addition to casinos, there is online gambling. The gamblers are vulnerable to alcohol abuse and prostitution. The victims are the family members. The gamblers have less time with family members. They lie a lot and cheat.

The money got from gambling is not clean money. Although people willingly gamble their money they are manipulated into believing that they will make money. Some of these people are needy like widows. The person who wins rejoices at the expense of many who have lost.

Casinos exist to not only take your money but to keep as much of theirs as possible — both by offering games that are tilted in the house's favor and by having air-tight security measures designed to catch thieves and cheaters. It's common knowledge that just about every game you'll find in a casino is tilted in the house's favor.

According to Fox, "Anyone who's spent time in a casino knows they are designed to make sure you'll lose track of the time (and of the money you're probably losing). That means no windows and no clocks. "Two in the morning is the exact same thing as two in the afternoon," says Sal.

Some casinos have gone to desperate, and sexy, measures to keep you there and gambling. "They have stripper poles, they have party pits," Sal says. "You go to Vegas right now, it looks like a gentlemen's club. You see girls dancing on the poles. It keeps the guys at the table."

People who struggle with a gambling or shopping problem often hide their issues out of shame and a desire for secrecy. This often delays recovery and treatment and allows a gambling addiction to lead to other serious effects, including loss of jobs, failed relationships, and severe debt. Problem gambling is often associated with mental health problems, including depression, anxiety, and mood disorders. Gambling problems don't just affect mental health. People who have struggled with gambling benefit greatly from treatment and often also need family counseling and financial coaching to fully recover.

GOD DELIVERS YOU TO DELIVER OTHERS

Those who had gone through what others are going through are the best candidate to counsel them. We comfort others with the same comfort we were comforted with. There is no better ministry to the suffering than the one who has experienced the suffering. We are the sanctified (separated or set apart) vessels (temple of God) in which and through which He reaches out to the lost world. We live every day in His presence, and He lives in us to touch others through us!

Jesus is the greatest counselor because he went through what we are going through. "For we do not have a high priest who is unable to sympathize with our weaknesses, but we have one who was tempted in every way that we are, yet was without sin." (Hebrews 4:15). Jesus had compassion for all people who were oppressed. He reached out to them at their point of suffering. We have a tendency of looking into the history of the people who are oppressed or addicted. We try to assess how they ended up the way they are and blame them for allowing the situation to escalate to that extent. Use compassion to reach out to them without question. Whether they screwed up or the world screwed them up it doesn't matter. All they need is your compassion.

God uses people who have been delivered to rescue those who are still in bondage of the same predicaments. Whether you are in the valley or on the top of the mountain, God will give you some encouraging scriptures which you can share with others. You have to be inspired in order to inspire others. "There is no knowledge, no light, no wisdom that you are in possession of, but what you have received it from some source." Freely you received, freely pass it on to others. It is only as we develop others that we permanently succeed in our careers.

Be on fire in order to set others on fire. This is friendly purifying fire. "The human spirit is the lamp of the LORD that sheds light on one's inmost being" (Proverbs 20:27). The human spirit is a lamp that cannot light without oil. The Holy Spirit is the oil that lights up the human spirit (lamp). God put His Spirit in our spirit to illuminate our minds and to bring awareness of His presence. Jesus promised that "I will not leave you comfortless: I will come to you" (John 14:18). He sent us to light the world with His light: "Let your light shine before others, that they may see your good deeds and glorify your Father in heaven" (Matthew 5:16).

MARITAL RELATIONSHIP

I am going to kick off by discussing premarital counseling or the counseling that people need before getting married. There are two kinds of single people who seek premarital counseling. The first group consists of singles people staying together as if they are married people, seeking counseling in order to put right their relationship. Usually, I have two alternatives for such a couple: The first one is to separate, and go through regular classes regarding biblical marriage and get married while they understand what marriage exactly is. The second alternative is that if for some reason they can't separate due to the necessity of the children and other issues like health, I advise them to denounce sin, repent by turning to Jesus, and get married immediately or as soon as possible. By deciding to get married, they have realized that they are living in sin; they are trying to escape the grips of Satan. I don't want to be a roadblock to them. I tell them that "Go ahead and do it now."

The most important step in marriage is the first step – Choosing the right partner. If you fail to get it right at this stage get ready for a rocky relationship. The moment you marry the wrong person, there is no counseling that is likely to bring peace to your marriage. There are people out there who might be appealing from the outside but whose characters are stinking, and they made up their minds already never to change.

The most important point to know for anybody that is searching for a partner is that fulfillment does not come from your future spouse. True fulfillment comes from God. If you are not fulfilled when you are single, you will never be fulfilled even after getting married.

Know yourself, and know what you want. Be honest with yourself – why is that so hard? The heart is deceitful. The heart of a person can be corrupt, or it can be good and helpful, depending on what has been put into it, and whether it is being led by the truth...... One way to be led by the deceitful heart is to give no energy to seeking the Kingdom of God and his righteousness. That is when you can be confused not knowing the difference between what you want and what you need. "You lust and do not have. You murder and covet and cannot obtain. You fight and war. Yet you do not have because you do not ask. You ask and do not receive, because you ask amiss, that you may spend it on your pleasures." (James 4:2-3).

Discover your calling or ministry and your career first then choose a spouse that will be comfortable with what you are called to do. This will help to avert future conflicts with your future spouse when they are uncomfortable with what you are called to do. It is good for a couple to share their calling and ministry. When couples choose to unselfishly serve others together, they experience peace, contentment and a deeper bond that strengthens their marriage.

Marry a person that loves God more than you. Ladies, don't ever allow a man to bypass God to win your heart. Make him come through God and obtain God's permission to have your heart. In days past and still happens today, a sincere gentleman would ask a young lady's father for his permission not only to court his daughter but also to marry his daughter. I still believe in doing it this way and even if you don't have an earthly father, ladies, you have a heavenly Father. Make him obtain your daddy's permission. Don't settle for less.

We live in a sex-oriented society whereby everything is defined by sex. Know your value. It is embarrassing when most men view women as sexual objects. A decent woman should resist being treated as a sexual organ to satisfy a man. Women can offer more than sex because they are equally intelligent as men. They can be good teachers, lawyers, doctors, managers and etc. When men sexually objectify women, it means that they are misogynists, haters of women. Women have the power to stop such myopic male characters. Sex is a big slice from the pie of intimacy but sex shouldn't be used to define us. Apart from sex, men and women can individually do great things. And together, united in marriage they can do greater things.

Be specific regarding what you need. Outline ten things you are looking for in your future spouse. Definitely, it is difficult to meet a person that meets all of the ten requirements. If you get somebody that can meet seven out of the ten requirements, that is good enough.

Never go on a date with a person unless you feel that there is a possibility of getting married to him or her. Dating should be limited to marriage only. It will help you from getting hooked up to the wrong characters. Most people I talked to who are going through bad marriages say that at first, they were not interested in engaging themselves in a serious relationship but eventually, they were hooked up or manipulated by their dates. If you don't see a person as a potential partner in marriage, cut it short as quickly as possible in order to avoid any future regret.

Dating time is examining time. There are some irregularities and misbehavior that are going to pop up during the dating period. These are red flags that should not be ignored. Make sure that you address them immediately. Don't expect them to disappear in the future. Expect them rather to increase in case you get into a serious relationship. In fact, people hide much during dating time in order to entice you. After marriage, they pull out their true colors without fear. During dating time they will put on the best cologne or perfume to hide the stink from you. Dating time is not just fun time; it is serious examination time. If there is something that can be fixed, do it. Remember that you marry them for who they are, and who they will be. After marriage, there is little you can do to fix the abnormalities.

Take time to study your future spouse. There is no need to rush going into a relationship. When a person rushes you, chances are he or she is hiding something from you that could be disclosed given the time. Take it slow, uncomplicated, sure, stable, consistent, and no rush. You deserve a person that is sure of you, and that you're sure of. It takes time and proper observation. Even if it requires an investigator; it is worth doing. Check everything including their driving records, background checks, criminal records and etc. The employers ask for the same things before they employ you. But marriage is by far greater than employment. Remember that you are going to trust this person with your life and future.

Don't fall in love with the face and body. Fall in love with the spirit, heart, and character. I like this quotation: "My dad told me that, "Her mindset will raise your children. Not her body and good looks. Choose wisely". Don't focus on external appearances only. Some good things come to us when wrapped in a non-appealing way. If the strength of the relationship is based on external performances like beauty and good sex it is doomed to fail because those external things fade away with time.

Get to know a person thoroughly well. Some people say that they fall in love the first time they met. I am not saying that it is impossible, I am saying that it is unusual. People don't fall in love but grow in love. Everything that falls gets broken and everything that grows gets stronger! Build your relationship beginning from friendship. Build friendship first. When you marry your best friend, he or she will make the best partner in love.

Look for the chemistry between you. Your future relationship is going to be sustained by the chemistry you feel in courtship. When you pick your future spouse sit down with him or her and discuss your future together. The more you talk the more you are going to know each other. Discuss your likes and dislikes, your vision, your finances, the size of family you want, where you are going to stay, your health, and etc. All these things need to be discussed and addressed in order to avoid future confusion. It is important for both of you to be on the same page.

God forbids a believer to get married to a non-believer. Don't be unequally yoked with a carnal person. Two horses that are not of the same size will not plow the field. A believer is in union with Christ. Wherever you go, you go with Him. There is a union of souls involved in physical sexual activity. Whenever you unite with the unbeliever sexually there is a spiritual consequence. Several people have been tricked into believing that the people they are dating converted to Christianity. Most people will agree to become Christians just for the sake of marrying you, after the wedding, they go back to the world. The bottom line is that never date a nonbeliever. Period.

The solid foundation of any marriage is established during the dating time before marriage when you are getting to know each other. At any cost avoid any sexual intercourse before marriage. Sex must be saved within the boundaries of marriage. If your partner is forcing you to have sex before marriage, it is a red flag; you need to reconsider before entering into a lifetime covenant relationship with that person. It is a clear sign that he or she does not respect the sanctity of marriage. Even after you are married, he or she will have sex outside marriage because he or she does not respect the sanctity of marriage.

Never date a married person. I know there are some confused people out there who believe in breaking up marriages in anticipation of getting married to one of the couples after divorce. Never even think about doing such an evil act. Elder Stephen Huston said that the law "Do not kill" applies also to killing somebody's marriage. Listen to the words of Jesus: "Anyone who divorces his wife and marries another woman commits adultery, and he who marries a divorced woman commits adultery." (Luke 16:18).

I want to give one of the most important pieces of advice to all single people. You may ignore the rest but you cannot afford to fault on this one: Ask God to show you the right person. I like this quotation "Ladies, if you run after God as you run after a man, God will give you a man you won't have to run after." This advice applies to men too. As I said, marry somebody that loves Jesus more than he or she loves you. This is how you put on your marriage a divine value.

If you believe that you have the right person, never be afraid to pursue him or her aggressively but with restraint. Some people need a little pressure to get on board. Some people do experience fear when falling in love—because it's really scary to be that vulnerable! When you're falling in love, you have the possibility of getting hurt. Some people instinctively run away from serious relationships because they're too afraid of that possibility of heartbreak. Again, it's easier for them to choose to abstain than to go through a possible rejection. Do things to prove to him or her that everything will be OK.

Respect your body by dressing decently. Dressing code matters. People are going to respect you judging the way you dress. Dress appropriately in public places. Your body is sacred. Respect it and do not defile it in any way. Through your dress and appearance, you can show that you know how precious your body is. By dressing properly, you can show that you are a disciple of Jesus Christ and that you love Him. Make sure that the parts of the body that are reserved for your husband or wife are properly hidden from public view.

Learn to dress modestly. To dress modestly is to show propriety in the way you dress. To be modest is to be unpretentious or to have an accurate estimation of oneself. Immodest clothing is any clothing that is tight, sheer or revealing in any other manner. Young women should avoid short shorts and short skirts, shirts that do not cover the stomach, and clothing that does not cover the shoulders or is low-cut in the front or the back. Young men should also maintain modesty in their appearance. Avoid sagging pants. Sagging is a manner of wearing trousers or jeans that sag so that the top of the trousers or jeans is significantly below the waist, sometimes revealing much of the wearer's underpants. You can use ornaments but don't be obsessed with them. Do not disfigure yourself with tattoos or body piercings. Young women, if you desire to have your ears pierced, wear only one pair of earrings. It is descent. I want to emphasize that beauty comes from within. There is no more beautiful countenance than that of a woman or a man who has Jesus Christ in their heart.

I recommend that both of you get tested of sexually transmitted diseases. Never be afraid to know your status. Advanced science has made it possible for an HIV-negative person and HIV-positive person to stay in a relationship without the possibility of infecting each other. I know a couple who got tested before marriage, and one of them tested positive for HIV. They discussed it and agreed to go ahead and get married. Today, they have two kids, all of their kids tested negative, and even the parent who tested negative is still negative. So, don't be afraid to get tested. Discuss it with your future spouse. There are times when the unexpected become acceptable. Love conquers all fear.

I want to end by saying that there are biblical principles in place regulating a healthy marriage. Dating time is reserved to study your future spouse to see if he or she respects the biblical marriage. Dating time begins when the two of you meet and extends all the way to that moment when both of you stand before a priest to say your vows. You have the right to change your mind even at the very last moment before you say "I do take him or her as my husband or wife------". But After you say your vows, what is done is done; it can't be undone. You can't change your minds about the person you have married because you can't change your vows. Therefore, choosing the right person to marry is the first but the most important step in your future marriage. Do it right. When you miss it, you mess up the entire marriage. And it will be tough to fix the damage. You might have a great wedding, but a great wedding does not guarantee a great marriage.

Marriage: Marriage is one of the institutions ordained by God on the earth to establish His virtues on the earth. The idea of marriage comes from heaven to the earth as opposed from the earth to heaven. There is a Divine family whereby God is the Father to the Son. God chose the Israelite to be his people, his nation, his children. And so they are his children, a family established through the covenant God ratified with Abraham. We are sons and daughters of God because we adopted into the Divine family by the grace of God. We are welcomed into God's family as joint heirs because of the love of God for us. As sons of God who have been adopted into His family, we are now truly alive. We aren't being led by the forces of evil. We're being led by the Holy Spirit. He's providing us divine counsel. He's speaking to our hearts and our minds. He's illuminating the truth of the Scriptures to us. He's pointing us in a direction that is for God's glory and our good.

The Father and the Son are masculine. The grammatical gender of the word for "spirit" is feminine in Hebrew (רוּחַ, rūaḥ), neuter in Greek (πνεῦμα, pneûma) and masculine in Latin (spiritus). The neuter Greek πνεῦμα is used in the Septuagint to translate the Hebrew רוּחַ. The pronouns used to address the Holy Spirit, however, are masculine. God is a husband to Israel. Jesus is the Bridegroom, the Church is a bride.

Marriage is a relational covenant between a man and a woman. Each person involved in the covenant gives himself or herself as a gift to the other. The body says to the other body that everything I have is yours. Marriage is like emptying one vessel into the other ending up with one full vessel. This is the idea "The two become one". The grace takes two different substances and comes up with a cocktail of one usable mixture. I want to say that when we marry the couple, we pronounce them as the two becoming one. Spiritually, the two souls are sealed in the covenant of oneness. But practically, to be one is the process that has to be worked out daily. The couple has to prove that they are actually one in their actions.

The first two chapters of the book of Genesis are about God creating all things. Several times God says "It is good." One time God says "It is not good". And one time God said, "It is very good". After God created Adam, He said it is not good for man to stay alone. After God pulled Eva from the sides of Adam, He said "It is very good." Adam looked at Eva for the first time and he said, "You were made from me". Eva looked at Adam for the first time and said that "I was made from you". Adam looked at Eva for the very first time and he saw something that is the exact duplicate of his kind and he said "Wooh! Man" – meaning wo-man.

Love is the essence of any relationship. The first time the word "Love" is mentioned in the Bible is in Genesis 22:2. The Bible verse states, "Then God said, "Take your son, your only son, whom you love—Isaac—and go to the region of Moriah. Offer him there as a burnt offering on one of the mountains, which I will show you." You see, God instructed Abraham to prove his love for God by sacrificing something he loved most. The lesson is that love involves making sacrifices. Sacrificing is the highest form of worshiping. We become like what we worship. When we worship Jesus, we love what He loves in the same way He loves. We see people in the eyes of Jesus. Jesus looked at people through the lens of compassion. He loved people unconditionally.

God establishes order on the earth through families, Churches, and governments. There is the head of the church, the head of the family, and the head of the government ordained by God. In the King James Version of the Bible, Romans 13 reads, "Let every soul be subject unto the higher powers. For there is no power but of God: the powers that be are ordained of God." But God also holds those leaders accountable to honor Him with the authority He gives them.

The Bible says clearly that man is the head of the family as Christ is the head of the Church. "Wives, submit to your own husbands, as to the Lord. For the husband is the head of the wife even as Christ is the head of the church, his body, and is himself its Savior." (Ephesians 5:22-23). It is instructive to compare this with the partly similar passage in 1 Corinthians 11:3. There "the head of the woman is the man," as here; but "the head of every man (individually) is Christ," considered in His human nature; and finally, "the Head of Christ," as the Son of Man, "is God." There, accordingly, "headship" is simple lordship; the woman is subject to the man, the man is subject to Christ alone; Christ as the Son is subject to the Father.

According to the scripture, a husband is put in a strategic position in decision-making. But it does not make him a dictator. Somebody said that the husband is the head but a wife is the neck that turns the head. A husband should always consult his wife before making an important decision. In case of disagreement, a husband should consult Christ through prayers and make a final decision. I want to say that a husband is not married to his decision; he is married to his wife. It means that his decisions are binding but not permanent. There is always room to adjust his decisions.

"Wives, submit yourselves unto your own husbands, as unto the Lord." The scripture instructs wives to submit "as unto the Lord." Our Lord demands perfect obedience from us. A wife is instructed to submit to her husband in the same way. The calling to submit is limited to her husband. It is not an instruction given to all women to submit to all men. It is an instruction given within the context of marriage. God gave this commandment of women submitting to the husband because God created man. He knows that He created in man the masculine personality that is quenched by submitting. He created the opposite gender (woman) with a tender personality of submission in her to satisfy the masculine personality. Again, the requirement to submit should not override your conscience. If a husband requires you to do things that are contrary to the scriptures, you have the right to refuse. The Bible clearly says that we should obey God rather than men (Acts 5:29). This rule is a golden one for all people, in all circumstances, and all times.

A husband is instructed to love his wife as Christ loved the Church. "Husbands, love your wives, just as Christ loved the church and gave himself up for her to make her holy, cleansing her by the washing with water through the word, and to present her to himself as a radiant church, without stain or wrinkle or any other blemish, but holy and blameless. In the same way, husbands ought to love their wives as their own bodies. He who loves his wife loves himself" Ephesians 5:25-28). The keywords are "and gave himself up for her". The Church is the bride of Christ. Our bridegroom loved us more than Himself. He demonstrated His love to us by stretching out His hands and He was nailed on the cross in our place. It is called sacrificial love. This is the kind of love a husband must show to his wife practically. I don't know a wife that will refuse to submit to a husband that loves her sacrificially. I want to emphasize that the calling to the wife to submit and a calling to a husband to love is unconditional. You don't stop submitting and loving just because your spouse is not doing their part. Do your part regardless, and you will be blessed. The working formula is "Love as unto Christ" & "Submit as unto Christ".

Children are instructed to submit to their parents. Fathers as heads of the family are supposed to bring up godly children. "Fathers, do not provoke your children to wrath; instead, bring them up in the discipline and instruction of the Lord" (Ephesians 6:4). It denotes the exasperation produced by arbitrary and unsympathetic rules. Elsewhere, the Bible instructs us "Let the word of Christ dwell in you richly, teaching and admonishing each other in all wisdom, singing psalms, hymns, and spiritual songs with grace in your hearts to God." (Colossians 3:16).

Ephesians 5:21 - "Submit to one another out of reverence for Christ". "Submit" means "to give over or yield to the power or authority of another." Ephesians 5:21 isn't telling us to yield to another person. It is telling us that we yield to Jesus! When we do that, we give Him the authority to guide us and show us how to live—not my will, but His. As we study this passage of Scripture on the biblical teaching of marriage and family, we can use the analogy of a pair of scissors to define the roles. Just as a pair of scissors need two halves to function properly as a whole, so does marriage. We've seen that Paul is very fair and balanced in the way that he addresses the people involved in these relationships. For instance, he talks first to the wives, then to the husbands; he talks to the children, and then he talks to the parents. "Do nothing out of selfish ambition or empty pride, but in humility consider others more important than yourselves. Each of you should look not only to your own interests, but also to the interests of others" (Philippians 2:3-4).

Love is the bond that holds all relationships together. Whenever I am privileged to counsel a couple involved in a serious conflict threatening their marriage, the first question I ask is that "Is there any love for each other saved pertaining to this relationship." If they answer "Yes" I proceed with the counseling. As long as there is a dose of love for each other, there is a brick to build on the relationship. If they answer "No" I divert my attention to teach them what love is, and what love is not.

You should purpose in your hearts to love each other. Feelings for each other are real but feelings change. The love of the heart involves the will that never changes regardless of the change of the feelings. "Remember love is the richest of all treasures. Without it there is nothing, and with it there is everything. Love never perishes, even if the bones of a lover are ground fine like powder. Just as the perfume of sandalwood does not leave it, even if it is completely ground up, similarly the basis of love is the soul, and it is indestructible and therefore eternal. Beauty can be destroyed, but not love."

The biblical ministry of counseling is that of reconciliation. A counselor's primary duty is to protect the marriage in place. He or she must do everything possible to reconcile the warring parties. He or she must do everything possible to keep the couple together except in case of violence. In case there is violence, a counselor may recommend separation but not divorce. A counselor is not a judge to pronounce a guilty sentence and authorize divorce. God alone has the right to unite and separate marriage. Jesus said, "'For this reason, a man will leave his father and mother and be united to his wife, and the two will become one flesh' Therefore what God has joined together, let no one separate." (Mark 10:9).

Marriage is the greatest union among humanity. Marriage is made to depend, not on laws, or contracts, or religious ceremonies, but on the divine union. Strictly speaking, that constitutes or should constitute, marriage. Such union may not be broken at the will of man. Jesus said that "Now I tell you that whoever divorces his wife, except for sexual immorality, and marries another woman, commits adultery." (Matthew 5:23). Our Lord here enunciates the law which was to obtain in his kingdom, which, indeed, was simply the reintroduction and enforcement of the primitive and natural ordinance. The sin of all illicit intercourse, whether in adultery, or concubinage, or prostitution, is that it separates that union from the relations and duties which the divine order has attached to and makes. Even in this situation, various measures must be taken to preserve the marriage before divorce is authorized.

I want to say that there is no such thing as a perfect marriage because of the reality or existence of the fallen nature. There is no perfect marriage because you are not perfect. The number one problem is you. There is no perfect marriage because there is no such thing as a perfect person. Every relationship needs to be perfected by grace. Marriage is a work in progress. There is always a need to add something to beautify it. In the same way, there is a need to paint and repair our houses.

Working together in agreement is the overcoming power in a marital relationship. The first place to work together is in the area of praying. They say that a couple that prays together stays together. Praying together is a two-cord knot that cannot easily be broken. I usually compare marriage to a house with two doors – a front and a back door. A husband is the gatekeeper of the front door. A wife is the gatekeeper of the back door. They work together as a couple through prayers to keep the enemy locked out of the house. It is a spiritual war whereby praying and resisting temptation are prominent. Make praying your priority and resist temptation. Praying magnifies God in your relationship. The Lord is the strength of your lives to keep you going even when you are overwhelmed by the circumstances. Pray even when you don't feel like praying. Prayer is the warm bread waiting for you in the oven whenever you wake up. Partake of it. Share it with the family.

Study together; immerse yourselves in the Word of God. Remember that you are two different individuals brought together into a union of one by the grace of God. The grace will sustain the union as long as both of you abide in Christ. The Bible is God's instruction for both of you to sustain unity and ironing out your differences. Certainly, there is going to be disagreement because you are different personalities and both of you have different desires. In such a situation open the Bible so that the Spirit of God finds for both of you a common solution. There should never be any disagreement regarding the Word of God. Other ideas which are not scriptural, should be discussed amicably. Never forward an idea for discussion without first figuring out the compelling problem it will solve.

The couple involved in a marriage covenant should learn to solve their problems amicably. The Bible says that "Be angry, yet do not sin." Do not let the sun set upon your anger" (Ephesians 4:26). There is justifiable anger. "He that will be angry and not sin let him be angry about nothing but sin." The first check is to beware of sinning; to keep your anger clear of bitterness, spite, malevolence, and all such evil feelings. We are prone to a hot temper. Anger quickly attracts sin in the same way garbage attracts rats. Keep your anger in check so that it does not cause you to sin. Take your trash out. Don't let it stay overnight. Make it a habit to resolve the discords before you go to bed.

As I said, learn to solve the discords as they surface. Never let the little things that bother you go unsolved. When little rocks accumulate, they are likely to build a big mountain. Whenever you let those little grievances go unresolved, one day they will erupt into an explosion of the volcano.

And when the volcano speaks powerfully, everyone looks for a safe place to escape! It is wise to avoid living on the brink of a volcano crater.

God intended marriage to be a union of two people. Jesus unites the consciences of the two people to become one by the sprinkling of His blood. It means they are under obligation to seek the guidance of God through prayers in their lifetime journey of marriage. In case they are overwhelmed, they have a choice to consult the clergy or priest or any qualified marriage counselor for biblical guidance. These are stakeholders because they have the interests of God to keep the union of marriage in place, because what God united let no man separate (Mark 10:9). Unfortunately, social media lifted privacy and opened the way for every friend and multiple mutual friends to be counselors of other people's marriages. Some of these are on social media for comedy, sarcastic and some are Nuts with a capital "N". The best way to minimize the intrusion of such unwarranted pollution in your marital affairs is to keep the affairs of your marriage off Facebook and WhatsApp. Remember that not all people are well-wishers, this includes relatives and friends. They post or reply to your postings with nice and impressive messages but behind the walls, they are working for your demise. Hope I am helping somebody.

Communication is the key to a strong relationship. Communication is a two-way street – Both of you have to work on improving it. "You got to build with somebody who wants it as bad as you do. A power couple is two hustlers. Not a hustler and a leach." Study each other in order to perfect your communication. It would be a lie to say that men and women are the same. They are different in terms of their biology, and they show differences, on average, in terms of their personality and interests. It is important to study your spouse. I am going to elaborate on some of the common words that women use when communicating with men. The intended message is from the spoken words. For example when your lady says this to you, "Do whatever you want." it means absolutely do not do whatever you want. Under no circumstances should you do it. You will regret it.

When your lady says "I don't care." She does dare. She cares immensely. So pay attention. This can also mean that there is a consequence if you continue to ignore her.

When your wife casually says "It doesn't matter." Absolutely times

118

a million, it does matter. Women like to pretend that they're oftentimes giving you a choice when really they've already made the choice they would like for you to concur with abundantly clear and are just waiting for you to verbally confirm it. If you veer from her clearly previously identified choice, it's curtains for you.

When you see her bothered and she says "I'm fine." Meaning, she's totally not fine. This is one of those phrases that is intended to lure in the man, wanting him to show concern or curiosity in why she has said 'I'm fine' when she clearly does not seem fine. "I'm fine," is usually code for something like "I'm ticked off, and you better fix whatever it was that ticked me off."

When she comes to you in tears and she says "What is wrong with me?" She is not looking for your advice or opinion. She just needs to be comforted with a hug. Never try to counsel her at this moment.

When she is dressed and she is ready to go out, and she asks you "How do I look?" She is not asking for your opinion regarding her dress; she is asking for the highest compliment you can give. Never point out something wrong with her outfit.

When she says to you "We need to talk." Red flag! She is probably about to jump ship, leaving you to capsize without a life vest. Whatever it is she's about to tell you is not just a simple talk, it's serious business.

When she asks you "Who were you talking to?" She has in mind a person of the opposite sex. She is suspicious. Trouble is brewing.

When you ask her to hurry up and she says "Just give me a minute!" Women don't intend to lie about this, but we seriously underestimate the time it will take to finish getting ready. Five minutes turns into fifty in the blink of an eye, and honestly, their priority is not timekeeping but to look pretty as long as it will take to accomplish it.

Women, likewise need to study men in order to communicate better. Culturally, we do tend to raise boys and girls differently: Boys are rewarded for being tough and adventurous, while girls are rewarded for being good caretakers. This difference could have impacts on how people think, interact, and navigate the world.

Men are different from women in many ways. For example, your man needs to be respected. Men are most insecure about not being respected or valuable enough. Everything that comes from a wife to a husband must be wrapped in a package called respect. No man can stand a disrespectful woman no matter how beautiful she is. Your beauty becomes irritating when your character is ugly. The Bible instructs us to honor those who deserve the honor. "Honor is a foundation stone of everything in God's kingdom. honor is not optional, It is deserved, expected, and demanded."

A man needs to be encouraged positively. Never tell your man something he can't do well. Just look for the things he can do well and encourage him. A man wants to look like he is the only hero in front of his wife. He wants to conquer territories but not to be conquered. Don't expose your husband's weaknesses to your family and friends. It will bounce back at you. You are each other's keeper (Ephesians 5:12).

Be polite to your husband. Never use attitudes and moods to communicate to your husband, you never know how your husband will interpret them. Defensive women don't have a happy home (Proverbs 15:13).

Men don't appreciate being directed by women. When your husband is driving don't rush to tell him that he has lost direction. Mute it and wait a little bit; he will figure out by himself that he is lost. That is the right time for you to swing in with your idea.

Never compare your man to other men. Openly comparing your husband to another man sends a message to him and the world that he's not good enough. Comparing your husband to other men can seriously undermine your relationship. If you attack his Ego, his Love for you will diminish. If you're "jokingly" lusting after another man and finding your man inadequate, this topic is really no joke. It can set your husband up to feel as though he can't win. Men do not often talk about feeling inadequate, but if they're honest, they're most insecure about not being respected or valuable enough. If your husband joked about your body, you'd probably take it very hard because so many women feel insecure about their bodies. Be aware of how your joking may make him feel.

Never ill treat your husband's friends because you don't like them, the person who's supposed to get rid of them is your husband (Proverbs 11:22).

Give your man space whenever it is necessary. Often, men want to sit alone, relaxing their minds. When he sits down relaxing don't ask him what he is thinking. Sometimes all he needs is his space. He's not trying to push you away, men need time to reflect, relax and reconnect that is why men need space, so they can come back and give their best to you.

Women are "naturally" better at talking about their feelings than men do. It takes a little bit of pressure for a man to express his feelings to you. Men are not "naturally" more logical. Given the fact, it's important not to make assumptions about what your man is and isn't capable of based on his gender, nor to pigeonhole him into certain stereotypes. Don't assume how he feels about things just because he's a man.

Trust is the Jewry in your marriage that is not worth losing. Being truthful is therefore the most important investment in your relationship. Honesty is the first chapter of the book of wisdom. When two people agree to get married, they open up to each other without the possibility of hiding anything from each other. There should be no hidden secrets. Yes, every person deserves privacy, including married people but avoid lying to your spouse because it will hurt your relationship in the future when the truth comes out. I am not talking about hiding a piece of chicken from your spouse but hiding some significant information pertaining to the covenant of two becoming one. For example, hiding from your spouse the children from your past relationship. Another example is hiding your income and assets from your spouse.

According to DJ Hejtmanek, transparency is a worthy goal. Don't allow fear to silence you. Feeling vulnerable should never keep us from sharing the truth. Fear silences our voice. Resist it. Feeling vulnerable often causes us to shrink back into insecurity. Step forward. Jesus brought light out of the darkness. Carry His light into the scary places of your own life. He is faithful to shine His clean, white light and dispel the darkness in our shadow-lands. Then go forth in transparent victory. Let your life become an open book declaring his grace, His transforming power, and His amazing love.

I want to say that it is not healthy to share all your past relationships with your husband unless there are children involved. There are things that you don't just share without praying for the right timing. Know when to come out clean. Remember that good communication takes into account what you say, how you say it, when you say it and why you say it. Pray for godly wisdom. Don't give your spouse more information than he or she can handle mentally.

Whatever you do, avoid telling your spouse lies. The Bible warns that "Let no man deceive you with EMPTY WORTHLESS LYING words:

for because of these things comes the wrath of God upon the children of disobedience. Be not you, therefore, partakers with them. (Ephesians 5:3-7). The term "Empty worthless lying words" is in reference to not being truthful regarding what we say, and what we don't say or hide from our spouses.

Truthfulness is a great portion of integrity. Integrity means to be sincere even in the things you do in secrecy. The power of integrity involves building a life without the possibility of compromising. Losing integrity can cause serious impairments affecting overall relational performance.

Patience is a virtue. By calling patience a virtue, or state of moral excellence, it leads people to believe an ability to wait without agitation is an admirable quality. Patience is a skill that can be learned over time. The more we exercise patience, the less likely we are to become agitated when forced to wait for something. Mastering this virtue will make for a happier life. A moment of patience in a moment of anger saves a hundred moments of regret. There is going to be that tough moment that demands wisdom to resolve. Pray for patience in order to avoid overreacting. Patience is the game-changer. It makes you appear weak when you are strong, and strong when you are weak.

Patience brings endurance and perseverance. Pray to God to equip you with courage and perseverance. The Bible says that "Allow perseverance to finish its work, so that you may be mature and complete, not lacking anything." (James 1:4). Perseverance can be summed up to mean you're committed to your goal. Perseverance that's the key to a successful life. If you keep persevering long enough, you will achieve your true potential. Just remember, you can do anything you set your mind to, but it takes action, persistence, and the courage to face your fears.

Struggles are part of the marriage relationship because the vows made when getting married included loving your spouse in good and bad times. Embrace the good times with both hands in anticipation of tough times. God allows the struggle of life as an agent of growth, for, without them, we wouldn't have stumbled across our strength. We are placed in the struggles like a rough diamond and must be polished, or the luster of it will never appear. The daily struggles of life enable us to grow, develop resilience, & enhance our character and ability to endure! I want to warn that patience is not applicable in a situation where there is physical abuse.

In such a situation, an immediate separation is advised until the aggressive spouse proves that there will be no more violence and abuse. As I said, any counseling given should be intended to restore the marriage rather than to break it up.

This appeal is for the husbands: Fight for your marriage. Nothing good is ever easy to keep. Be ready to sacrifice everything (apart from your faith) for the sake of your marriage. The most important need of a woman is to be loved. Prove to her that nothing matters to you more than her. Never stop pursuing and courting your wife even after marriage. To court, someone comes from the word courtship. It describes the period of time before two people enter a relationship.... Simply put – courting is the time before a relationship starts when the couple gets to know one another, exchange gifts, and generally keep a respectful distance with little-to-no intimacy. Keep doing it even after she moves in to stay with you. If your relationship is becoming stale, revisit the old tricks during your early dating times. Add to your relationship various ingredients of romance. You need reminders. You need date nights that feel like the first time. You need romance and movie nights and sharing all of the memories you have together.

1) Give your wife a surprise call while at work
2) Bring home some flowers occasionally to surprise her.
3) Sex does not begin at night in bed; it begins the moment you meet your wife in the morning for breakfast. Make her feel relevant to your life and special too. Let her know that you are after her as a person rather than her body or sex. Be romantic to her.

As for a wife, respect your husband in privacy and in public. Let him know that he is in charge of the house. Your husband needs your attention. Even in a situation, whereby you have a helper or housemaid in the house, try to serve your husband instead of leaving him to the maid. Some housemaids have ended up taking over homes as housewives. They do everything that the housewives fail to do. Train your children to do the housework instead of a housemaid. "Many of us have indirectly trained the maid and left our children to be untrained and undisciplined. Your maid does all the cooking ...your children do all the eating ...when your daughters get married and can't cook and their marriages have problems you blame the devil. You start praying and going to crusades to save their marriage. It is disturbing".

Women have divided love after producing babies. Most women, after getting children make the mistake of taking the attention from the husband to the children. Yes, they are his children and he equally loves them too. But nature demands that a woman gives attention to a man in the house. "We know from research that a relationship that's not given attention will get worse," says Tracy K. Ross, LCSW, who is a couples and family therapist. She adds: "If you do nothing, the relationship will deteriorate — you'll be co-parents arguing about tasks. You have to put work into the relationship for it to stay the same, and work even harder to improve it."

Make yourself attractive and available for your husband. Some women make the mistake of giving up taking care of themselves the moment they get married. Remember that your husband is still a human being attracted to beautiful things. Always be that beautiful thing he is attracted to. If possible be available for your man. Never use sex as a bargaining tool to bring your husband to submission. It might make things worse. Some men are impatient, If they don't get sex from you, they go for it somewhere else. Never pretend to be sick for the purpose of denying your husband sex. You must give it to him how he wants it. Sex is very important to Men, if you keep denying him, it is a matter of time before another woman takes over your duty. No man can withstand sex starvation for too long (even the anointed ones). I want to say that both spouses are supposed to equally benefit from good sex. Unfortunately some women tend to think of men as the primary beneficially of sex.

1) Build sexual tension
2) Make sex more intense and satisfying.
3) Keep him thinking about you.
4) Be yourself but funny and exciting.

Don't be ashamed to be aggressive sexually. Talk to your man in a sexy way; men like it. Talk in a way that's both confident and effective, there are four factors that you need to consider…

- The Context
- The Tone Of Your Voice
- The Speed Of Your Voice
- What You Do While Talking sexy To Your Man

The three major causes of divorce are Adultery, finances, and struggle for power. I am going to begin with Adultery. Adultery destroys marriage absolutely. It might not be now but it is a sure deal. First of all, whether you are caught or not, once you get the third party involved in your marriage, you can't love your spouse as you are supposed to because there is divided minds, attention, and affection. Never let a third person come into your relationship. However much you are tempted to do it, just don't do it.

There is inconsistency whenever a third party comes into the covenant relationship of two people. An affair cannot be hidden forever. Soon or later it will be exposed. Even before it is exposed its effects are apparently visible. As I said, when you get involved in an extramarital affair you can't love your spouse as you are supposed to do. The love availed to the third party is not grasped from the air – It is transferred from your spouse to the third party. The moment you get involved in an affair, the affection for your spouse gradually diminishes.

An affair or cheating is when a married person gets involved in an improper relationship with another person outside the marriage covenant. All sexual activities (Flirting, kissing, and sexual intercourse) are limited within the context of marriage. Flirting or coquetry is a social and sexual behavior involving spoken or written communication, as well as body language, by one person to another, either to suggest interest in a deeper relationship with the other person or if done playfully, for amusement. When you do it with another person other than your spouse, it is considered to be cheating.

Some people say that watching porno without your partner knowing does not count as cheating. "But if your partner doesn't know you watch porn and they find out, it will make them feel uncomfortable and insecure." It is considered to be unfaithful to secretly watch porno because you eventually become a participant emotionally. There are those fantasies and imaginations seeing yourself in action and at times coming to a climax. The characters involved in action in porno videos are actors. In real life, they don't do as they act in porno. There is a danger of wanting your spouse to do what you saw the other person doing in porno videos. It can slowly affect your sexual life. Watching pornography is therefore another way of cheating on your spouse.

Lust is defined as a strong desire for something or someone that is beyond the moral boundaries as established by God. It means that God created in us exact limits of desires that are regulated by our hearts as opposed to our emotions. People lust for different things. Regarding relationship, lust is an intense or unbridled sexual desire – lasciviousness. Lust in all its nature is an abomination to God. "Dearly beloved, I beseech you as strangers and pilgrims, abstain from fleshly lusts, which war against the soul." Jesus warned that "But I say unto you, That whosoever looketh on a woman to lust after her hath committed adultery with her already in his heart." (Matthew 5:28). This is inclusive – both men and women. When you look at someone and go beyond looking and start undressing them or having the imagination of sexual encounters with them you are lusting after them. Just one look is enough. Resist the second and third look because they will take you the wrong way or direction. Dr. Billy Gram used to say that a bird can sit on your head but to allow it to make a nest on your head is deliberate negligence. I developed a habit, whenever I look at a beautiful woman, I thank God for the beauty of creation, and move on. No fantasizing, nothing. And it works!

Jealousness is one of the major causes of conflicts in marriage. I want to say that every person is jealous in one way or the other. In fact, the Bible says that our God is jealous. "You shall not bow down to them or serve them, for I the Lord your God am a jealous God, visiting the iniquity of the fathers on the children to the third and the fourth generation of those who hate me" (Exodus 20:5). It is holy jealousy without ill intentions. Jealous is a protective measure towards what belongs to you. Except that we should not let it escalate into abuse and control. When you are over-jealous your spouse sees mistrust. People don't want to be controlled. Give them a chance to prove you wrong.

The second major cause of divorce is the management of finances. Selfishness plays a major role. That is when the objective of getting married becomes what you can get out of the relationship instead of what you can invest in it. Be a giver not a taker. Takers strive to get as much as possible from others. They are not interested in contributing or add value to the pot of the relationship but to take as much as they can. Takers are not sincerely committed to a lasting relationship. According to research led by Yale psychologist Margaret Clark, most people act like givers in close relationships.

On another front, the economic crisis is reported to have a serious effect on the morals of the couple involved in marriage. A good example is when both spouses work full-time jobs. At times they work different shifts whereby they don't get value-time together as a couple. They don't have valuable time to raise their children in a godly way. We should never let money dictate our values. Remember that there are things that money can't buy.

Another challenge brought about by the economic crisis is when a husband and a wife work separately. I have no problem with a housewife getting a job. But it is improper to put your wife under another man's leadership, even at work. The Bible defines a woman as a weaker sex that should be protected by her husband. When you send your wife to work a job under the leadership of another man, you are putting her in the temptation of seeking protection from her boss. When I was in Bible college, Dr. Lester Surmall instructed me never to put my wife under the covering of another man. He warned me not even to rent my rooms to another family. It should be only one man and one wife under one roof. Today it is common to find a couple of families sharing one roof in order to share the bills. Dr. Lester Surmal used to say sarcastically "Yes, you will earn some money for the bills at the expense of your marriage."

The struggle for power is the third cause of divorce. It is caused mainly by ego and selfishness. Where there is selfishness there is no commitment. Consequently, there is a struggle regarding who controls who, and who controls what. In marriage, competition has no place. You were put together to compliment each other rather than to compete against each other. "Go into relationships with a positive expectation and looking for God's glory in others." The Bible clearly defines the roles of a husband and wife. We ignore it at our peril.

Somebody posted this article "The Father אלוהים formed the man first because he was created to be a visionary and so that he could become the recipient of all the information, revelation, and communication Father

אלוהים desired to share regarding humanity's relationship with Him and its "purpose" for being. Joel the prophet (nabi) affirmed this when he prophesied about the outpouring of the Holy Spirit (2:28) "And it shall come to pass afterward, that I will pour out my רוּחַ upon -all- flesh; and your sons and your daughters shall prophesy, your old men shall dream dreams, your young men shall see visions."

Men have built-in qualities enabling them to receive the vision and to bring it to pass. Note, this isn't any a common man, it's a man of רוּחַ guided by the Father. Old men will receive dreams and young men will see visions from God. It doesn't say women will see visions, it says women will prophesy. Ever notice when a lazy, irresponsible son is usually told by their mom like, "You'll grow up becoming a thief to feed your lazy bottom to the point that it'll become your job, etc..." And indeed though not all but mostly, it indeed comes to pass? this means, that women will speak of the things men see in visions. God's pattern is that man is given a vision, but the woman is there to make sure that he accomplishes it. Everything about the woman is designed to help him carry on his vision. Man and woman have each specific function. Some men have no vision because they're not committed to what the רוּחַ of God says to them. Without God's guidance, man cannot fully function in his purpose."

Now I am going to talk about the self-esteem of the couple. Self-esteem comes when you know that you are worth the blood of the Lamb. A spouse can easily lose their self-esteem in particular when they do things for their spouse in many ways and they feel ignored or not noticed. Do not give up doing good. Jesus is watching and appreciating you. Remember that He is an active member of your marriage covenant. And He is the best paymaster. He smiles at you even when nobody else does. Jesus is your first love. Who else would you rather sing over you? Only someone (Jesus) is in love with you. Respond to Him too in worship from your heart. And you will experience the peace that surpasses understanding.

Learn to appreciate your spouse. Above all, learn to appreciate God. Gratitude is a virtue. There is primary gratitude that involves the gracious goodness of God. Be thankful for who God is. The word "good" and God have the same root in English. God alone is good, and He is always good. This is enough to put a smile on your face. Then there is secondary gratitude involving the blessings of God in particular the family. Rejoicing in times of trials is radical gratitude. God created us and placed His joy in us that cannot be extinguished. Gratitude is supposed to be contagious. It is a good infection that should catch everyone in the family.

True happiness does not depend on the size of the family but on the size of the hearts of the individual members of the family; in the size of the sacrifices, they are willing to make for the sake of the family. And that's not just measured in words or gestures but in actions. Don't just talk, act. Don't just hear, listen. Don't just promise, prove. Don't just change, transform. Never give up doing good.

Forgiving is the key to a lasting relationship. "God's precepts protect us when we choose to forgive (yes, it's a choice we make), then God releases His forgiveness to us. Whether the sin toward us was great or small, withholding forgiveness is sin. (Even when we don't forgive ourselves!) Ask God to help you reach the point where you can choose to forgive, fully, from the heart. He will help us do what He requires. When we refuse to forgive, we become chained to our past and to our offender. Think ball and chain around your heart, weighing you down, constant and unrelenting."

Forgiving perfects our communication with God. Here are Jesus' own words in Matthew: "For if you forgive others their trespasses [their reckless and willful sins], your heavenly Father will also forgive you. But if you do not forgive others [nurturing your hurt and anger with the result that it interferes with your relationship with God], then your Father will not forgive your trespasses." (Matthew 6:14-15).

If you're going through a valley or a storm right now, extend your roots deeper into the good soil of God's presence. Jesus is there waiting to comfort and counsel. His love is all-sustaining and his forgiveness complete — even when it's ourselves we need to forgive.

Do not avenge yourselves, beloved, but leave room for God's wrath. For it is written: "Vengeance is Mine; I will repay, says the Lord." On the contrary, "If your enemy is hungry, feed him; if he is thirsty, give him a drink. For in so doing, you will heap burning coals on his head." (Romans 12:19-20). Forgiving is not taking the offender off the hook but handing them over to God. It is regaining your freedom – Free from grudge and hate due to somebody's offense. Forgiving is standing aside yourself as a mere spectator, and allow God to preside over your case as a credible judge of all.

Learn to solve your problems peacefully with honor. Obstacles either define us, destroy us or strengthen us. In case of discords sit down in your bedroom to solve them. Never shout at each other in front of your children. Correct each other in private. Defend each other in public. Keep your personal matters off social media. Never think about humiliating your spouse in public. Regardless of the situation, stand by your man or woman in public. If there is nothing good to say about your spouse in public just keep quiet.

I am going to end by addressing the issue of abuse in marital relationships. God's design for marriage never included abuse, violence, or coercive control. Even emotional abuse can bruise or severely harm a person's heart, mind, and soul. Although domestic violence can take place in any intimate relationship, the great majority of it is perpetrated by men against women. The issue of abuse should be addressed immediately. In case of violence, separation is recommended. At times the victims of abuse do not acknowledge it. "The path to seeking knowledge on abuse starts with understanding what abuse is. When those people affected by abuse see the situation more clearly, they are more likely to begin healing from the hurt and to help provide safety information for others."

HOW TO OVERCOME LONELINESS

Loneliness could be defined as isolation and can leave you feeling empty and without hope. Periods of loneliness are hard to understand. Sometimes it can feel like no one seems to care. I am going to discuss this topic from the spiritual and psychological points of view. Depending on how you cope with loneliness, it can be used positively and negatively. Loneliness does not necessarily mean that you are alone. As for the believers, Jesus is ever with us. He never forsakes us. I usually advise the overseas missionary who feel like strangers in a foreign land to know and to believe that they are not alone. Jesus is with them. He promised to watch their going out and coming in. And His promises never expire. He knows their tomorrow.

Don't get bored because our God is never boring. Certainly, heaven is not boring. During His earthly ministry, wherever Jesus went there was a commotion. We may not see Him with our physical eyes but He is still having the same impact wherever He is. He promised to be with us up to the uttermost ends of the earth (Acts 1:8). "Jesus returned to us in the presence and the power of the Spirit". We are never alone.

You have dual citizenship. You are what God called you to be in eternity. Act as you are called to be. Do what angels are doing in heaven. They are busy singing, praising, and worshiping God. We can learn a lot from the angels as we see how they worship God. If we can emulate what we learn from the angels, perhaps we can draw closer to God in our own worship as we emulate the worship taking place in Heaven right this very moment. And this can be a liberating truth.

Solitude is another spiritual practice that can help us grow closer to

God. If seeing and hearing from God is your goal, then solitude is the answer. It's what we need in order to quiet our souls and our minds long enough to hear His gentle whisper. Jesus often retreated to a solitary place to pray (see Mark 1:35 and Luke 6:12). He invited His disciples into solitude to rest (Mark 6:31-32). In the Old Testament, both Elijah and Moses retreated into solitude to hear from God.

Some of the famous biblical characters were lonely. David, who penned over 73 chapters of the Psalms, identifies with your loneliness. As a book of songs, the Psalms offer a breadth and depth of varied emotions. Some of the songs in Psalms were sung publicly, some privately. Some were written by worship leaders for the temple. Others were written by Moses and Solomon. David, however, is the Psalms' main author. And although he had great talent, he struggled with deep spiritual battles. In Psalm 68:5-6, King David writes, "A father to the fatherless, a defender of widows, is God in his holy dwelling. God sets the lonely in families, he leads out the prisoners with singing; but the rebellious live in a sun-scorched land." Even a quick glance at Psalm 63: 1-12, in your English Bible, shows an ancient Hebrew pattern; David uses seven different means to praise and worship God (seven as in a complete set) as antidote to loneliness.

Psychiatrists counselors advise their clients to do certain things in order to avert loneliness. Things like walking outside and watch the sky. Biblical counseling instructs their clients to lift up their eyes and praise God. We are challenged by our culture to never stop learning to use a few extra percentage points through life; but in a vastly more strategic way, God is saying through David— why not start employing more and more of your capacity to worship God? Regularly use your lips, your tongue, your hands, your will, your mouth, your mind, and your intellect to the max in seeking to offer worship to God. We need a new generation of God-hearted, Spirit-empowered, Christ-seeking worshipers. Believers like David used every Psalm 63:2 tense of life to describe his pursuit of the Lord. He says this has been my past pursuit: So I have looked for You in the sanctuary, To see Your power and Your glory. One of the most fundamental truths from this Psalm is that God can satisfy us to the very core of our existence and being. Loneliness hides the future in a cloud of mystery. But God reveals His faithfulness even in the dark. Listen to what

David writes: *Psalm 16:9: Therefore my heart is glad, and my glory rejoices; My flesh also will rest in hope.*

Richard J. Foster says in his book Celebration of Discipline: "The purpose of silence and solitude is to be able to see and hear." If seeing and hearing from God is the goal of solitude, then I must be willing to ignore distractions. Ignore distractions by withdrawing to a secret place. In pursuit of solitude, I started taking solo walks around our neighborhood. It was difficult to keep my earbuds at home and resist the temptation to listen to a podcast. Those friendly voices are a companion in my ear when I'm trying to make space for solitude. Instead, I turned my attention to the flowering bushes along the sidewalk, the seagulls squawking overhead, the rhythm of my breath."

Loneliness does not necessarily mean being alone. "Loneliness lies. When it creeps up, you could be surrounded by people in a coffee shop with tears right behind your eyes. Even the act of holding back tears back causes aching pain." Jeremiah was surrounded by people but he was lonely. The book of Lamentations is sandwiched between the books of Ezekiel and Jeremiah. This unusual book properly follows the book of Jeremiah the prophet and priest because it was written by him. It is the "Lamentations of Jeremiah" as he wept over the city of Jerusalem following its desolation and captivity by Nebuchadnezzar. In the Septuagint version of this -- the Greek translation of the Hebrew -- there is a brief notation to the effect that as Jeremiah went up on the hillside and sat overlooking the desolate city, he uttered these lamentations. Jeremiah felt lonely because he was ignored by the people he was sent to help.

On the negative side, people feel lonely when they are ignored and abandoned by their families and close friends in particular when they are no longer beneficial to them. Parents feel lonely after their children move out of their homes. Moms are stuck at home with empty nests without their young children.

Christians are lonely in this corrupt world. Christians are tramped down (bashed) by the insensitive people of the world and bureaucracy every day. We are partly to blame for the bashing because we have not represented Christ as we are supposed to do. We have made ourselves a good target for the world to mock. The petty bickering and fighting are causing us to lose our saltiness. For example, the Church is still divided upon political allegiances and prejudice as the world is. We are supposed to become members of a new race, overcoming petty prejudice, and giving our ultimate allegiance to the Lord as opposed to politicians. Although we are not exempted from persecution, the bashing we see today is self-inflicted; it is bash and crash. The Bible warned us against losing our saltiness. In this case, losing saltiness applies to what is absolutely useless due to incompetence.

I am going to elaborate on the loneliness that is encountered by overseas missionaries. Missionaries pursuing their overseas calling feel lonely due to separation from their families, friends, relatives, and familiar places back home. I would not recommend missionaries to go into those remote areas alone without a team structure in place because it is very hard to have times of fellowship. It is possible to go to a place where people look at you as a stranger. Not being able to share heart to heart with anyone on the field can be very lonely. Have a structure in place whereby you can fellowship with the indigenous Christian people. It helps to break up the loneliness if your mission organization has planned times of fellowship and prayer. If not, start creating your own fellowship, times of prayer with strong Christian natives, and mentor relationships where someone challenges you with God's Word to keep you growing.

Therefore go and make disciples of all nations, baptizing them in the name of the Father, and of the Son, and of the Holy Spirit, and teaching them to obey all that I have commanded you. And surely I am with you always, even to the end of the age." (Matthew 28:20). God's promise that He is with you to the very end of the age. It means that He will be with you until He physically returns to be with you. The appearance of Christ in the flesh is the beginning of the last age of the world. Here the context determines its significance as stretching forward to the end of the age, or aeon, which began with the first Advent of the Christ and shall last until the second.

Open up to the indigenous people where you are positioned. Some of the natives may not be believers but they are curious to know what you are doing. Build a strong communication chain with the indigenous people. When people realize your mission they are glad to provide you with some of the essential information you need that enables you to stay strong and healthy during your mission work. Hook up with other missionaries in the neighborhood and remote areas. Meet with them often and share your testimonies. If you have your family around, give your kids opportunities to play with other missionary kids or with nationals from strong Christian homes.

We are social animals. No one ever succeeds without the help of others. The beauty and joy of this world are meaningless if you don't have somebody to share with. Fellowship is an important aspect of our faith. I like this quotation from Cathy in Guatemala: "Living in remote areas is a sacrifice, the needs are great, and not many are willing to do it. But if you look for ways to find creative fellowship and make spiritual and emotional refreshment a priority, you can do it. Don't let a year of depression bring you to the point where you realize you need fellowship. Build it into your ministry. Don't feel guilty being gone for two or three weeks at a time every two or three months. It's much easier to know your needs and plan for them than to have to get counseling and be off the field for a large chunk of time. We are all human. It is God's ministry. He can do it with or without us. He chooses to use us. Don't try to be a superhuman. God is the vine, we are the branches. He is our source for strength so that we can soar like eagles."

There is induced loneliness due to isolation. Some people are lonely because the world has been so unkind to them. Some people won't like you regardless. On the positive side, some people will never like you because your spirit irritates their demons. On the negative side, bad characters can artificially cause others to isolate you.

Loneliness can be caused by bad habits and can cause bad habits. If you're feeling lonely, it often also means you've built some habits into your daily life that might be making you feel closed off from the world. Some of these habits can be a result of hard work. That is when you have no time for others. Also, great wealth can make you lonely. Most agree that money helps when things are dire. If you are worried about food, warmth, or shelter, having some cash is decidedly beneficial. However, wealth can attract you, at best fake friends, whose priority is to exploit you.

"Two new studies offer conflicting evidence, one suggesting that people with higher incomes spend less time socializing, and another suggesting that they feel less lonely. People with higher incomes, less inclined to rely on family for material or logistic support, delegate their social time to more deliberate—perhaps even strategic—relationships. Could higher-income people be prioritizing friendly hangouts or professional networking over "family obligations?" This study doesn't answer that question, nor does it address the relative importance of connections with friends versus family to overall happiness. However, most would agree that dedicating more time to social relationships, of the family or friend variety, is likely to result in stronger, more authentic connections, less likelihood of loneliness, and a bigger boon to happiness. The second study looked at loneliness, the presumed antithesis of feeling loved and a sense of belonging, and a factor that correlates with less happiness. The researchers define loneliness as "a perceived discrepancy between desired and actual social relationships; a perceived lack of control over the quantity and especially the quality of one's social activity."

Know who you are in Christ and love the new person you are becoming, and love others. We need each other. We can do what any other creations (animals) cannot do because of our capacity to communicate with God and with others. As long as we can communicate and discuss issues, there is nothing we can't solve. Our capability is in God that strengthens us. God is going to use some of your brains, muscles, and time to accomplish His plans on the earth.

Intriguingly, some people have a tendency of withdrawing by exuding negative emotions – sending a clear message that they aren't ready to engage in any social activity. The more solitary, the more friendless, the more isolated you become. Self-reliance bestows benefits but it is not easy to build and sustain them. Secretiveness should have limitations. Going public is beneficial. Given the fact, it is not good to talk to the public about your problems unless you trust them. Minimize the extent of your secrecy. Utterly hiding issues to yourself might result in severe depression. People who hide everything to themselves see themselves as the primary enemy. They take revenge on their bodies in retaliation. The visible evidence is self-harm like self-cutting, overeating, over-shopping, sexual addiction and etc. Self-harm is also referred to as non-suicidal self-injury (NSSI). However, self-harm can cause more damage to someone's health and safety than they may have intended and can also cause accidental suicide. Some people who self-harm may only do so once, whereas others self-harm frequently and for many years. These are signs of depression.

Obsession with the Internet can be a cause of loneliness to ourselves and others. A recent experimental study by Robert Kraut et al. (1998) found that greater use of the Internet decreases communication within the family, diminishes the size of the subjects' local social networks, and increases feelings of loneliness and depression. Spend your time with the family. There are things you can learn from the elders that cannot be found on Google. Social media can cause loneliness in many other ways. For example, when you see and read the postings of others regarding families, relationships, achievements and etc, and you start feeling not measuring up. You start feeling like others are way up there and you are down here. Loneliness exaggerates the lies fed on you instead of the reality.

Stop comparing yourself with others or trying to be what you are not. God created you beautiful. Self-esteem is appreciating who you are. Be yourself, no one is like you. God made you to be you not someone else. "We live in a pathologically dissatisfied world. And I'm going to tell you why. Because we love to compare --- Go around the world and discover that people aren't happy with their bodies. Filipinos want to be fair-complexioned like Westerners, and so buy bleaching stuff. Westerners want to own bronzed bodies like ours, and so purchase tanning lotions. Those with moles have them removed, while those who don't strategically implant beauty spots. Some people want to shed a few pounds to look like Ally McBeal, while others want to gain some baby fat to look like Drew Barrymore" ~ Paul Alowo

Negative habits are the major cause of loneliness. Bad habits drive people away. Take an inventory of your life, your thoughts and where you're headed. "Check yourself. Sometimes you are the toxic person. Understand that you make mistakes. You hurt people. Apologize. That is growth, understanding that there are things you need to work on. That is enlightenment, striving for continuous improvement instead of faking perfection."

But not all people isolated have bad habits. People love to put labels on lonely people, and these are among the most common: Crunchy, crazy, mentally sick, selfish, sleazy, cruel, ego-maniacal, and etc. If you identify yourself with any of these bad habits there is still hope. Counteracting these habits starts with praying, then making choices to change your lifestyle, and your thinking patterns, even just a little bit at a time will make a difference. If you can't reverse your behaviors by yourself seek help from your pastor.

As I said, people love to put labels on lonely people. Before you isolate somebody, find out the truth. False allegations are the most chronic form of mental abuse. When people can't kill your dreams and purpose, they will try to assassinate your character. "Character assassination" is the slandering of a person usually with the intention of destroying public confidence in that person. It is the act of lowering one's character in a bid to ruin the character of others. One mistake you should never make is to allow yourself to be recruited by someone, to hate another person who hasn't wronged you. Don't inherit other people's enemies: It is a total lack of education and enlightenment when you automatically make your friend's enemies your own. Avoid taking hasty conclusions because of what others are saying about someone else. Ironically, what people say about others, says a lot about them. "The things you say about others, say a lot about you! I can tell a lot about a person by what they choose to see in others."

If you are a victim of character assassination, reject the lies of the devil. Work on bringing forth the real person whom God created you to be. Work on your character. God alone can establish your character so that it follows you even in your grave and it lives on the earth even after your demise. When God establishes the character, it is indestructible.

Disability can be a cause of loneliness. When you are disabled people are likely to ignore you. There is a misunderstanding that the disability affects everything about the disabled person. I don't see it as a lack of empathy from his peers as much as I see fear of the unknown.

The Lord is God of the physically healthy and the mentally strong, but He is also the God of the physically disabled and the mentally handicapped. He is sovereign over the fragile and feeble as well as over the adroit and mighty. The Bible teaches that every person conceived in this world is a unique creation of God (see Psalms 139:16), and that includes the disabled and the handicapped. Disability, like any other sickness is attributed to the work of the evil one. A natural question is why God allows some people to be born disabled or handicapped or why He allows accidents that bring about a disability or handicap later in life. This issue falls under the umbrella of a theological/philosophical debate known as "the problem of evil" or "the problem of pain."

Why are some people handicapped? The answer is found in the curse of sin. Every person born into this world has death sentence over his or her head. We are born to die. Every day we celebrate our birthdays, we are celebrating a year closer to our graves. Disability is one of the sicknesses that torment us in this world to death. We are are all disabled or handicapped in one way or another. "The need for eyeglasses indicates impaired or "handicapped" vision. Dental braces are a sign of imperfect teeth. Diabetes, arthritis, rosacea, a "trick" knee—these can all be considered disabilities to some extent. The whole human race lives with the reality of imperfection. Everyone experiences less-than-ideal conditions. We are all broken in some way. The handicaps we live with are simply a matter of degree."

God allows some people to be disabled or handicapped is that God will glorify Himself through it. When the disciples wondered about the man born blind, Jesus told them, "This happened so that the works of God might be displayed in him" (John 9:3). When the same disciples later wondered about Lazarus' sickness, Jesus told them, "It is for God's glory so that God's Son may be glorified through it" (John 11:4). In both instances, God was glorified through the disability—in the case of the man born blind, the temple rulers had incontrovertible proof of Jesus' power to heal; in the case of Lazarus, "many of the Jews who had come to visit Mary, and had seen what Jesus did, believed in him" (John 11:45). Every human being is and can be useful. Disability is not inability. Do not deny yourself an opportunity to show what God can do in you and through you for His glory. Remember that if you are a child of God, disabilities and handicaps are temporary. Those conditions are part of this fallen world, not the world to come. God's children—those who by faith in Christ are made children of God (John 1:12) — have a new body awaiting them that will not suffer from any predicament. They have a bright and glorious future.

Aging is another cause of loneliness. As we age, we have a tendency to think passion and zeal are reserved for the young. We feel there is less need for us because others are carrying the torch. As a result, we quit dreaming, and we disengage ourselves from all social activities. I want to say that no matter your age, God isn't finished with you! Keep on dreaming big time.

You are not identified by your body. The weakened body is just a container of the real you. God uses the real you.

God uses us regardless of our age. The key to being used by God is availability. The calling to seek God is extended to all people regardless of their age. Your days are not over. They are just beginning. Your season of fullness and fruition blossoms now. You are not very old to be isolated because your age-mates are still socially active. The Psalmist prayed that "Even when I am old and gray, do not forsake me, my God, till I declare your power to the next generation, your mighty acts to all who are to come." (Psalms 71:18).

There is no time when you are useless. God never says that He doesn't want anything from you because of your age. He treasures you the same way at all times. You are a steward of every moment of time that you are breathing. You are still in a sound mind for a reason. "God is calling each of us regardless of our age to step out of the shadows, to rise and take our places in the Kingdom. Shoulder to shoulder, men and women. Into positions of authority in the secular realm, in business, in technology, in the arts and entertainment, in His Church. Into rank and file formation as foot soldiers to fulfill Kingdom strategies. All stations, all walks of life."

It is possible to mistake boredom with loneliness. Life can be boring with or without people around you. Never be afraid to try something new, because life is boring when you stay within the limits of what you already know. Creativity is opening up new doors and doing new things. Make changes around you. Move the furniture around. Go out for dinner instead of regular kitchen cooking. If you have a spouse talk to him or her about making life more exciting. Use some humor because it is terribly rude to tell people that they are boring. Do things together that you don't normally do and have fun when life is just flat-out boring.

Loneliness is not a virtue. Loneliness is not an entity; loneliness is the absence of the joy of the Lord. It is caused by other factors as we have discussed. The good news is, we can reverse all the negatives of life and the bad habits and start reversing our feelings of loneliness too. A key to dealing with loneliness is to maintain closeness in your personal walk with God and, if married, your spouse. Simply making these two vital relationships your top priority will keep you from a host of other problems.

It is possible to be loved but not notice it. At times, love has to be discovered. "Peter turned and saw the disciple whom Jesus loved following them, the one who also had leaned back against him during the supper ---- 21 When Peter saw him, he said to Jesus, "Lord, what about this man?" (John 21:20–21). John is called the disciple whom Jesus loved, not because Jesus showed favoritism but because John discovered the love of Christ more than other disciples. We are related to God evenly but our love for Him varies. We know God by our intimate relationship with Jesus Christ. The covenant relationship involves our loyalty and submission by embracing God's moral authority. Spiritual discipline is attained by dedication through devotion. Devotion is not intended just to increase the amount of head knowledge of the scriptures but to enable us to discover the love of Christ availed to all of us equivalently. The enrichment of discovering the love of Christ for you is discovering the love for others in you (1 John 4:20).

Life may not be the party we hoped for, but while we are here we might as well dance. Get out and engage people. "If we make choices to engage, even when we don't want to ... it's possible that we may feel less lonely. This may be something as small as going outside for a walk or calling a friend, or something as major as taking on a new hobby or trying to date or go to meet-ups." I want to warn you that don't choose a company out of desperateness. It is possible to embrace the wrong characters in a bid to beat loneliness, and you end up in a disaster. I compare it to jumping from a hot pan to fire. Choose wisely whom you associate with. People are either God-sent to inspire you or Satan-sent to drain you. Choose your circles wisely. Pray and act on the truth. It is not the truth that you hear but the truth that you know that will set you free. Beautiful people are searching for beautiful people. As you elevate your frequency you will meet beautiful new people with the same mindset. Choose quality over quantity. Swing into action now. Be the initiator.

Naturally, we are social animals. It is unnatural to admire staying alone. They say that "The human heart is a theater of longing." We long for companions to counter loneliness. Our longing for family, friends, colleagues, and even strangers is core to human survival. Survival is akin to happiness. No one except you is responsible for your happiness and the happiness of others. "Life is ten percent what happens to you and ninety percent how you respond to it." You can turn a sour environment into sweetness. You can turn a bitter relationship into better. Every relationship has to be cultivated and nurtured. "Be the one who nurtures and builds. Be the one who has an understanding and a forgiving heart, the one who looks for the best in people. Leave people better than you found them."

Remember that there is no person without flaws. Learn to accommodate people in their weaknesses without compromising your basic values. It is good to love people but there is the side effect of being vulnerable. At times we are hurt by the very people we love most. Keep on loving regardless. Loving is the noblest thing to do even though loving the unlovable causes tumors in our soul in particular when our efforts to love are frustrated. Those wounds are left for us to suffer for the rest of our lives. I struggle many times in that pain but that does not stop me from loving because it is my nature to love. "The beginning of love is to let those we love be perfectly themselves, and not to twist them to fit our own image. Otherwise, we love only the reflection of ourselves we find in them."

The best way to find love is to find God. Have you ever grieved over "lost time" or "wasted time" while engaging others in friendship? Remember that there is no time wasted whenever you are stepping into your calling. Loving others is to be who and what God crafted you to be from the very beginning. Nothing is ever wasted or lost with God. The Lord is never on the wrong side of time. He's always on the right side and on time, and so are you. Remember that God uses what appears to be a myriad of delays and wrong turns for His glory. So, never get discouraged.

If you don't love yourself as you love others it is because you are loving the old version of yourself. It is impossible to love your old self. Learn to love yourself by discovering your image in Christ. Your new nature is love. Your old nature is contrary to your new nature. Your old nature projects the unlovable character. Being loved continuously when you believe that you're unlovable is like throwing salt on a wound. It stings like acid. You want it desperately, instinctively knowing deep down you were wired to need it. But the more love is given, the more unworthy of love you behave, constantly trying to find ways to make up for the void and pain that reside like a monster inside your heart.

The major reason we stay away from people is that we are offended by them. "What it takes to offend you is all it takes to defeat you!" There is truth in this statement. That's why Jesus taught us how not to get offended by exercising forgiveness. Today may we give our forgiveness freely so we are not trapped, broken, or defeated by an offense. The Word of God is the cleansing agent to wash in daily. I like this prayer: "Lord, your Word is the salt in my wound. Your Spirit is the breath in my nostril. Your purging makes me uncomfortable, but rejuvenates me."

The antidote to unfairness is fairness. The question is how do you achieve fairness in the corrupt world? There is always going to be shocking negativity. It is your response to negativity that can make a difference. Remember that people love at their level of consciousness. Choose your battles wisely...every battle is not for you. Although you will need to fight some, others are only a distraction. True love is awesome, and you deserve not just to have it but to give it. Don't settle for anything less. "Facts – settle for less, and less is exactly what you'll get!"

Give generously. "Generosity is giving more than you can, and pride is taking less than you need." The Bible says that it is more blessed to give than to receive. When you light somebody's candle with your candle, your candle doesn't go off but it shines brighter. "There is no exercise better for the heart than reaching down and lifting people up."

Love all but trust a few. As I said, don't desperately choose companions or partners out of fear of loneliness or to be alone. Acknowledge that to be alone does not necessarily mean loneliness. "We are all born alone and die alone. Loneliness is definitely part of the journey of life." There is a difference betterment to be alone and 'loneliness'. Loneliness is not just to be alone because you might be living with several people and still be lonely and unseen. Loneliness is a condition of the mind. Loneliness is a psychological defect and it is real. Loneliness expresses the pain of being isolated and ignored. A true believer is never alone because Jesus never forsakes us even in times of trouble. One of the most extraordinary things about God is that He wants to be found and it is His desires that we experience His presence. He is ever knocking in search of us. Through His Son He has made a way for us to have fellowship with Him, to grow in our relationship with Him, and to grow in our intimacy with Him.

It is hard to find sincere friends. It is tough to trust people in particular if you have been betrayed in the past times. "Any chronic fear, anxiety, or resistance to life tends to correlate highly with your self-perceived inability to handle unknown impending chaos. In other words, if you don't think you are fit to handle life, life will scare you." Discard the spirit of fear. Be discerning. Sometimes the reason you get the wrong people in your life is that you make wrong choices. If you can't trust your judgment ask God for a gift of discerning. Sometimes the problem isn't with others but with you. "It is easy to distrust others when you have repeatedly broken your trust with yourself." Tell yourself that you're going to stop going for the wrong characters. Don't pick a carbon copy of your ex-friends. Learn from the past but don't dwell in the past. Never let your past determine your present and future. Dark thoughts flourish in a dark environment. Come out of the darkness and begin afresh in the light. You can pick up the broken pieces and excel. You know that you will heal eventually and build an even better life. There are still great people out there. Just be positive and careful.

"When you have an excellent spirit everything becomes excellent. You will live an excellent and fulfilled life. Excellent spirit will make you great, an excellent spirit will make you thrive in every area of your life, will make you productive, will direct your future, will open closed doors, will make you dream big, an excellent spirit will make you creative, will make you bold and steadfast, an excellent spirit will influence your culture, will influence your character, will influence your integrity and above all, every thing will be done for the glory of God."

Start by discovering your mission, vision, goal, and passion. Go public with your vision. "Public faith means going public with what's in your heart, with humility and respect for others, as we speak of the truth of the gospel." People are normally attracted to other people with whom they share the mission and the goals. You will definitely make great friends in this way.

People are going to be attracted to the uniqueness of ideas. It doesn't matter what you do, so long as you change something from the way it was before you touched it into something that's like you after you take your hands away. People are curious to learn new things. "The greatest legacy one can pass on to one's children and grandchildren is not money or other material things accumulated in one's life, but rather a legacy of character and faith." A person with a legacy is never forgotten. "The worst feeling is not being lonely, it's being forgotten."

It is important to make friends and to keep friends. Don't make friends at the ruins of the old friends. The best way to make friends is to be a friend. "You can make more friends in two months by becoming interested in other people than you can in two years by trying to get other people interested in you." We are a big family of God but we must be friends too.

"Self-aggrandizement is the maelstrom of baser instincts – disfigured people." If you are serious about making friends stay out of the limelight. Focus on others other than yourself. Sacrifice your ego for the sake of others. "Talk to someone about themselves and they'll listen for hours."

Be a peacemaker. First and foremost, make peace with yourself. "The life of inner peace, being harmonious and without stress, is the easiest type of existence." When things change inside you, things change around you. Make peace with others. People do not want want to hear criticism and judgment always.

Be nice in order to attract the attention of others. The little things of charity you do to others matter. Be beautiful inside and express the same beauty to the outside. "Actions speak louder than words, and a smile says, 'I like you. You make me happy. I am glad to see you." A smile is a curve that sets everything straight. A smile with love behind it has so many positive effects on us: It stimulates the brain, makes you come across as friendly, and brings joy to the people around you.

Listening to others is one of the ways of attracting people to you. Listen even to those whom you don't agree with. "You can't win an argument. You can't because if you lose it, you lose it; and if you win it, you lose it." If you have a good sense of humor and a good approach to life, instead of arguments, that's beautiful. If you don't, practice it anyway. I know some people who would provoke arguments and they quickly back up by saying "I don't want to argue". If you don't like argument why did you start it in the first place?

If you don't have friends examine yourself in particular your attitude towards others. Jealous people are hard to be friendly with. You must acknowledge that we are different, and the blessings of God come to us at different levels and seasons. Just because it's your friend's time to shine doesn't mean it is yours. Jealous people are blind to reality. Ironically, at times you are better off than the people you admire. You simply can't see it because your focus is on others.

I want to end by saying that most of our loneliness is due to life's struggles. These are things that we face alone and we try to push them off our backs but they keep on coming back with different velocities. Negative emotions like loneliness, envy, and guilt have an important role to play in an unhappy life you are currently experiencing; they're big, flashing signs that something needs to change. Surrender yourself and your burdens to Jesus. You must acknowledge that you are little people in the big arms of God. Whenever you are alone, you are not lonely because there is an invisible hand of God providing, protecting, and comforting you. "Before God ever let you get in the storm you are in now (loneliness, anxiety, depression, financial burden, whatever it may be), He already knew what He was going to do to bring you out of that storm!"

Proverbs 16:6-7 – "When a man's ways please the Lord, he makes even his enemies to be at peace with him" The inner peace is never enforced, it is imparted in humbleness, and it conquers by love. "True humility is not thinking less of yourself; it is thinking of yourself less." John the Baptist is the most humble person. He said concerning Jesus that "He must increase, but I must decrease" (John 3:30). The heart is restless until it finds its rest in Christ. Reconciling with God means reconciling with your neighbor. The vertical relationship with God is justified by the horizontal relationship with the neighbor.

"Lord, be in the frequency, vibration, and energy of mine today! Today is my day."

HOW TO SOLVE CONFLICTS IN OUR CONGREGATIONS

Christians are adopted in the family of God. The Divine family is supposed to be the opposite of secular dysfunctional families. Yet, conflicts are real even among the children of God. It is estimated that there are many wars among our congregations and individually Christian families as it is in the secular organizations. Many congregations and Christian homes are wracked by conflicts rather than permeated with the sweet aroma of the peace of Christ. I want to say that conflicts are going to be there regardless. But we must know how to solve them. The old nature is the source of conflicts. The problem is that some Christians try to discipline themselves from outside without addressing the stiffness of the heart. True humbleness and humility must begin from within the heart and must be expressed outside in our deeds. We need peace with God in order to have the peace of God. It is when you cease to be at war with God, that you cease to be at war with yourself, and with others.

The Holy Spirit is given to unite us as opposed to dividing us. The unity of the Holy Spirit is evident in the writing of the scriptures. The Holy Spirit is the author of the Scriptures. The Bible was written in the period of 1600, by about 40 writers, from different backgrounds, and different geographical locations but with the same message. We should give the Holy Spirit an opportunity to unite us as He provided the unity and unit of the Scriptures.

The Bible says that the Holy Spirit distributes the gifts of the Holy Spirit and the ministries of the Holy Spirit for edification. "And He Himself gave some to be apostles, some prophets, some evangelists, and some pastors and teachers, for the equipping of the saints for the work of ministry, for the edifying of the body of Christ, till we all come to the unity of the faith and of the knowledge of the Son of God, to a perfect man, to the measure of the stature of the fullness of Christ; that we should no longer be children, tossed to and fro and carried about with every wind of doctrine, by the trickery of men, in the cunning craftiness of deceitful plotting, but, speaking the truth in love, may grow up in all things into Him who is the head—Christ— from whom the whole body, joined and knit together by what every joint supplies, according to the effective working by which every part does its share, causes growth of the body for the edifying of itself in love." (Ephesians 4:11-16). "Our spiritual gifts are strengthened when we work together in unity and love …this is why the enemy tries so hard to sow division and strife …he realizes the power in unity and what the Church would be capable of if we walked in obedience to our Father's heart together in one accord …how sad that we can't see it …Father forgive us!"

There are different reasons that cause discords. The main one is that people are offended either by the church leadership or by other members of the congregation. We are naturally not compatible with pain and patience. Yet God calls us to a life of humility because He works through it to develop our characters. The other main reason is that we are naturally stubborn people. We want things our way. That is why the greatest miracle of salvation is found in your mirror. Every time you look in the mirror thank God for His grace that saved a wrecked sinner like you.

Why are people offended? Seemingly minor issues like attention, neglect, lack of recognition, some are very private such that they don't what to be publicly recognized. The main reason people get offended is that all of us have egos. The human ego is selfish and corrupt. It is the fallen nature of humans not wanting to know the truth and lack of respect for others. For example, elevating some believers above others creates a mentality of second-class citizenship whereby a person feels systematically discriminated against within a congregation. Jesus warned against establishing places of honor for some people depending on their external appearances. The ground of the sanctuary is supposed to be leveled whereby all people are treated the same. Jesus descended from the highest point on the universe (heavenly throne) to the lowest point on the earth of serving (Matthew 20:28). All Christians are followers of Christ to His lowest place of servanthood. The culture of the world puts celebrities and rich people on a pedestal by establishing for them high places of honor in public places. By doing so, they judge the poor unworthy of such places. It is the spirit of servanthood that can maintain the unity of the unit of the church.

Koinonia (/ kɔɪnoʊˈniːə/) is a transliterated form of the Greek word κοινωνία, which refers to concepts such as fellowship, joint participation, the share which one has in anything, a gift jointly contributed, a collection, a contribution. One of the major causes of conflicts in our congregation involves the people who come to fellowship with wrong motives like to be entertained, to use the church to meet their lust for the flesh, and etc. Such are carnal Christians and they are the recipe of confusion because they have selfish interests. We live today in a society of me, myself, and I. In this me, myself, and I society, we see God's Word being fulfilled that stated that men will be lovers of self more than God. The sad thing is that this behavior has crept into our churches. In many of our churches today, church services have been changed from heartfelt worship to entertainment. Churches that once focused on sound doctrine, prayer meetings, and Bible study, now compete against one another like businesses for new members. In an attempt to increase numbers, they advertise things that have nothing to do with God's Words or God's commands.

In our congregations, there are some dwarf believers who are not ready to mature in faith. They seem to be passionate about attending church but they are not ready fully to engage their hearts into spiritual maturity. They are at the edge or stagnant. Ultimately, when you're at the edge, you have to go forward or backward. The nightmare is the vice of the backsliding believers who tend to drive the rest of the congregation their way. The sad news is that some of those who are backsliding never admit that they are backsliding although they are living a nightmare in the darkness of the soul. The problem is that they are very contiguous if they are not confronted or even isolated.

There are some people who don't stay in one church permanently. They keep on moving from one church to the other. After causing problems in what they consider to be their home church, they comfortably move to another church. They are trouble makers wherever they go. "Although there are good biblical and theological reasons for leaving a church, people need to be very patient, very thoughtful, and gain counsel from elders when it comes time to ask the question as to whether or not they should leave the church. And really, it all centers on the ordinary means of grace and whether those ordinary means of grace are active in the church." I suggest that a pastor be investigative. He should ask the person willing to join his congregation, where he has been going to church, the names of his pastor, and why he is leaving that church. If possible he should contact the former pastor for a recommendation.

Rumors are very destructive to any congregation. Most schism do not happen because of what is taught on the pulpit but on what is said outside the pulpit. Being a pastor is tough because you can hear all kinds of rumors against you and against others. Not because you entertain them but they find a way to come to you in form of prayer requests, confessions and testimonies. People have a tendency of exaggerating something spoken. Others have a tendency of prematurely judge even when they don't have a full picture of what happened. No wonder the doctrine of confessing our sins to each other publicly is no longer implemented. The reason is that the confessed words will escalate into fierce fires of rumors. The tongues of some believers are already set on fire to pollute the whole congregation with rumors. Of course it is not the fire of the Holy Ghost; it is the odd fire. Ironically, those who spread rumors and those who entertain rumors are guilty of the same offense. "Always remember... Rumors are carried by haters, spread by fools, and accepted by idiots."

Resist being a vessel used by the devil. Ask Jesus to make you a channel for His love to flow through. Don't just pretend to love others. Really love them (Rom. 12:9). "God's love has been poured out into our hearts through the Holy Spirit" (Rom. 5:5) As John 15:6 says, when we're not abiding in Christ, our efforts are like sticks put into the fire and burned. They accomplish nothing. People come to attend church with a huge empty heart that demand to be filled with love. Give them the love of Christ. It us only when they invite God in their heart that real change comes. After they are changed, the love of Christ in them must be activated daily and passed on to others. Love must keep on flowing from one vessel to the other leaving no room for hate and division.

Jesus told Peter that feed my sheep (John 21:17). It is interpreted as

"Feed My lambs; be a shepherd to the weak ones of the flock; feed these weak ones." A pastor is not supposed to beat up his congregation with the scriptures but to feed them to grow. Understanding the difference will make the difference. This is what it means to be guided and to guide others.

It is estimated that two-thirds of the people that leave the church are willing to return to church if they are approached cordially and re-invited to church. A pastor must be flexible to reach out to them. "Hearts that bend will always mend."

The conduct of the clergy can cause division and hence schism. Satan is smart. He knows how to kill many birds with one stone. No wonder Satan targets preachers. A dent on the character of a preacher is likely to affect almost all members of his congregation. The church leaders must take precautions to be holy. Also, the members of our congregation should be educated that a pastor is not a super-spiritual giant up there who can't fall into temptation, and who is without flaws. They should be aware that a pastor is a natural man like them. Pastors have emotions like the rest of the people. They need to be loved. Express your love to them regularly. Pastors need prayers from all members of the congregation because they have great responsibility and accountability. They need the shield of our prayers so that God protects them from the evil one.

We should work together to remove the weeds of negativity. Negative feelings are the byproduct of ongoing spiritual warfare. Often we consider them to be mere feelings and ignore the fact that we are under spiritual attack. Child of God, the day you accepted Jesus Christ as your Lord and Savior, you automatically signed a contract to engage in spiritual warfare against Satan. The Bible is a story of the conflict between good and evil. God alone is good. The moment the goodness of God becomes your new nature through Jesus Christ, the forces of evil are provoked to attack you. His aim is to attack Christ in you. It doesn't matter whether you acknowledge the spiritual warfare that is in progress or not. You are under attack. Thank God that He does not allow Satan to do what he wants to do as he wants it to be done. Otherwise, we would have been overwhelmed in a moment of time. God has Satan on a leash. He gives us the Divine power to restrain the devil and render him ineffective.

We fight from victory to victory. When you become a child of God you acquired the character and nature of Christ – It is a sin-free zone where Satan cannot trespass. As long as you walk in the new nature (Spirit) and in the character of Christ (holiness) you are safe and secure. It is the responsibility of God to protect you. But you must walk within His boundaries of protection. Some of the benevolences of salvation are that you can communicate with God by the power of the Holy Spirit. Also, you acquire an antenna to discern the signal of Satan in whatever form he may try to approach you. You have the power in the name of Jesus Christ to overcome. Jesus gave every believer on earth the authority to use His name. The transfer of this type of authority in our world today is what is recognized in legal terms as "The Power of Attorney". A Power of Attorney is the authority that is given to another person, so as to act on behalf of the issuer in legal or any other matters. The terms of the transfer of power are always included in the document that transfers that power. And how powerful that transfer is, will be determined by the value in it that is put in place by the issuer. The Bible is the document that clearly highlights the transfer of authority to the believers. Every sentence inside it with the red ink, where Jesus reveals the transfer of such authority to the believers itemizes the transfer itself.

Satan attacks the Church with weapons of mass deception. We are instructed to counter his attacks by picking up our weapons of spiritual warfare which are mighty through God to the pulling down of strongholds, tearing down arguments and every presumption set up against the knowledge of God. Our weapons are not carnal but spiritual – Word, prayer, faith, and of course the name given above all names – the name of Jesus. "For our struggle is not against flesh and blood, but against the rulers, against the authorities, against the powers of this world's darkness, and against the spiritual forces of evil in the heavenly realms." (Ephesians 6:10 – 12). The scriptures define the nature of our adversary. We are fighting against the spiritual powers and principalities in high places. The prince of the air controls all of the earthly institutions, apart from the Church, whom he is fighting against. We are in a fierce spiritual battle. It is a truceless war with the spiritual powers of evil themselves. We are instructed to put on the whole (full) armor of God as opposed to pieces of the armor to engage our archenemy. Putting on the full armor is standing in the full power, strength, and protection of God. That is when we put our trust in the wisdom of God that defies the wisdom of man, and that cannot be defeated.

Paul portrays the nature of our fighting as wrestling. It is up-close and personal combat. There is a possibility of being hit by the enemy in the face where it hurts most. But regardless of the firepower of the enemy, we are called to stand because we have the upper hand. We stand in the righteousness of Christ as opposed to our own righteousness. We guard our minds with the helmet of salvation and the sword of the Spirit, which is the Word of God. We use the belt of truth to put our armor together. We hit back the enemy by the Word (Truth). We defend ourselves from the flaming arrows of the evil one by the shield of faith. We stand in the shoes of the gospel. We are instructed to be strong in the Lord and in His mighty power through prayers and supplication in order to secure our victory. The scripture calls us to put on the armor and stand. To stand is to faithfully put to use everything God has rendered to us. It is important to note that praying and the Word are the two major weapons of convection at our fingertips to use in our spiritual warfare. Jesus is the Word that became flesh (human) to be demonstrated for us to obey. The Word is not just informative but formative and transforming. In John 6:63 Jesus confirmed this point when He said "The Words (Rhema) that I speak to you are Spirit and they are Life. ... The Word in your mouth is the sword of the Spirit. This is not a calling to pastors alone but to each and every believer.

The Church of Jesus Christ, despite all of its appalling failures and sins, is the greatest force on earth for good and the only threat to Satan's kingdom. It is the only group of people on the planet feared by the god of this age (Satan). No other religion poses any threat to Satan. None. Just the Church. Satan trembles when he hears God's people praising their Lord. Even the weakest saint on his or her knees surely strikes fear in the enemy camp. No surprise that the Church is always under attack.

"Satan is most effective in the church not when he comes as an open enemy but as a false friend; not when he persecutes the church, but when he joins it; not when he attacks the pulpit but when he stands in it." Whenever we give the wrong characters access of the pulpit we give the devil a platform to cause confusion. Satan uses the church goers as his mouthpiece to create disorder in church. In particular the people who have nothing to do. They are the major cause of conflicts. They are found of backbiting and bad mouthing those who are actively serving. My advise is that "Get busy doing something." While the saying, "idle hands are the Devil's workshop" is not found in the Bible, it is a wise one and in line with biblical truth. To be idle is to be lazy or to avoid work. Idleness is not the same as resting, which the Bible commends. Rather idleness is doing nothing when you should be doing something. It can often result from having no specific goal or purpose. The Bible says that "A worker's appetite works for him because his hunger drives him onward. A worthless man digs up evil, and his speech is like a scorching fire. A perverse man spreads dissension, and a gossip divides close friends" (Proverbs 16:26-28).

I know there are some people out there who claim to be Christians but who avoid going to church because they were offended by other believers. Satan tricks many believers to think that since they don't have to go to church in order for them to be saved they can as well stay away from the church. Abstaining from fellowship is the first step towards backsliding. Fellowship is biblical. "For where two or three gather together in My name, there am I with them." (Matthew 18:20). Also, the Bible encourages us never to stop getting together "Let us not neglect meeting together, as some have made a habit, but let us encourage one another, and all the more as you see the Day approaching." (Hebrews 10:25).

"Not forsaking the assembling of ourselves together, as is the manner of some…". This passage is often cited to rebuke those who "miss church," but it has a deeper meaning. The book of Hebrews was written to a group of Christians who had "endured a hard struggle with sufferings" (Hebrews 10:32). They were "exposed to reproach and affliction" (Hebrews 10:33). They witnessed their brothers and sisters being thrown into prison. They themselves "joyfully accepted the plundering of [their] property" (Hebrews 10:34). It sounds like to me this letter was written to Christians who experienced the "great persecution against the church in Jerusalem" (Acts 8:1). Back then, these Jewish Christians endured this persecution with joy and faith. But now, decades later, their joy and faith seem to be wavering. Some of them are ready to abandon the way of Jesus. The book of Hebrews is written to prevent that falling away. It is written to show that our covenant with Jesus is better than the old covenant. Jesus is a better high priest, who entered a better tabernacle, to offer a better sacrifice, and give to His people a better inheritance. To abandon Jesus would be the worst mistake anyone could ever make. I want to emphasize that going to church does not make us Christians. But withdrawing from church or stop attending church is the first step towards abandoning our faith.

Don't let bitterness disengage you from fellowship and hence nullifies your access to God's promises. If we walk in forgiveness we will not hold a grudge. "Life appears to me too short to be spent in nursing animosity or registering wrongs." To be wronged is nothing unless you continue to remember it. Unforgiving greatly hinders your spiritual maturity by isolating you. Jesus taught to forgive endless without keeping records of wrong. "Then Peter came to Jesus and asked, "Lord, how many times shall I forgive my brother who sins against me? Up to seven times?" Jesus answered, "I tell you, not just seven times, but seventy-seven times!... (Matthew 18:20-22). Seven is a number of God meaning complete. Forgiveness keeps no record of wrong. It is a calling to forgive others completely or indefinitely. It is forgiving others forever.

Paul teaches us how to reconcile to each other: "Your Father in heaven is not willing that any of these little ones should perish. If your brother sins against you, go and confront him privately. If he listens to you, you have won your brother over. But if he will not listen, take one or two others along, so that 'every matter may be established by the testimony of two or three witnesses.'... (Matthew 18:14-16). Talk directly to the culprit instead of talking about him with others. Take two people who are spiritually mature than you for accountability. Each and every step must be taken in the direction of restoring the offended person. Our fellowship is not like a justice system trying to expose the wrong and punish them. It is intended for reconciliation. Jesus knew Judas as the traitor but Jesus did not expose him. In fact, Jesus did not call Judas the son of perdition until Judas left the fellowship and went to betray Jesus. Regarding everything we do, we are supposed to restore the wounded brethren instead of shooting them down by condemnation.

If everything possible has been done in vain to reconcile the culprit, the elders must confront him or her and rebuke him or her. If they don't yield to a rebuke, the Bible says that they should be treated as a heathen. "And if he fails to listen to them, tell it to the church. And if he fails to listen to even to the church, let him be to you as the pagan and the tax collector" (Matthew 18:17). Elsewhere, Paul wrote that "Now we command you, brethren, in the name of our Lord Jesus Christ, that ye withdraw yourselves from every brother that walks disorderly, and not after the tradition which he received of us" (2 Thessalonian 3:6.14,15). The traditional law enjoined that a Hebrew might not associate, eat, or travel with a heathen, he was to be virtually excommunicated. Light does not mix with darkness but expels darkness. "-----10 and try to discern what is pleasing to the Lord. 11 Take no part in the unfruitful works of darkness, but instead expose them. 12 For it is shameful even to speak of the things that they do in secret. 13 But when anything is exposed by the light, it becomes visible, 14 for anything that becomes visible is light." (Ephesians 5:10-14). Turn on the light of the Word brighter, and Satan will free. Satan is like roaches. He is afraid of the light. Turn on the light and you see how roaches run for cover!

Another cause of conflict in our congregation is ego. During the earthly ministry of Jesus, there was discourse among the twelve Apostles concerning who is the greatest in the kingdom of heaven, and the mutual duties of Christians (Matthew 18:1). The apostles made the inquiry in the present tense, as though Christ had already selected the one who was to preside over the others. Jesus invited a little child to stand among them. From the boy's trustfulness and submission, He draws a needed lesson for the ambitious apostles. "But Jesus called them to him and said, "You know that the rulers of the Gentiles lord it over them, and their great ones exercise authority over them. 26 It shall not be so among you. But whoever would be great among you must be your servant" (Matthew 20:24-26). In the secular world, everybody looks for an opportunity to be the boss over the other. Jesus said that "It shall not be so among you". In the kingdom of God, the greatest is the servant to others. Even so, the Son of God came to serve, not to be served (Matthew 20:28).

"Then the mother of Zebedee's sons came to Jesus with her sons and knelt down to make a request of Him. "What do you want?" He inquired. She answered, "Declare that in Your kingdom one of these two sons of mine may sit at Your right hand, and the other at Your left" (Matthew 20:21). James and John were one of the chosen three who had been witnesses of the Transfiguration (Matthew 17:1). The favor which had already been bestowed might, in some degree, seem to warrant the petition. Jesus explained that it is God's decision who takes the seats of honor in Heaven, "Those places belong to those for whom they have been prepared."

A comparative spirit is alive in the church today. To walk in our true identity, we have to let go of comparison. It is a challenge for many of us today. We compare our callings to others' callings. Worse, we spend much of our lives being compared to how well we measure up to societal norms. Our God isn't in comparison business at all. The fruit of the Spirit is the eternal value place on the soul. God, evenly determines our success by the fruit of the Spirit, regardless of our callings. He designed us each uniquely but the ground of the cross where we stand is evenly leveled. No one stands on a higher ground than the other. Given this fact, we must acknowledge the sovereignty of God. God has a right to bless as He wills. Jesus tells the Parable of the Laborers in the Vineyard. The lengthy parable is found only in the gospel of Matthew 20: 1-16. The landowner, whose decision to pay all the workers the same was an act of mercy—not injustice—represents God, whose grace and mercy are shed abundantly upon those of His choosing. "For he says to Moses, 'I will have mercy on whom I have mercy, and I will have compassion on whom I have compassion.' It does not, therefore, depend on man's desire or effort, but on God's mercy."

We must learn to revel in a diversity of tastes, creative expressions, giftings, and cultural differences in the Body of Christ. The problem is that some work hard to impress others. When we let go of trying to appease and please everyone but God, we will find our genuine selves. "Walking in our unique design brings a fresh wind of authenticity that is attractive, appealing, a magnet to those who need a Savior, and a desire to be their truest and best selves. Only Jesus can transform our lives like that! I'm so thankful. Are you walking in your true design, friend?"

When we begin walking in the fullness of who God designed us to be, our fresh aroma will attract others to Jesus. "------then make my joy complete by being like-minded, having the same love, being united in spirit and purpose. Do nothing out of selfish ambition or empty pride, but in humility consider others more important than yourselves. Each of you should look not only to your own interests but also to the interests of others." (Philippians 2:2-4). We take care of each other because Jesus takes care of us.

The Bible gives the following definition of the Church (the body of Christ): "There is one body, but it has many parts. But all its many parts make up one body. It is the same with Christ. 13 We were all baptized

157

by one Holy Spirit. And so we are formed into one body. It didn't matter whether we were Jews or Gentiles, slaves or free people. We were all given the same Spirit to drink. 14 So the body is not made up of just one part. It has many parts. 15 Suppose the foot says, "I am not a hand. So I don't belong to the body." By saying this, it cannot stop being part of the body. 16 And suppose the ear says, "I am not an eye. So I don't belong to the body." By saying this, it cannot stop being part of the body. 17 If the whole body were an eye, how could it hear? If the whole body were an ear, how could it smell? 18 God has placed each part in the body just as he wanted it to be. 19 If all the parts were the same, how could there be a body? 20 As it is, there are many parts. But there is only one body." (1 Corinthians 12:12-27). We are the body of Christ. We ear supposed to function as a body. The body has levels of organization that build on each other. Cells make up tissues, tissues make up organs, and organs make up organ systems. The function of an organ system depends on the integrated activity of its organs.

We are adopted into the Divine family, which is holy and spotless. We are not adopted into the dysfunctional families of the earth but the heavenly family that is pure. Resist having issues that are not compatible with the kingdom of the glory. The Bible says that "Blessed be the God and Father of our Lord Jesus Christ, who has blessed us in Christ with every spiritual blessing in the heavenly realms." (Ephesians 1:3). It is the thanksgiving for the Divine ordination to the blessings of the grace. Here we have 1) the Author of our blessings (God). 2) Their nature and sphere. 3) The Medium through whom we have them. The scripture says "every spiritual blessing" – meaning all of the spiritual and natural gifts are needed to build up the body of Christ (Church). We should in particular exercise the gifts of exhorting and encouraging each other. "And let us consider how we may spur one another on toward love and good deeds, not giving up meeting together, as some are in the habit of doing, but encouraging one another—and all the more as you see the Day approaching." (Hebrews 10:24). The strict meaning may simply be--let us take note of one another, to stimulate one another to good works. The good works are rewards (gifts) of our salvation.

Today's prayer: "Lord, Trusting is a tonic for mind and body, and the antidote to solitary, yet we are allergic to it. The only one that can truly satisfy the human heart is the One that created it. In every human heart, there is a round hole that can only be filled by the endless love of God. Lord, your love is extravagant for it accommodates a sinner like me who barely merits it. Receiving Jesus Christ is making Him my sin-bearer in exchange for life eternal. Enormous enlargement of an object gives it a personality it never had before. Embracing the cross is the maximum enlargement of life. It is a conviction that life can continue indefinitely. Changed lives begin with changed hearts. Eternal life is when God, by His grace, puts His life into the human hearts on basis of the human faith. Death is putting human life in the human hands and trusting in human resources. Lord, I seek Your counsel. Relieve me of unbelief because unbelief is the synthesis of crisis. Wash my soul with the joy of your salvation. In the name of Jesus, Amen.

Today's prayer: "Lord, you said that "When the enemy comes in like a flood God's Holy Spirit will raise up a standard against him. When the enemy shall come in, like a river the Spirit of God will make him flee." (Isaiah 59:19). Please help us to Remain fixed on the target and not distracted by skirmishes in the fray. Entering Your rest in perfect peace tunes us into the frequency of Your Spirit that never fails. You have the answer for every question – the blueprints and strategies that will move us into position and are being formed within us even now. Amen."

1. We may make our plans, but God has the last word (Prov.16: 1).
2. If you pay attention when you are corrected, you are wise (Prov. 15:31).
3. If you try to make a profit dishonestly, you will get your family into trouble. Don't take bribes and you will live longer (Prov. 15: 27).
4. Intelligent people want to learn but stupid people are satisfied with ignorance (Prov. 35: 14).
5. When wise people speak, they make knowledge attractive but stupid people spout nonsense (Prov. 15: 2).
6. If you stay calm, you are wise but if you have a hot temper, you only show how stupid you are (Prov. 14: 29).
7. If you oppress poor people, you will insult the God who made them; but kindness shown to the poor is an act of worship (Prov. 14: 31).

8. Wisdom is in every thought of intelligent people; fools know nothing about wisdom (Prov. 14: 33).
9. Pride leads to destruction and arrogance to downfall (Prov. 16:18).
10. Your will to live can sustain you when you are sick but if you lose it, your last hope is gone (Prov. 18: 14).

Think seriously about these ten lessons and see how they can transform you into a different human being. Remember that temptation is ordained testing by God to prove our faithfulness.

COUNSELING THE PEOPLE WHO ARE IN GRIEVING

Death brings out the best and worst in families. A good counselor prepares the people to cope with death, to have a decent burial for their beloved, and to get ready to face the after-death trials. When death occurs, the family members and close relatives start discussing the cause of death and what could have been done to prevent it. After death, there is finger-pointing, blaming, and other fights between family members and relatives. "It can feel like a secondary loss. There is a situation when you're trying to cope with the death of your loved one, and suddenly your support system is not only unsupportive but a source of additional stress."

Naturally, there is nothing in life that can prepare us for the death of a loved one. Whether death results from a sudden accident or a sustained illness, it always catches us off-guard. Death is so deeply personal and stunningly final, nothing can emotionally prepare us for its arrival. With every death, there is a loss. And with every loss, there will be grief. Culture tells us to move past this process quickly. Take a few days, weeks perhaps, to grieve, but don't stay there too long. Grieving can make those around us uncomfortable. Friends sometimes don't know what to do with our pain. Loved ones struggle to find adequate words to comfort our aching wounds. A good counselor finds the answers in the Bible. He or she should be ready to answer the questions that a grieving person hides in their heart. I am going to outline some of the questions that go on in the minds of a person that has lost somebody very close to them.

* If only the deceased could have one more day, one more memory together, one more moment.
* It is like a piece of the heart of the grieving person is missing.
* A grieving person feels pain, and they think that the pain would not go away.
* As a hiker that walks up a steep mountain and stops to catch a breath… worn out from the journey, so is a grieving person's life, day after day.
* So many things racing through the minds of a person grieving; they wish that things you would have been differently..
* Some having regrets and feel guilty; they wish they could have done something to prevent the death experience of their beloved. They wish they could do something to bring back the dead relative.
* They feel lonely walking through life without the presence of their beloved.
* Some don't for sure know where the soul of their dead relative is. His body's still here, so why isn't he?
* What's it like "up there" without a body?
* Where is "up there?"
* In some cases days seem like they are getting a little easier, only to stumble upon a trigger and reliving it all over again.
* Then there is this question: "why me?" question to God.
* Why do bad things happen to good people?

These are big questions for a small mind. A good counselor must be prepared to answer the above questions from the biblical point of view. Death is cruel and evil. We may not be intellectually equipped with all of the answers regarding why God allows evil, but we are spiritually equipped with all the answers we need regarding the origin, causes, and eradication of evil. The Bible has the moral answers to all of our spiritual, physical, and emotional needs.

The scariest thing is not the death of the physical body but what dies inside us while we are still alive. Satan kills primarily by stealing our faith, love, and hope. Why? "Faith makes everything possible. Love makes everything beautiful. Hope makes everything real with certainty." God uses death as a means to bring about brokenness. The body of Jesus was broken in order for it to be ours. God's plan is to break us before He gives us a way to be used in His kingdom—most probably as Jesus broke the five loaves of bread and two fishes before He gave them away to feed the masses (Matthews 14:13-21). I want to say that is OK to grieve for the dead. Death is still heartbreaking but it is sometimes God's way to bring about brokenness. "Sometimes God will wreck your plans to save your life. Appreciate the detour".

Death is universal. It applies to all people although it comes to us at different times, in different ways, and in different packages. The Bible says that the wage of sin is death. The Wages of Sin originates from the starting of the biblical verse Romans 6:23 "For the wages of sin is death, but the gift of God is eternal life in Christ Jesus our Lord." The presence of sin cost us this physical life. God is holy and He cannot fellowship with unholiness. Sin polluted us rendering us good for nothing. God could have eliminated the corrupted body by eliminating Adam, and the human race would have been in nonexistence. Or, God could have eliminated every soul at conception because every person is born in this universe contaminated with sinful nature. The Bible says that "Surely I was brought forth in iniquity; I was sinful when my mother conceived me." (Psalm 51:5). We are born in this corrupt world corrupted deserving to be trashed but the grace of God preserves us. Therefore the question is not why does God allow bad things to happen to good people (because there is no such a thing as a good person in accordance with the standard of God) but why does God allow good things to happen to bad people.

God's love, mercy, and grace made for us a way out of this predicament of death. According to the Bible, "Sin entered the world through one man, and death through sin, and in this way death came to all people because all sinned. For sin was in the world before the law was given, but sin is not taken into account when there is no Law. (Romans 5:12-13). Sin entered mankind by Adam. Every person is born with the sinful nature inherited from Adam. The sinful nature causes the individual sins of which we are individually accountable. The mercy of God gave us the Law for accountability. The Law brings awareness of sin but does not eliminate the consequences of breaking the law, which is death (Romans 7:7). The Law demands absolute justice. "The sting of death is sin, and the strength of sin is the law. (1 Corinthians 15:56). Death is represented as a venomous serpent. The strength of sin is death. The demand for restitution was a significant part of the law that God gave to Moses. It was a seasonal sacrificing of animals to wipe away the sins of that particular season and maintain the communication of God flowing.

The reality is that no man could keep the Law in its totality during their lifetime. The Law was given to us as God's mercy leading us to God's grace that we receive through Jesus Christ. The Law in its deathful aspect is annulled, and the sinful soul delivered. Jesus, finally defeated death in our lives when He became a permanent perfect sacrifice for us. He doubles as the ultimate High Priest and perfect sacrifice. The cross became the greatest altar on the face of the earth where His body became the Lamb that takes away our sins. His resurrected life that cannot suffer death became ours. "When the perishable has been clothed with the imperishable and the mortal with immortality, then the saying that is written will come to pass: "Death has been swallowed up in victory." "Where, O Death, is your victory? Where, O Death, is your sting?" (1 Corinthians 15:55).

Jesus was not a high priest from the tribe of Levi or a Levite but from the highest order of Melchizedek. Melchizedek is an old Canaanite name meaning "My King Is [the god] Sedek" or "My King Is Righteousness" Jesus, our High Priest, entered not the holy of hollies covered by the curtains made by man but entered once for all the holiest place in heaven to present His sacrifice once forever. "We have this as a sure and steadfast anchor of the soul, a hope that enters into the inner place behind the curtain, where Jesus has gone as a forerunner on our behalf, having become a high priest forever after the order of Melchizedek." (Hebrews 6:16–20).

Sin came to us through one man (Adam). The love and justice of God made one man (Jesus) pay for the wages of our sins (death), and by His righteousness, we are acquired eternal life. "So then, just as one trespass brought condemnation for all men, so also one act of righteousness brought justification and life for all men." (Romans 5:12-18). The sin which has such wide and disastrous effects was Adam's. So that it is strictly legitimate to compare his fall with the act of redemption. It is strictly true to say that by one man (Adam) sin and death entered into the world, as life and grace entered by another man's obedience (Jesus Christ). In either case, the consequence was that of one man's act. Jesus Christ restored everything we lost in Adam. He defeated death on our behalf. "Therefore being justified by faith, we have peace with God through our Lord Jesus Christ" (Romans 5:1). Faith brings justification; justification brings peace—peace with God, through the mediation of Jesus. Jesus paid the ransom of our sins by dying on the cross. His resurrected life became our life eternally. The person who has accepted Jesus Christ as his personal Savior is identified with Christ in all that He has accomplished. The believing sinner is joined to Jesus Christ in His death, in His burial, and in His resurrection. This is our vital union with Christ. This is the means whereby we walk in the newness of eternal life. (Galatians 2:20).

The soul of a born-again believer is reunited with Christ. Paul said that "I eagerly expect and hope that I will in no way be ashamed, but will have complete boldness so that now as always Christ will be exalted in my body, whether by life or by death. For to me, to live is Christ, and to die is gain" (Philippians 1:21-22). To live is Christ.--This, of course, means "Christ is my life," yet not in the sense that He is the source and principle of life in us, but that the whole concrete state of life is so lived in Him that it becomes a simple manifestation of His presence. The scripture emphasizes that Christ is our very new life. Elsewhere, the Bible says that "For you have died and your life is hidden with Christ in God. When Christ, who is our life, is revealed, then you also will be revealed with Him in glory." (Colossians 3:3). If Christ is the principle of life in us, then whatever we think and say and do, exhibiting visibly that inner life, must be the manifestation of Christ.

Paul said that nothing can separate from the love of God, not even death. "No, in all these things we are more than conquerors through Him who loved us. For I am convinced that neither death nor life, neither angels nor principalities, neither the present nor the future, nor any powers, neither height nor depth, nor anything else in all creation, will be able to separate us from the love of God that is in Christ Jesus our Lord." (Romans 8:37-39). Paul speaks of God's predestination of believers to glory, his purpose is to encourage them to persevere in holiness on the ground of their assurance of God's eternal purpose concerning them.

Jesus said that God is the God of the living (not of the dead). "Even Moses demonstrates that the dead are raised, in the passage about the burning bush. For he calls the Lord 'the God of Abraham, the God of Isaac, and the God of Jacob.' He is not the God of the dead, but of the living, for to Him all are alive." (Luke 20:38). Jesus Christ is our life effectively and efficiently. Paul said that "For to me, to live is Christ and to die is gain." (Philippians 1:21). All life, in the truest, highest sense of that term, depends upon our relation to God. We live to Him, and in Him. Life is a precious gift from God regardless of where we are (as for believers, heaven or earth). God equally loves the departed saints as He loves the saints who are still living on the earth because we are one body (Church). While we are still on the earth, we are called to number our days but God alone can number our lives because the greatest dimension of life is eternal. Although this world is not paradise, heaven begins here on the earth; we can experience heaven on earth the moment we are regenerated. Planning for the end begins now rather than later. In order to finish well, you must start well. Beginning well is responding to the gospel, and then continuing in your convictions by exercising the discipline of Christian life till our bodies will be glorified. God alone, by His grace, can take you from where you are to where He wants you to be. The sum of our lives is within the frame of His parameter. Christ must be magnified or glorified in our bodies, whether by life or by death. Spiritually, we must live for Him, and die in Him. A person is never ready to live until they are ready to die. Only a person that is ready to die in Him and for His name's sake can say "For to me, to live is Christ and to die is gain."

How to cope with grieving? When you lose someone you care about, it can be numbing. The vacuum you feel from losing someone is normal. Grieving a loved one is not easy. Maybe your grief has left you feeling hopeless and broken or maybe you feel angry and confused. Whatever emotions you are experiencing, it's okay. You are not alone in this grieving process because God is still here for you and loves you. God wants you to be confident in Him, regardless of the situation. Praying boosts our confidence in God. "You can't face the day until you have faced God in prayers". Many times in Scripture, God's people are encouraged to seek the face of God. The Hebrew word for "face" in the Old Testament is often translated as "presence." When we seek the face of God, we are seeking His presence. When we approach God in prayer we are seeking His face. "The *Lord* wants us to humbly and trustingly seek His *face* in our *prayers* and in our times in His Word. It requires intimacy to look intently into someone's *face*."

Suffering is not from God but at times God allows sufferings to keep us close to His throne. Paul had a thorn in the flesh. "And lest I should be exalted above measure by the abundance of the revelations, a thorn in the flesh was given to me, a messenger of Satan to buffet me, lest I be exalted above measure. Concerning this thing, I pleaded with the Lord three times that it might depart from me. And He said to me, "My grace is sufficient for you, for My strength is made perfect in weakness." (2 Corinthians 12:7-10). The Bible is not specific regarding what kind of thorn Paul had in his flesh. Most probably it was inspired so that we can fill in the blank all kinds of thorns we have in us. This includes injuries, rejection, sicknesses, death and etc.

God used Peter and Paul tremendously in the ministry of healing. Acts 20: 7 -12, we are told about Eutychus, a man Paul raised from the dead at Troas. The young man had fallen into a deep sleep and fallen from a height that led to his death. Paul raised him from the dead soon thereafter. The Bible says concerning Peter that, "---insomuch that they even carried out the sick into the streets, and laid them on beds and couches, that, as Peter came by, at the least, his shadow might overshadow some one of them" (Acts 5:15). But Peter could not heal the fever of his mother-in-law. The fifth documented miracle of Jesus was the healing of Simon Peter's mother-in-law and was recorded in several of the Gospels including Luke 4:38-41. "Now Simon Peter's mother-in-law was suffering from a high fever, and they asked Jesus to help her. So He bent over her and rebuked the fever, and it left her." None of the apostles could heal this simple fever but Jesus. The ministry of working of miracles is not something we can earn; it is a gift that is bestowed to us by the grace of God in accordance to the Divine will and purpose. As far as our subject is concerned, God at times allows some bad things to happen to us, not because He is angry with us but to teach us some spiritual virtues and discipline and to grow our faith. We are God's beloved children. And we should trust God that He has no ill intention against His children. We should praise Him even regarding the things that we don't understand. The bottom line is that we shall fully comprehend when we cross over.

The fact that we really don't know what Paul's thorn was turns out to be both merciful and instructive to us. It's merciful because, given the various possibilities, we all can identify with Paul to some degree in our afflictions. It's instructive because what Paul's thorn was isn't the point. The point is what God's purpose was for the thorn. You have your own thorn in the flesh, or if you live long enough you'll be given one (or more). Yours will be different from mine, but its purpose will be similar. For we are given thorns that significantly weaken us in order to make us stronger. "Pain insists upon being attended to. God whispers to us in our pleasures, speaks in our consciences, but shouts in our pains. It is his megaphone to rouse a deaf world." (C S Lewis).

"Deep calls to deep in the roar of your waterfalls; all your waves and breakers have swept over me." (Psalm 42:7). The Hebrew word for deep is "tehowm" and it carries the meaning of a surging mass of water, water making a commotion or noise, wave following wave without intermission. A grieving person is exhausted of strength and courage to do even the things they normally do. They need strength. Strength to think straight. Strength to feel hope. Strength to make some wise decisions. Strength to make the next positive move. Strength call on the Lord. Strength greater than their own grieving heart. But they have to learn strategies to put themselves under the waterfall of God's grace and power. This is one of the great purposes of Christian counseling: learning biblical strategies of availing ourselves of divine strength when we are utterly depleted and passing it on to others.

The book of Philippians is known as one of the jail epistles. Paul wrote this book in times of suffering while languishing in the dungeon; a jail in a cave hole in Rome, with no toilet but a bucket, with one small opening on the roof serving as ventilation. Today we call the book of Philippians the book of joy. "I can do all things through Christ who strengthens me." (Philippians 4:13). The "can-do" attitude is in reference to the strength amidst sufferings. Christ gives us the strength to not only endure the tough times but also to grow during them. We aren't meant to just slog through the pain; we're meant to see our faith blossom right in the face of our battles. God equips us with the armor we need to stand firm. Trials are called tests because it is during our weakest moments that we discover our strength in the Lord.

Suffering applies to all people at different times and to different degrees. God is not the source of evil but He might allow evil to happen to shake things up. He shakes things up to remind us that we don't belong to the temporal comfort of this world. He shakes things up to put "order" in its rightful place. When death happens to a family, it is not a unique situation. It is appointed for every person to die. The right question to ask God is not why death has happened but why is any person still living when it is appointed for every natural man to pay the wages of sin, which is death. The answer is that every air we breathe in it is because of grace. To a believer, death is not the end but the beginning of life in a new dimension. It is always darkest before dawn.

Is it OK to be angry with God? God is never wrong even when the happenings don't make sense to us. God is not the cause of our miseries even though they cannot happen unless He allows them. In the first place, God did not have to do anything beneficial for a sinful man. A corrupted soul is compared to the bad meat, that is good for trashing. Every good thing that God does for a fallen man is because of grace. It means that none of us get what we deserve from God. The grace of God is at work even in bad times to refine us into the perfect finished product. When we can't see the work God is doing through tragedy and pain, let's remain faithful in trusting God's wisdom, judgment, and timing. May I always be reminded of this unequivocal fact.

God is good all times. It is His nature to be good. Questioning the goodness of God is adhering to your old nature. Often, we tend to follow our hearts, and to believe our own hearts to be true. Yet we willingly forget God states that the heart is "deceitful above all things and desperately wicked" (Jeremiah 17:9). So, to have the knowledge of God, our heart would be the last thing we would want to follow. Renewing your mind is the first step in unfollowing your corrupt nature, and it is a process involving a lifestyle. It is called to be led by the spirit.

"God is good, even when life doesn't feel good. Pray for well-seasoned faith that will stand firm, with abundant joy, in this difficult season. "So now, beloved ones, stand firm, stable, and enduring. Live your lives with unshakable confidence. We know that we prosper and excel in every season by serving the Lord, because we are assured that our union with the Lord makes our labor productive with fruit that endures" (1 Corinthians 15:58).

Grieving is good but it should not be prolonged to the extent it becomes destructive. Grieving should be positively handled and used to shift your minds from the current situation to God. Jonathan was the son of King

169

Saul who was in line to inherit the throne. 1 Samuel 18:3, Jonathan made a covenant with David. That covenant was a serious promise in front of God that they would always be friends. Jonathan repeated the sacred name of God, which appears as 'LORD' in English translations, 5 times in these verses. He wanted to emphasize that he had made these covenant promises with God, and not merely with David. Therefore, Jonathan's covenant with David was now part of Jonathan's relationship with God. In these matters, Jonathan considered himself responsible to God. Their friendship was not just something that they had chosen to do. God himself had made them friends, so that David could become Israel's king. David grieved the loss of his close friend Jonathan. After which he wrote, "My soul makes its boast in the Lord; let the humble hear and be glad." (Psalms 34:4-5, 8,2).

Not once in the Bible does it say that worry about it, stress over it, or, figure it out. But over and over it says "trust in God". God picks up the broken pieces and uses them for His glory. Where it is utterly broken, God sees mending. Where there is complete disorder, God sees order. Where there is oppression, God sees deliverance. Where there is bondage, God sees freedom.

I like this posting "If people just took it a day at a time, they'd be a lot happier." Happiness begins now, at the moment you are in regardless of the circumstances. A butterfly lives only for 14 days but still flies joyfully capturing many hearts. The fact that life is short does not hinder it from capturing the attention of many with its beauty. Don't let the pains and problems of life make the beauty of life fade. So give life your best, and live and beautify other people's lives. "The mystery of human existence lies not in just staying alive, but in finding something to live for." It is possible to be happy about the wrong things. Jesus gives you a reason to be happy for the right thing. And this is the only thing that matters. I don't know about you but I get a warm fuzzy after reading these remarks."

Our blessed hope is in the advent of Christ. The word blessed can mean "happy" or "beneficial"; our hope is "blessed" in that Jesus' return will be an amazing, joyful experience for the believer in Christ. We will be blessed beyond measure when we see Christ. The trials of this life will be over, and we will see that "our present sufferings are not worth comparing with the glory that will be revealed in us" (Romans 8:18). The "blessed hope," then, is the joyful assurance that God will extend His benefits to us and that Jesus Christ will return. We are waiting for this event now.

For the trumpet will sound, the dead will be raised imperishable, and we will be changed. "in an instant, in the twinkling of an eye, at the last trumpet. For the trumpet will sound, the dead will be raised imperishable, and we will be changed. When the perishable has been clothed with the imperishable and the mortal with immortality, then the saying that is written will come to pass: "Death has been swallowed up in victory." (1 Corinthians 15:53).

Today's prayer: "My sacrifice, O God, is a broken spirit; a broken and contrite heart you, God, will not despise (Psalm 51:17). Naturally, it's hard asking someone with a broken heart to fall in love again. But God builds his kingdom with materials of broken hearts. A broken heart is the one that is humbled under a sense of pain and sin and sees the need to repent. Jesus is the Rock. "Whoever shall fall on that stone shall be broken; but on whomsoever it shall fall, it will grind him to powder." (Luke 20:18). "Lord, you approve and accept my sacrifices of sincere repentance. Therefore, it is not the broken heart that kills, but the unbroken pride. You alone can water my desert and cause it to blossom. In the face of oddity and adversity, grant to me the decency to embrace sanity. "When peace like a river, attendeth my way, When sorrows like sea billows roll, Whatever my lot, thou hast taught me to say: It is well, it is well, with my soul."

Today's prayer: "Lord, the realization of my own flaw is the beginning of sanity. I have one life to live that will determine my life forever and I must live it to the utmost. I am not scared of adversity because no matter how long the night lasts there must be a dawn. Indeed, one is never ready to live until they are ready to die. Jesus Christ is the light that dispels fear, provides assurance and direction, and engenders enduring peace and joy. He is the unchanging power in the ever-changing world. The greatest reward by Christ is more Christ. I want more of Him because I can't get enough of Him. I have decided to settle for nothing less than Christ. And I am convinced that when everything seems to be falling apart, I am not falling apart. My prayer today is that I must decrease so that He increases."

"For we brought nothing into the world, and we cannot take anything out of the world." (1 Timothy 6:7).

"'He will wipe every tear from their eyes. There will be no more death or mourning or crying or pain, for the old order of things has passed away." (Revelation 21:4).

"I consider that our present sufferings are not worth comparing with the glory that will be revealed in us." (Romans 8:18).

"The LORD is close to the brokenhearted and saves those who are crushed in spirit." (Psalms 34:18).

"Come to me, all you who are weary and burdened, and I will give you rest. (Matthew 11:28-30)."

"Blessed are those who mourn, for they will be comforted." (Matthew 5:4).

PRAYERS THE BEST THERAPY

For true Christians, prayer [Gk: "proseuche"] is "communion with God". Through prayer, we actually experience a relational experience with God. The quality of our prayer life then determines the quality of our relationship with God. Prayer is talking with God. Prayer is listening to God. Prayer is enjoying the presence of God. It can take many forms. For example—Praising, worship, confession, repentance, thanksgiving, praise, waiting (silent, and listening), and petition (asking for things).

Praying is therapeutic. Begin your prayers by praising God. The Bible instructs to magnify the name of the Lord. "I will praise the name of God with a song; I will magnify him with thanksgiving." (Psalms 69:30). We magnify God for our sake instead of for God's sake. The bigger our God is to us, the smaller our problems become. The Bible calls us to experience the joy of praying unceasingly. "Rejoice always, pray without ceasing, give thanks in all circumstances; for this is the will of God in Christ Jesus for you." (1 Thessalonians 5:16-18). Praying without ceasing is praying always. It is basically having the mindset of praying. Praying is having a valuable time with God. In real life the more time you spend with your lover the more you look like them. The same applies to prayers. We are related to God intimately through Christ. The more time we spend with God in prayer, the more we look like Him. "Lord, When I am empty I just come to You and You fill me. When I am thirty, I just come to You, and you quench my thirst. When I am hungry, I just come to you, and you feed me. When I am sick, I just come to You, and I am healed. When I am lonely, I just come to you in prayers, and I am never the same."

Praying is communicating to the holy and all-powerful God who created all of the visible and the invisible things. We believe in the infinite creator. By virtue of creation, He is an intelligent designer. By wisdom, He made everything beautiful and placed them exactly where He wanted them to be so that they operate as He designed them. But the corruption of sin tainted the beauty of creation. Praying initiates restoration. Praying begins with the sinner's prayer of confession to God, repenting, and asking Jesus to save you. A new beginning involving a new nature and character is initiated.

The cross became an absolute divine inspiration revisiting the Law with the blazing and amazing grace to make our ways straight. The final sacrifice was made at the altar of the cross. We don't have to carry with us animal sacrifices in order to approach the holy God. When we are born again, our sincere prayers become the sacrifices that we present to God. Praying should begin by offering to God a sacrifice of praise, even in those hard times when we don't feel like it. We don't praise God for the trials we are going through, we praise Him in trials. It is our pleasure to praise God because of who He is.

The Bible answers the most asked questions: How to go to God – Jesus says He is the way. How to live – Jesus says I am the life. How to know – Jesus says I am the truth. Jesus instructed us how to let Him into our hearts through prayers: "Ask, and it shall be given you; seek, and ye shall find; knock, and it shall be opened unto you" (Matthew 7:7) Praying is the first step in walking in your God-given purpose. "The day your knees become too far from the ground, that is the day your crown will fall from your head."

After we are adopted into the Divine family by His grace, we start on the process of sanctification. The Holy Spirit indwelling us guides us in our prayers through the Scriptures. We are called the people of the book (Bible). But God is the hero of the book. God wrote this book with the ink of His own blood! We are heroes of the Christian faith even though to different degrees. A hero is someone who does what must be done and needs no other reason. That is what we are supposed to be.

We are supposed to consult God in prayers before we talk to anybody about our problems. The mistake people make is to talk to others about their problems before talking to God. God is closest to us. It means that our arms should be wrapped around prayers first – Talk to God first before you talk to other people. Jesus is God and man – two natures in one person. As God, He knows everything about us. As a man, He knows how we feel because He experienced what we are going through. Therefore, God is our number one counselor. The Bible says "Where no counsel *is*, the people fall: but in the multitude of counselors *there is* safety." (Proverbs 11:14). There is nothing wrong with seeking counsel from other people but they must be praying people. Often, we can be very demanding, especially when it comes to what type of friends we have and who gives us counsel or instruction, and understandably so. There is nothing worse than a person with zero experience rashly offering advice as if they are the voice of authority in a situation they cannot relate to. Our problems are moral and spiritual. Jesus is most qualified as a credible counselor.

Jesus unburdens us the burdens of the world. It doesn't mean we are free from the trials of life. God wants us to be people of value in His eyes and in the eyes of people. "We are hard pressed on every side, but not crushed; perplexed, but not in despair" (2 Corinthians 4:8). Made weak by time and fate, but strong in will to strive, to seek, to find, and not to yield. Circumstances and cultures are subject to change but no cultural change will make us compromise because we are glued to the unchanging truth. We are more than conquerors in Christ that loves us and strengthen us (Romans 8:37). We are ordinary people serving an extraordinary God. Show me a hero, and I will show you someone who has given his or her life to something bigger than oneself.

A born-again person has two natures – The physical and the spiritual. Praying begins in the spirit. Praying is not limited by the physical. Praying is engaging the physical things with the heavenly things. We do not initiate praying, God does. God initiates praying by calling us to pray. Whenever we pray we are responding to God's calling to pray. The Lord's Prayer, which is a model of our praying given to us by our Lord, begins with hollowing the name of the Lord. It is an instruction for us to begin praying by honoring the name of the Lord, to whom we pray, with humbleness and humility from within to outside. When we approach God with reverence, great things begin to approach us. "Therefore, since we are receiving a kingdom that cannot be shaken, let us be thankful, and so worship God acceptably with reverence and awe, for our God is a consuming fire." (Hebrews 12:28-29).

We as humans are particular, picky, demanding, and selfish. We want things how we want them, the way we want them, and when we want them. Praying begins in the spirit and ends in the spirit. "Pray in the Spirit at all times, with every kind of prayer and petition" (Ephesians 6:18). The opposite of praying in the spirit is praying in the flesh. That is when we pray with wrong motives or when we are entangled with other acts of the flesh like strife, unforgiveness, bitterness, hate and etc. We are called to pray in the spirit all the time. At all seasons. No period of life should be without it - youth, middle life, old age, all demand it; no condition of life - adversity, prosperity, sunshine, desolation, under sore temptation, under an important duty, under heavy trial, under all the changing circumstances of life.

Pray in faith and persevere in prayers by faith. Faithful prayer invites God's powerful response (John 14:12-14; 15:7-8). Faithful praying begins in a relationship with God. Praying is entering the presence of God and talking to Him as the Father within the nature and character of Jesus Christ. Faithful prayer flows and syncs from the transformed heart that is adjusted to the teachings of Jesus and is expressed in the words. It is praying as Jesus would pray when our words match the character of God. Praying is two-way communication. We talk to God through prayers, and He talks to us during prayers. God listens even in a situation when you can't hear Him. There is no voice of a child of man lifted to heaven, which is not heard by the Father who is in heaven. God hears all of our prayers but listens to those who listen to Him. "When you talk to God, He listens. We must listen to Him too." There is a time for us to stop talking and say to God that "Speak, Lord, I hear." Listening to God involves heeding to His will.

Praying is keeping the communication line with God alive. Imagine not talking to your loved ones or someone close to you for a day, week, month, or even year. How your heart longs to talk to that person and commune with them, to hear their voice, and be in their presence. How much more do you think God's heart yearns to talk to you? To meet you in that secret spot and have one on one time with you. How much do you think His heart yearns for that lost sheep to come home or that prodigal son to come home to Him? We cannot even fathom the Love of God. So God longs to commune with you. The question is – does your soul thirst for Him?

Knowing that we belong to God and going and stay in His presence is therapeutic. We should approach the throne of God without fear because God is our ally. We should carry everything to God in our prayers. God gave us abilities to do a lot of things. But He wants us to consult Him even regarding the things we can do. We are supposed to pray and go ahead and do them. We should not ask God to do something we can do. Again, it is advisable to ask God to do the things that we can't do and to dedicate to God the things that we can do before we do them.

It is comforting to know that God is near to us than anybody because we abide in Him and He abides us. It costs us nothing to talk to Him. There is no conversation more important than talking to God. Prayer is the most important conversation of the day. It also the easiest and quickest way of talking to God. Prayer moves faster than the speed of light. It reaches God even before we say it because He knows our hearts and thoughts. Now that's pretty powerful and well worth comprehending! Yet we don't pray as often as we are supposed to pray.

Make it a habit every day to start a new page of your story. Make it a great one by praying. When praying becomes your habit, the blessings of God become common and natural. Pray both in good and bad times. Pray when everything feels good. Pray when it seems like all is crumbling right before you. Pray hardest when it's hardest to pray. Regardless of your situation, remember two things – God is with you and He is in control. There's always an unseen hand working on your behalf. Don't underestimate the power of prayer and the power of God. Praying is therefore the right thing to do. The more you practice doing what is right, the more natural and habitual it becomes. Do it even when it is tough to do it. Remember that it takes commitment to do tough things.

When we pray, God heals the total man (spirit, body, and soul). Great joy can break forth if we embrace the treatment He is initiating within us – body, soul, and spirit. You have been redeemed, you are being delivered (sanctified), and you will be transformed! Remember that the moment we get saved we acquire a new nature and begin a process of preparing us to acquire the new bodies that cannot suffer sickness, depreciation, and even death. The process ends in putting on the stature of Christ. When we shall see Him we shall be like Him. No more pain. The only scars in the kingdom of glory will be in hands and feet of our Lord.

Have you ever wondered why the Lord wants us to pray? After all, He controls everything, and His plans won't fail because of our lack of praying. Yet amazingly, through prayer, He allows us the privilege of being involved in His work. Prayer connects inadequate people to an all-sufficient God (John 15:7-16).

"Prayer isn't an action you do. Prayer is the way you live." One of the reasons for prayer is that it teaches us to depend on God. That's why Philippians 4:6 tells us to talk with our Father about everything. James 4:2 adds that sometimes the reason we don't receive it because we haven't bothered to ask. However, this doesn't mean we'll automatically receive whatever we request. God isn't subservient to us—He works all things after the counsel of His will, not ours.

Another reason we should pray is that God wants us to bear much fruit. If we abide in Christ and His words abide in us, our requests will align with His will, and we'll receive what we ask (John 15:7). Then our faith will be strengthened to trust Him in even greater ways. And the more we rely on Him to provide, protect, and guide us, the deeper our relationship with Him will grow.

Intercession prayer is a therapy. Get your minds off your worries by praying for others. Pray for others with such awareness that others are praying for you. The intercessors of God are assigned to you, and you don't even know them but they have got you covered, most probably compared to the invisible angels who surround us. Those of us who have experienced God's love must freely share it. Praying is sharing God's love. Every believer is supposed to get involved in the intercession ministry. "When you light a lamp for someone else, it will also brighten your path."

Supplication is praying for others to access the goodness of God. We are supposed to share God's unconditional love by praying even for our enemies. Pray even for your enemies positively. It doesn't mean approval or endorsing their behaviors. It means abundant faith manifested by unconditional love. Ask God to work on them and to give them time to repent. "Patience with others is love and respect. Patience with self is confidence. And patience with God is faith".

Psychology deals primarily with emotions. Christianity is different from psychology in such a way that our healing begins in our spirit and is manifested in our emotions. "According to psychology, sometimes people need to vent and get it out of their system. I stopped venting and started praying because I don't need sympathy I need strength."

Jesus is the truth – It means that He is the absolute standard upon which reality depends. I want to emphasize that praying is not changing God's will because God's will is perfect, and needs not to be changed. God will not change His mind to contradict the Word that He has already spoken and wrote it down in the Scriptures. Absolute surrendering involves the will of a person. Surrendering the will is coming to the end of yourself. Before you surrender your will, you have not sincerely surrendered to Christ because every time you surrender something else, other than the will, there is something left to surrender. The love of God gives it all. The lust of the flesh keeps it all. Absolute surrendering is committing your spirit to His Spirit.

Praying is to know the will of God. The highest form of praying is finding the will of God in particular when the will of God is against ours. Praying is finding out what God is doing and getting into it. Praying is not to ask God that our will be done but His will to be done. In the Lord's Prayer, we are instructed to pray for God's will to be done on the earth as it is done in heaven. In heaven everybody says "Yes" to God; nobody' says "No" to God. It must be no different on the earth. Once again, you cannot know the will of God unless you talk to God in prayers and you allow God to talk to you in His Word (Bible). Praying is motivated by the Word of God and is measured by the will of God. The Bible is not just a book about information but transformation. The Word of God is the unchanging will of God written to all generations. "The Bible is not a menu that you can ask the waiter to take out, add, or change some items: It is what is!"

If our petitions are not glorifying God, they are not from the minds of Christ. We need the minds of Christ (renewed minds) to scan our petitions. It means that our prayers must be sanctified by the Holy Spirit through the Word of God. A new heart demands a new mind. Each and every prayer must be intended to shape us in the image of Christ.

Praying is not just addressing God with the list of things you want Him to do but addressing Him with the list of things He wills you to do. It is praying for the things you are willing to do for His glory. Basically, praying is asking God to do what He has already made up His minds to do or sanctioned. The Bible is God's manual of a list of things to do. Reading the Bible demands action: Read it with an attitude to do everything instructed instead of selectively choosing what to do.

I want to emphasize that absolute surrendering involves the will of a person. God created us for Himself. He saves us unto Himself. He created us to fellowship with Him. He saves us to fellowship with Him and to worship Him. Worshiping is part of praying.

Praying is therapeutic to a hurting soul. When we pray we can be instantly overwhelmed by the surging faith, strength, and a flash of enlightenment, expelling the cloudy specters blurring our minds. Humble yourself under the mighty hand of God; in due time you will be lifted up and honored before a watching world.

We are all in a process of receiving. Trust God, and He will faithfully lead you through the process, and you will be strengthened as you go. It is not going to be easy but God will go with you through it to strengthen your faith. The Bible says that "so that the proven character of your faith— more precious than gold, which perishes even though refined by fire—may result in praise, glory, and honor at the revelation of Jesus Christ." Your faith is to glorify Jesus even in times of trials. He will not allow a problem to come to you without a solution. "I have learned to trust God. I asked for wisdom. He sent me problems to solve. I asked for peace. He sent me turmoil in order to find peace. I asked for courage. He sent me difficult times to overcome. I asked for prosperity. He sent me tasks of choice. I asked for love. He sent me strangers to love."

Praying is therapeutic to the painful anxiety which is inevitable in all who feel alone in mere self-dependence amidst the difficulties and dangers of life. The Bible says that "Do not be anxious about anything, but in every situation, by prayer and petition, with thanksgiving, present your requests to God. And the peace of God, which transcends all understanding, will guard your hearts and your minds in Christ Jesus." (Philippians 4:6-7). Prayer and supplication with thanksgiving.--By "prayer" is meant worship generally, so called (as in common parlance now) because in this state of imperfection praising must be its leading element, as worship will be in the perfection of the future. All we shall do in heaven is worshiping, no prayer requests.

God is all we seek. We want each of our prayers to be our expression of longing for Him and His will. We can forego many things, but we cannot forego His presence. "One thing I ask from the Lord, this only do I seek: that I may dwell in the house of the Lord all the days of my life, to gaze on the beauty of the Lord and to seek him in his temple" (Psalm 27:4).

Praying is therapeutic when you are struggling with self-forgiving. "The LORD is like a father to his children, tender and compassionate to those who fear him. For he understands how weak we are; he knows we are only dust" (Psalm 103:13-14). One of the names of God is Erech Appayim, the One who, because of His goodness and tenderness, is not easily angered. We need to remember this when we've made the same mistake repeatedly. He will still respond to us with no impatience. Because God is so good and tender, He "suffers long and is kind" (1 Corinthians 13:4).

Biblical counseling/prayers

Biblical counseling is opened and sealed with prayers. Prayer is the greatest force we know to help us to overcome when the odds seem impossible. We shouldn't pray last but first. Praying psychologically convinces the person you are counseling that your source is God. A great majority of people claim to be Christians but in actuality, they do not represent Christ. Praying identifies us with the One to whom we pray. Prayer is irresistible. People might ignore what you say but nobody can resist your prayers.

Praying is the means of picking up the frequency of the voice of God. Hearing directly from God will equip you to have a healthy and more intimate Love Relationship with Jesus Christ and to sense your Heavenly Father's activity in and around your daily life. Empowered by His Holy Spirit you can live the victorious life God has created and designed you to live!

Pray for your clients to open up. In some cases, the reason people can't open up is that they are scared of admitting their fears or concerns to themselves. If there is something, that is causing them stress or worry, vocalizing it can make it feel more real. "Praying brings reassurance that God is working behind the scenes for their betterment. Stress makes them believe that everything has to happen now. Faith reassures that everything will happen in God's timing." Praying allows them to wait and see why God made them wait.

Praying is the best medicine to heal the wounded. Praying restores confidence in both parties involved in counseling. Usually, I ask my clients to pray over what they are going to say. It is easy to extract a prayer of confession from a person you are counseling. Confession. We all mess up. Deep down, we know it. That's why we feel sorry when we've done something wrong or failed to do what is right. Confession is the act of admitting our guilt, regrets, and confusion to the One who wants to help us make it right or move on. We join the rest of the human race in saying "God, have mercy on me, a sinner." (Luke 18:13) And He will.

I usually break up the interview with my clients whenever they become emotional in order to pray over them. When we pray God convicts the people whom we are counseling. Few people are willing to accept to own the bad things. God tests us by revealing to us the nature of our hearts. God alone who knows the hearts of all men can convict a person of wrongdoing. "Even before a word is on my tongue, You know all about it, O LORD." (Psalm 139:4). It means that my tongue cannot utter a word which thou dost not altogether know. Conviction is when the passion of the heart tells the mind what to do. Conviction is useful when it is converted into conduct.

When we are counseling, we should expect testimonies of true accusations, false accusations, and a playing victim attitude. We need to mature in the area of discerning. We need to pray for our clients to have a clean conscience. Conscience growth means something truthful is growing inside the heart. It means Jesus is at work. "When Jesus was accused He uttered not a word. When others were accused He spoke up. We need to know when to zip up & to speak up. God is our defender."

We need God because without God we cannot..... And without us, God will not........ There are things that we cannot do without God's intervention. And there are things that God won't do without our participation. We invite God to intervene in our situation through prayers. When we talk to God, He talks to the situation bothering us, and there is change.

Some of the questions that people need an answer to:

Is divorce unforgivable sin?

Some orthodox Christians believe that divorce is an unforgivable sin. This view is not as common as it once was. After all, a large percentage of Christians have been divorced. Common "sins" such as divorce usually make poor candidates for the unforgivable sin since such a position would disqualify many Christians from eternal life.

Those who say that divorce is an unforgivable sin quote Malachi 2:16, where God says, "I hate divorce." Those who quote this verse usually overlook the fact that this Scripture lists other sins which God also hates, such as pride, lying, and discord (Prov 6:16-19). Elsewhere, God said that Jacob I loved Esau I hated. (Malachi 1:3; Romans 9:13). Jesus said that "If anyone comes to Me and does not hate his father and mother and wife and children and brothers and sisters—yes, even his own life—he cannot be My disciple" (Luke 14:26). The word "hate" in these cases when used by God means to love less.

God divorced Israel (Jeremiah 3:8-10). It was a spiritual divorce but it is still a divorce. God's divorce for Israel was for a limited time. God is not yet done with Israel. God will return to Israel when the time of the gentile is over. There are many sins recounted in the Hebrew Bible but none are ever called unforgivable sins. In the Book of Matthew (12: 31-32), we read, "Therefore I say to you, any sin and blasphemy shall be forgiven men, but the blasphemy against the Spirit shall not be forgiven." The unforgivable sin is rejecting the Holy Spirit to activate your salvation.

Divorce was not in God's original plan of marriage. Jesus recommended divorce due to the weakness of human flesh. Jesus said, "Moses, because of the hardness of your hearts, permitted you to divorce your wives, but from the beginning, it was not so" (Matthew 19:8). Elsewhere, Jesus said "It was also said, 'Whoever divorces his wife, let him give her a certificate of divorce.' But I say to you that everyone who divorces his wife, except on the ground of sexual immorality, makes her commit adultery, and whoever marries a divorced woman commits adultery." (Matthew 5:31-32). Also, "But I say to you that everyone who divorces his wife, except on the ground of sexual immorality, makes her commit adultery, and whoever marries a divorced woman commits adultery" (Matthew 5:23); "And he said to them, "Whoever divorces his wife and marries another commits adultery against her" (Mark 10:11).

"And Pharisees came up to him and tested him by asking, "Is it lawful to divorce one's wife for any cause?" He answered, "Have you not read that he who created them from the beginning made them male and female, and said, 'Therefore a man shall leave his father and his mother and hold fast to his wife, and the two shall become one flesh'? So they are no longer two but one flesh. What therefore God has joined together, let not man separate." They said to him, "Why then did Moses command one to give a certificate of divorce and to send her away?"---- "He said to them, "Because of your hardness of heart Moses allowed you to divorce your wives, but from the beginning, it was not so" (Matthew 19:3-8).

Paul's teaching about divorce: "But if the unbelieving partner separates, let it be so. In such cases the brother or sister is not enslaved. God has called you to peace" (I Corinthians 7:15).

"----(but if she does, she should remain unmarried or else be reconciled to her husband), and the husband should not divorce his wife" (1 Corinthians 7:11).

"To the married I give this charge (not I, but the Lord): the wife should not separate from her husband (but if she does, she should remain unmarried or else be reconciled to her husband), and the husband should not divorce his wife. To the rest, I say (I, not the Lord) that if any brother has a wife who is an unbeliever, and she consents to live with him, he should not divorce her" (1 Corinthians 7:10-12).

For a married woman is bound by law to her husband while he lives, but if her husband dies she is released from the law of marriage. Accordingly, she will be called an adulteress if she lives with another man while her husband is alive. But if her husband dies, she is free from that law, and if she marries another man she is not an adulteress" (Romans 7:2-3).

According to the above scriptures, divorce is authorized in case of adultery. Having sex with another person outside a marriage covenant is adultery. This applies to separated couples too. If the petition before the court is not finalized, if one or indeed both partners have met someone new and wish to pursue a relationship having sexual intercourse with someone else does amount to adultery. "Accordingly, from a legal perspective, if either were to engage with a new partner sexually, prior to the grant of the decree absolute, this is classed as adultery."

Although, there are scriptures authorizing divorce, God hates divorce. I suggest that divorce should be the last step to be taken after all other steps of saving the marriage have failed. Walking away from your marriage may be the easiest choice, but it will have the heaviest impact. When the two are united in marriage, they become one. Trying to separate the two is compared to separating two pieces of wood glued together. Each piece of wood goes with particles of the other piece. The two pieces will never be the same.

Typically, children are the innocent victims of divorce. And too often, parents who divorce are so involved with their own problems that they are unaware of the needs of the children. This is a dilemma of great magnitude for many children. How are they supposed to decide? After all, they do love mum and dad. But now they have to decide on a preference. Even if the parents decide which parent the child is to live with, the situation is far from good. The child might ask himself, why doesn't mum or dad want me to stay with them?

The effects of divorce on children include emotional trauma. A child may begin questioning if he is to blame for the parent leaving. This kind of loss can cause a child to question his own self-worth, and worry that the remaining parent will also leave. This is one of the many different effects of divorce on children. No matter what happens. A divorce is in most cases neither fair nor equitable for the child.

Not all people can handle divorce in the same way. One of the spouses is going to be the victim of divorce. Divorce can bring on PTSD, specifically symptoms like night terrors, flashbacks, and troubling thoughts about the divorce or marriage. These symptoms can become exacerbated by reminders of the divorce and seriously affect one's day to day life. In a divorce, there is the first, immediate trauma, and then the longer-term trauma which may not fully resolve until long after the legal divorce is over. Somebody said that the only trauma worse than divorce, on some life events scales, is the death of a child.

What is the unforgivable sin?

Spiritually speaking, people are worried about the destiny of their souls. The most asked question is that of the unforgivable sin. In the Book of Matthew (12: 31-32), we read, "Therefore I say to you, any sin and blasphemy shall be forgiven men, but the blasphemy against the Spirit shall not be forgiven. "Most Christians have wondered at some point in their life if they have committed the unforgivable sin. I have personally talked with Christians who were divorced, got an abortion, or committed adultery, and thought that maybe they had committed the unforgivable sin. Others think that suicide is an unforgivable sin. They say "If a person commits suicide, then they are going to hell." Then I have talked with some who believe that the unforgivable sin is rejecting God. They believe that if you are a Christian and you go back to living like you aren't a Christian, or if you curse Jesus, or deny that you ever knew Him, then this is the unforgivable sin.

Actually, there is a sin of grieving the Holy Spirit. The Bible says "And do not grieve the Holy Spirit of God, in whom you were sealed for the day of redemption." (Ephesians 4:30). Elsewhere, the Bible instructs us not to extinguish the Spirit. (1Thessalonians 5:19). But all of these are not unforgivable sins. Given this fact, we should avoid grieving the Holy Spirit. There is implied a personal relation to a Divine Person, capable of being "grieved" by our transgressions, partly as sins against His perfect holiness, partly as suicidal rejections of His unfailing love. In the description of this effect of sin we have the needful complement to the view hitherto taken of its effect, as marring our unity with men; for that unity is always in God, through the Holy Spirit working out in each soul the image of Christ. "There is one Body" only because "there is one Spirit." Sin vexes the one, but grieves the other.

I am going to explain what I believe to be the unforgivable sin according to the scriptures. What is sin? The Bible says that sin is the breaking of the law. "Everyone who practices sin practices lawlessness as well. Indeed, sin is lawlessness." (1 John 3:4). The Moral Law consists of Ten Commandments. Jesus taught us the greatest commandment. "Jesus said unto him, Thou shalt love the Lord thy God with all thy heart, and with all thy soul, and with all thy mind. This is the first and great commandment." (Matthew 22:36-40). Since the greatest commandment is loving God, the greatest sin should be not loving God with all thy soul, and with all thy mind. In the Old Testament, Love invaded the earth. The Father came to redeem mankind and He was rejected. In the New Testament, Grace invaded the earth. The love of the Father sent the Son to redeem mankind and He was rejected. The love of God sent the Holy Spirit as the last chance at your fingertips to embrace salvation. Rejecting the Holy Spirit to regenerate your soul is therefore the unforgivable sin.

Often, people ask me if they have committed the unforgivable sin. A person that has committed the unforgivable sin has no conviction and sees no need to repent. As long as you still have the conviction towards righteousness, which is the absolute work of the Holy Spirit, you have not committed the unforgivable sin because the conviction in place is intended to draw you back in the sheepfold of Christ.

When you have committed the unforgivable sin, conviction ceases. That is when the Holy Spirit gives up on you and you become absolutely yourself. When the gospel is preached to you, it will have no impact at all on your soul. It will be most probably like one of the bedtime stories of your grandfather. You have a seared soul that is not sensitive at all to the things of God. Compared to a seared scar on your arm whereby all senses of feeling are dead. Paul warned against the seared conscience. "---influenced by the hypocrisy of liars, whose consciences are seared with a hot iron." (1 Timothy 4:2).

The people who committed the unforgivable sin don't have the peace of mind. As long as you have the peace of God you are fine. Peace is the most wanted thing in the world, just next to life. Genuine peace does not come from the surrounding. Real peace is the inner peace of the mind. As C S Lewis said that "God cannot give a happiness apart from Himself, because it is not there." It is there only when the God of peace from inside becomes the peace of God surrounding you. "And the peace of God, surpassing all understanding, will guard your hearts and your minds in Christ Jesus." (Philippians 4:7). It is the peace which God gives, which flows from the sense of His most gracious presence, and consists in childlike confidence and trustful love. This peace passes all understanding; its calm blessedness transcends the reach of human thought; it can be known only by the inner experience of the believer. Basically, grace precedes peace; peace comes after grace. You will never attain peace until you attain grace. Don't let anything steal that peace.

Sin is missing the required mark of the righteousness of God. All sins are offensive to God. But there is a different degree of sinning. For example, the sin of sexual immorality is a sin against the body which is the temple of God (1 Corinthians 6:18-20). Given this fact, all sins can be forgiven if there is sincere repentance. It is genuinely acknowledging that you have sinned, turning away from that sin, and turning to the righteousness of Christ. Ask the grace of God to cover you. Walk in the light of grace knowing that you are forgiven. The Christian life is the lifestyle of a repented heart. This is what it means to love God wholly heartedly.

Can I lose my salvation?

Everyone needs to be saved from the corrupt nature and the curse of sin. Salvation is when God introduces eternity in our hearts. We were created for eternity, and we are redeemed for eternity. Salvation is complete in our redemption the moment we accept Jesus Christ as our Savior. But He must be our Lord too. Salvation is therefore experienced in three stages: Jesus justified us before God by His blood. It means we go before God in the very holiness of God (Christ). He is sanctifying us by His Spirit through the Word. It means God introduces His character in our hearts and asks us to cooperate in the process of sanctification. A redeemed soul freely inclines towards sanctification because its new nature is to be holy. The word 'holy' means to be separated or set aside for God. This is the evidence of the saved person. Then, when He returns, He will glorify us into the fullness of His stature. It means when He comes for us we shall be like Him from inside to outside.

To be born again is to acquire a new nature (spirit) of Christ. Jesus said that "If anyone loves Me, he will keep My word. My Father will love him, and We will come to him and make Our home with him." (John 14:23). The thought of God as dwelling in the sanctuary and among the people was familiar to the disciples from the Old Testament Scriptures (see, e.g., Exodus 25:8; Exodus 29:45; Leviticus 26:11-12; Ezekiel 37:26). Here our

Lord is laying down the principle of relation – the law of close intimacy, the conditions of higher knowledge. The keeping of the Word is a certain consequence of holy love. "And my Father will love him. And the divine family will come and make the human heart their home through the Holy Spirit." When the Holy Spirit checks in our hearts, He never checks out. He comes to stay permanently as long as we let Him stay. He will not forcefully stay where He is not wanted.

As long as we are in the sheepfold we are safe and secure. It is the responsibility of the Savior to protect us and to defend us from the devour. Jesus said that "My sheep listen to My voice; I know them, and they follow Me. I give them eternal life, and they will never perish. No one can snatch them out of My hand. My Father who has given them to Me is greater than all. No one can snatch them out of My Father's hand." (John 10:27-29). I like this quotation: "Your faith will not fail while God sustains it; you are not strong enough to fall away while God resolved to hold you". Dr. R C Sproul compares our security in Christ with a dad that puts the arm of his little kid in his arm to help the little kid to cross the street out of fear of heavy traffic. The security of the little kid is in the grip of the dad. The little kid is safe as long as the grip of the dad is in place.

"My sheep listen to My voice; I know them, and they follow Me." According to the scripture, Jesus gives us the responsibility of hearing (heeding) His voice, following (walking in His footsteps), and staying (abide) in the sheepfold. We are safe and secure as long as we are in the sheepfold. Jesus will not force us to stay in the sheepfold. He respects our free will before we are born again and after we are saved. Jesus said that "As the Father has loved Me, so have I loved you. Remain in My love. If you keep My commandments, you will remain in My love, just as I have kept My Father's commandments and remain in His love." (John 15:9-11). The key sentence is "Remain in my Love". It is a calling to abide in Him constantly. This is something we decide to do or not to do.

God gives us a gift of faith purposely to overcome Satan. For whatsoever is born of God overcometh the world: and this is the victory that overcometh the world, [even] our faith." (1 John 5:4). The world in this case is not in reference to the physical nature of the universe and its beauty but the corrupt world system. I want to emphasize that our greatest enemy is ourselves or our old corrupt nature that freely inclines towards the corrupt world system. Jesus introduced the cross as a means of killing 'self' within us. The weakened corrupt nature from within constantly tries to unseat the new nature from the throne of our hearts to draw us in the old corrupt ways. We overcome the world by the Word. Jesus said that "The Spirit gives life; the flesh profits nothing. The words I have spoken to you are spirit and they are life" (John 6:63).

Jesus said that "Whosoever eats my flesh, and drinks my blood, hath eternal life; and I will raise him up at the last day" (John 6:24). Jesus gave his flesh to eat, not through any physical process, not through any sacramental rite, but through the Spirit to our spirit. It is when by the power of the Holy Spirit, the Word finds residence in us and permanently stays. The liberating truth is when God's Word becomes our conscience. That is why the Word became flesh or physical (John 1:1). His body ascended so that His Spirit can descend to inhabit our hearts. Our physical and everything about us inside-out is not mindless labor but gigantic labor of love! This is what it means to be filled with the Spirit.

Clarifying on the grace

God made one man from dust and created him a living soul by breathing life in his nostrils. The rest of human beings came from that one man called Adam. According to the Scriptures, there are only two men, two races, and two genealogies. "So it is written: "The first man Adam became a living being;" the last Adam a life-giving spirit." (1 Corinthians 15:45). Our genealogy from the man (Adam) is an extended death sentence on the earth until we are justified in the heavenly courts by one man called Jesus Christ. By the act of disobedience of one man (Adam), all were condemned. By the act of obedience of one man (Jesus), all are justified before God. The first Adam became, by his disobedience, a mere living soul, and from him, we inherit that nature; the second Adam, by His obedience, became a life-giving spirit, and from Him, we inherit the spiritual nature in us and hence eternal life.

The condition of sinning is inherited from the first man (Adam) who represented all mankind. The sinful nature within us causes us to sin. We sin because we are sinners by nature. The Law is bad news of condemnation to the unbelievers. But the grace is the good news of God's forgiveness extended to us. God, unconditionally forgives those who come to Him with a sorrowful and repentant heart. "Therefore, there is now no condemnation for those who are in Christ Jesus" (Romans 8:1). The damnation brought about by the presence of sin is lifted. The condemnation which in the present and final judgment of God impends over the sinner is removed by the intervention of Christ, and by the union of the believer with Him. By that union, the power and empire of sin are thrown off and destroyed.

I want to clarify that the first sin was committed by Adam but we are not accountable for the first sin of Adam. The original sin inherited from Adam causes our individual sins of which we are accountable. Sin enters us in multiples ways in particular in what we see, taste, touch, hear and smell. But sin has one exit – the confession of our sins by the mouth to our Lord. It must be sincere confession leading to repentance. God demands the confession of our sins and the repentance of the sincere heart in order for forgiveness to be ours. Repentance is turning from your ways and turning to God's ways. It is turning to God seeking direction to live the way He created you to live.

The antidote to sin is grace. There is no human effort or ritual that can eradicate sin. Everybody knows that grace is the unmerited favor of God or getting what we don't deserve. But this is not all that grace is. Often, I am tempted to believe that grace cannot be fully comprehended or contained in our finite minds, in the same manner, we cannot contain God in our tiny minds. My professor used to compare various definitions of grace to three blind men who were asked to define an elephant by touching it. One blind man touched the trunk and came to the conclusion that an elephant is like a tree. The second blind man touched the belly and said that "Now I know an elephant is like a huge wall." The third blind man touched the tail and said, "I am convinced that an elephant looks like a rope". None of the three blind men had the true definition of the elephant. The grace is much bigger than we tend to define it.

Salvation is not just getting a ticket to go to heaven; there is the abundant life that comes with salvation beginning from now. Jesus said that whosoever drinks of His water will never thirsty again (John 4:14). It is not an external supply, which must be sought to meet the recurring physical want, but it is the inner never-failing source, the fountain of living water, which satisfies every want as it occurs. Everything that God does for a fallen man is by His grace. The best definition of grace is that it is the divine influence on the human heart: Grace transforms the heart by the Holy Spirit. Then the grace sanctifies the human heart by teaching us to obey the commandments of God. Jesus divided the Ten Commandments into two parts – Loving God and loving your neighbor (Matthew 22:37-40). It is because the first four commandments define how to love God, and the last six define how to love your neighbor. In fact, it is one law of loving God proven by the way we love our neighbors.

I want to emphasize that we are justified by grace alone (not by our works), but we are called to grow in grace (2 Peter 3:18). Our good works are the proof that we are saved. Remember that salvation is divided into three parts – Justification (we are declared to be innocent by faith in the finished works of Jesus); sanctification (God in union with man's obedience transforming our characters from inside to the outside); glorification (acquiring the final stature of Christ by God). The grace allows the Holy Spirit to dwell in us. The Holy Spirit sanctifies us through the Word of God. This ministry of the Holy Spirit guarantees the security of the believer "until the day of glorification."

On Mount Sinai, God wrote with His finger ten moral laws on two tablets of stones, revealing the depth of man's depravity, and handed them to Moses for people to observe. (Exodus 20:1-17). Although all the people promised to do everything written down in the Law they failed miserably. The Israelites represented mankind in the same way Adam represented mankind. The Bible says "So the law became our guardian to lead us to Christ, that we might be justified by faith." (Galatians 3:24). The role of the Law is rather a higher kind of guardianship to the grace. We are not under the Law because we are called to a higher standard of living than the Law – A standard that cannot be attained by human efforts. We are called to manifest the life and righteousness of God, which can only be attained by our relationship with Jesus Christ. We are saved by grace through faith. "For by grace you are saved through faith, and this not of yourselves; it is the gift of God" (Ephesians 2:8).

The laws are in place to restrain the lawbreakers. We are sinners under grace. We can sin because the sinful nature is still in us but our desire changed from wanting to sin to wanting to be holy as God is holy. The Holy Spirit is our restrainer. He convicts us of righteousness. Love is the motivating factor in our relationship with God. We don't observe the Moral Law out of fear of the consequences of not observing it. We are not worried about going to hell because Jesus saved us from it. We strictly observe the Moral Law because of our love for God. It is the same thing as you won't cheat on your spouse out of fear to be caught but out of love for your spouse. Love conquers and alters all. God loved us in Christ. "See what great love the Father has lavished on us, that we should be called children of God!" Children of God are of the same nature and character as God. And that is what we are!

It is important to note that Jesus Christ did not come to win the love of the Father for us. It is the love of the Father that sent Jesus to die for us. Every one of us has the ability to resist God's *grace*. But none of us can hold out against God once He sets His *love* upon us. The saving grace of God is effectually applied to those who have accepted Jesus Christ as their Lord and Savior such that no natural force can undo what the supernatural work of the Holy Spirit has done in the salvation of sinners.

There is no man so good that if he places all his actions and thoughts under the scrutiny of the laws, he would not deserve banishment. We are sinners but dressed in the robes of righteousness. The only way a sinner can be certainly sure of the forgiveness of sins is to stand before God in His imputed righteousness. Grace allows a sinner to stand before God in the imputed righteousness of Christ. We go to God with the resume of Christ. In normal life, it is challenging to build a resume that is pleasing to your boss. It is more challenging when it comes to God. But God says that He is pleased in nothing less than your faith (Hebrews 11:6). Our faith is in the righteousness of Christ. In Jesus Christ is the fullness of grace. "The Word became flesh and made His dwelling among us. We have seen His glory, the glory of the one and only Son from the Father, full of grace and truth." (John 1:14). The reality of the moral power and change wrought in those that believed recalls and is itself evidence of the reality of that in which they believed. Man came to be a son of God, because the Son of God became man. Our hope for redemption does not come from within us but from outside us; it is in Christ. There is no faith outside Christ.

God demanded that a perfect human being (sacrifice) saves the rest of the imperfect human beings. Jesus is not a seed of the corrupted man because He was conceived of the Holy Spirit. The sinless nature of Jesus Christ qualifies Him to be the only acceptable Savior to God. "For there is one God and one mediator between God and mankind, the man Christ Jesus" (1 Timothy 2:5). This scripture rules out the possibility of the authenticity of other false prophets who claim to be our guide to heaven. The mediator is the one that mediates the fallen man that needs to amend their relationship with God. Therefore, a mediator must be perfect in order to save others from their sins. Otherwise, he must save himself first before saving others. Surprisingly, all of the false prophets who claim to be sent by God to guide people to heaven cannot amend their own faults. They cannot save themselves; they need a Savior too! Why follow them?

God created Adam by breathing into him His life. Children of God have a new nature involving the resurrected life of Jesus Christ. "----when he had said this, he breathed on them, and saith unto them, Receive ye the Holy Ghost" (John 20:22). After the resurrection, Jesus was glorified. Receiving the Holy Spirit was necessary in order for the disciples to know Him and to communicate with Him in their conscience. This was the beginning of the supernatural life which makes Christian consciousness unique among religious experiences. This act created the conviction which was sealed on Pentecost. This being the most divine function of the Church and of the Disciples of Christ ever since. In the minds of the Jewish disciples who worshiped in the temple, it was like "the Spirit went from between the wings of the cherubim, and breathed upon them" by the decree, or order of the Lord." Life begins from the nostrils of God. God made man from the materials He already created (clay) and breathed into him life. The breathing of Jesus on His disciples was symbolic of the creation of man (Genesis 2:7), the conviction of which was accomplished and realized on Pentecost (the birthday of the Church) when God created a new life in them to dominate the old corrupted life. Regeneration means recreation. The creation and recreation of mankind did not take place without the Divine breathing. Unlike the plants and animals, man received his life from a distinct act of Divine breathing. It was not an in-breathing of atmospheric air, but an in-flatus from the Ruach Elohim, or Spirit of God that constituted to the image of God in man. Man became a living soul, not only capable of performing the functions of the animal life, of eating, drinking, walking but of morally thinking, reasoning, discerning, discoursing rationally as God, and worshiping God.

Our new nature is not compatible with the corrupt world. We are ambassadors of God in a hostile nation. The reason the world does not know us is that it did not know Him (1 John 3:1). The highest form of ignorance is when you reject something you don't know anything about. Spiritually, it is called 'lack of insight'. Sin is rejecting the love of God extended to us through Jesus Christ. God will honor your decision of rejecting Him by rejecting you. Again, this is not what I am saying; it is what the Bible says!

Salvation is God's grace. It is the gift of freedom from our sins that Jesus made possible by taking the punishment for our sins on the cross. This is one of the confusing scripture. "---and every tongue confess that Jesus Christ is Lord, to the glory of God the Father. Therefore, my beloved, just as you have always obeyed, not only in my presence, but now even more in my absence, continue to work out your salvation with fear and trembling." (Philippians 2:11-12). The scripture is an appeal to the believers who have the Holy Spirit residing in them to cooperate with the grace within them by manifesting the sanctified life out of them. We work out our salvation from the outside because God has already worked out our salvation from the inside. We are not called to work hard in order to earn our salvation but to work hard to manifest the fruits of our salvation that is already in place. "But grow in the grace and knowledge of our Lord and Savior Jesus Christ." (2 Peter 3:18). We are called to grow in grace. Growing in "the grace of our Lord" means growing in "the knowledge of our Lord." The Bible is our gym where we go to work out. We go to the scriptures to grow our faith. The scriptures are inspired and inspiring. They are inspiring only when we let the Holy Spirit be our teacher. Read the Bible with the right motives. I know some critics who read the Bible regularly to find mistakes. Ignorance looks for excuses not to change. A stiff-necked person looks for mistakes in the scriptures instead of embracing the truth. Poignantly, the inerrancy of the scriptures projects that whenever you find a mistake in the Bible, it is because there is a mistake in your life.

The grace is God's standard separating good and evil; it is God's standard of acceptance and rejection (Matthew 25:23). Grace divides the world into two human races: 1) The saved sinners who are under the grace.

2) The perishing world lost in their sins. In order for you to be saved, Jesus must be your Lord and Savior. I want to warn that there is a sizable number of people who claim to be born again, they accepted Jesus Christ as their Savior but deny Him an opportunity to be Lord over their lives. Jesus must be your Lord and the Lord of everything in your life or He is not Lord at all.

I am standing because of the grace, No one can stand apart from the grace. Grace is everything to a believer. When we pray, grace covers it all. When you pray and get what you want – That is God's direction. When you don't get what you want – That is God's protection. Either way, God is involved.

The grace has to be received and passed on to others. The grace is supposed to flow through you to others otherwise it might be revoked by God (Matthew 18:21-35). The golden rule says do unto to others what you want to be done to you. Jesus instructed us to ask for forgiveness from God as we forgive others. Spiritual forgiveness is not what you do but what you allow God to do in and through you by allowing His love and mercy to flow through you to others. Forgiving is not taking the offenders off the hook. It is handing the offender to God. Forgiveness is refusing to take the matter into hands and put it into the hands of the all mighty God. A righteous and just God promised to administer vengeance at His timing. It is acknowledging that God is in control of your situation.

What about tithing?

Tithing precedes the Mount Sinai incident when God handed the Ten Moral Laws to Moses. Abraham tithed before the Law was given to Moses (Genesis 14:20; Hebrews 7:2). Tithing is therefore not something new that came with Moses. Melchizedek is a type of Christ. The goodness of God precedes the Leviticus laws & Mount Sinai (Law). The Moral Law shows to us the impact of sin (deficit) and the required remedy that was not possible for any man to pay apart from grace. Justification is by faith, and that by faith alone. Righteousness is thus reckoned by God to the one who believes.

Melchizedek comes out to meet Abram when he returns from his victory. Melchizedek is grateful to Abram for defeating the enemies of Salem. In gratitude Melchizedek brings bread and wine and blesses Abram: "Blessed be Abram by God Most High, maker of heaven and earth." (Genesis 14:18-19). In return, Abram turns over 1/10 of everything he has just stolen back. Not one-tenth of his income but one-tenth of the loot. The way the story is told we know that he did it as an act of worship. It wasn't a duty. He did it out of gratitude.

God was the King of Israel. He instituted the uniformity taxation of ten percent to every Jew living in the Promised Land. Tithing was actively practiced during the ministry of Jesus even though the Scriptures do not specifically tell us that Jesus tithed. Jesus warned the religious leaders against the hypocrisy involved in their tithing: "Woe to you, teachers of the law and Pharisees, you hypocrites! You give a tenth of your spices—mint, dill, and cumin. But you have neglected the more important matters of the law—justice, mercy, and faithfulness. You should have practiced the latter, without neglecting the former. (Matthew 23:23).

The Bible recommends a cheerful giver regardless of how much is given. "The point is this: whoever sows sparingly will also reap sparingly, and whoever sows bountifully[a] will also reap bountifully. 7 Each one must give as he has decided in his heart, not reluctantly or under compulsion, for God loves a cheerful giver." (2 Corinthians 9:6-7).

"Being open-handed with our possessions (and our service and time) results in God being generous toward us. It's a lovely circle of grace. We give because we have freely received from God. He continues to bless us as we bless others. Financial giving has not been a difficult concept for me to grasp because my parents were good about teaching it when I was young. The principle of tithing, which is giving back to God a tenth of everything we earn, is simple when broken down in child-like terms. As a small child, my parents gave me a $1 allowance. Ten cents of that was for me to give at church." ~ D J Hejtmanek

Everything we have comes from God. It is all His anyway. We are stewards. He asks us to give back a small portion, the tithe, which simply means "tenth," for the work of his Kingdom in the earth. He also desires "offerings," which are gifts given freely for special purposes. "Bring the whole tithe into the storehouse, that there may be food in my house. Test me in this," says the Lord Almighty, "and see if I will not throw open the floodgates of heaven and pour out so much blessing that there will not be room enough to store it." (Malachi 3:10).

I want to say that tithing is a good practice in order for you to honor God with your finances. It is making a covenant or arrangement with God to become involved in your finances. Just make sure that when you make such a covenant you keep it all the way. I am not bound by ten percent. I give above ten percent cheerfully. I have a problem with some preachers who teach that the Moral Law (Ten Commandments) is an Old Testament issue that is not applicable in the New Testament, and yet they emphasize tithing.

"Each of you should give what you have decided in your heart to give, not reluctantly or under compulsion, for God loves a cheerful giver". (2 Corinthians 9:7). Give generously.

"If I give all I possess to the poor and give over my body to hardship that I may boast, but do not have love, I gain nothing." (1 Corinthians 13:3). Give from the spirit of love.

"Honor the Lord with your wealth, with the firstfruits of all your crops. (Proverbs 3:9)". Give the best to God, not leftovers.

"So when you give to the needy, do not announce it with trumpets, as the hypocrites do in the synagogues and on the streets, to be honored by others. Truly I tell you, they have received their reward in full" (Matthew 6:2). Give without expecting praises of men.

"But who am I, and who are my people, that we should be able to give as generously as this? Everything comes from you, and we have given you only what comes from your hand" (1 Chronicles 29:14). Give with awareness that everything belongs to God.

What about abortion?

A fetus or embryo in the belly of the mother is not a lifeless cell attached to a mother. A fetus is another life and the closest neighbor to the mother. The only difference between a baby outside the womb and a baby inside the womb is time. The law of loving your neighbor as you love yourself applies to the fetus too. A mother must treat another life in her belly as she wants to be treated.

The most dangerous place for a baby is in their mother's womb where the baby is at the mercy of the mother to live or not to live. The Bible says that the spirit of Antichrist is already here in the church (1 John 4:3). The word Antichrist means against or in place of Christ. The spirit of Antichrist is anti-people. It is anti-pro-life, pro-abortion, and pro-death. A Christian can't claim to be pro-abortion in any shape or form.

Abortion is primarily a legislative issue. The law of the country forbids taking an innocent life. However, when it comes to a fetus, the law is redefined. The courts sided with the government saying that a fetus is not a human being. This is when we bring in the Creator to tell us if a fetus is truly a human being. Gabriel foretells John's birth in this way: "For he will be great before the Lord. And he shall never drink wine and strong drink, and he will be full of the Holy Spirit even from his mother's womb." (Luke 1:15). Elsewhere, God said to Jeremiah that, "Before I formed you in the womb I knew you, and before you were born I set you apart and appointed you as a prophet to the nations." (Jeremiah 1:5). John was filled with the Spirit when he was still in the womb. Our souls/spirits are the eternal part of us. God knew us before we were born, while we were in the inward parts. He knew all our days. Now science says that there is light involved at the time of conception. "For the first time ever, scientists have captured images of the flash of light that sparks at the very moment a human sperm cell makes contact with an egg." Our Lord is light and life. He knew us when we were just a thought before he formed us.

Since you are God's breathe, God knew your spirit before you became human. We are God's breathe in the same way the Word is God's breathe. The popular phrase "abracadabra" is a modern mispronunciation of an original permutation of two Hebrew words from Strong's H1254 & H1696....*abara & kadavara*....meaning..." I will create, as was spoken". It should be correctly pronounced as *abracadavra* to mean: I will create as it was spoken....meaning I align my will to YHVH will to create what He has spoken into my scroll at my inception point of creation cornerstone.

Most young ladies who decide to abort their babies are not well informed regarding the dangers involved in abortion and the benefits of keeping the baby. Study shows that a sizable percentage of women who entered the abortion clinic to abort their babies changed their minds after they were exposed to the ultrasound and heard the fetal heartbeat.

There are various reasons out there given as excuses for killing a baby in the womb. According to one study survey, the reasons most frequently cited were that having a child would interfere with a woman's education, work or ability to care for dependents (74%); that she could not afford a baby now (73%); and that she did not want to be a single mother or was having relationship problems (48%). Nearly four in 10 women said they had completed their childbearing, and almost one-third were not ready to have a child. Fewer than 1% said their parents' or partners' desire for them to have an abortion was the most important reason. Younger women often reported that they were unprepared for the transition to motherhood, while older women regularly cited their responsibility to dependents. The decision to have an abortion is typically motivated by multiple, diverse and interrelated reasons. The themes of responsibility to others and resource limitations, such as financial constraints and lack of partner support, recurred throughout the study.

The confused ladies who do not seem ready to raise a baby should be introduced to other options. Adoption is a solution to unwanted pregnancy. The women who say that they decided to abort the babies due to lack of money to support them to go through pregnancy and raise the babies should be notified that there are many pro-life charities out there that are ready to help those mothers who are financially unstable. There is absolutely no reason given that is worth the death of the baby.

The young ladies who walk in the clinic to abort their babies should be informed about the severe consequences of their choices to kill the baby. These are some of the abortion risks to mothers: Death, future miscarriages, breast cancer, trauma. Abortion is a sin involving murdering the soul. You should do it with such awareness that you are answerable to the God who created that soul. God knew our souls before we were born. The soul you exterminate from the face of the earth cannot be exterminated from the memory of God who breathed it into existence. God will hold you accountable for your action. Whereas the world is applauding you with slogans of "women's right to choose," heaven is screaming "Murder!"

Our souls/spirits are the eternal part of us. He knew us before and after our conception, while we were in the inward parts. He knew all our days. Our Lord is light and life. Do you really believe Jesus, the Author of life would be OK with the taking of innocent life? Abortion is the work of the evil one who came to steal, kill and destroy. "Mary was in a very difficult situation especially within the context of her culture. Suppose Mary had aborted Jesus? Thank God she didn't even think about it. We need to support and help not only the Mothers in carrying their babies but afterward. Babies should be brought to the altar of the church to be dedicated to God. The members of the congregation should promise to help the parents to raise the babies – Spiritually, emotionally, physically, and financially.

What about same sex relationship?

God loves all sinners including homosexuals, fornicators, and, adulterers but He hates our sins. But we must acknowledge our sins. If we confess *our sins*, He is faithful and righteous to forgive *us our sins* and to cleanse *us* from all unrighteousness (1 Corinthians 11:31-32). As Christians, we believe with deepest sincerity that the embrace of homosexual practice, along with other sins, keeps people out of the kingdom of God. Same-sex relationship defies biology and theology. Biologically it does not fit. Even among animals, there is no male dog that will go to a male dog to have sex or a female dog that will go to a female dog to have sex. Theologically, it defies God's Moral Law. The most fundamental thing about our being is that we were created by God as His image-bearer. God created a male and female and united them to become one. And ordered them to multiply and replenish the universe.

The first appearance and application of something in the Bible is indicative of God's original intent. This is what's called the Law of First Mention. One of the first things God established was a marriage between one man and one woman. Look at how Adam responded after Eve was introduced to him: "This is now bone of my bones, and flesh of my flesh: she shall be called Woman, because she was taken out of Man." (Genesis 2:23). The Bible then goes on to say, "Therefore shall a man leave his father and his mother, and shall cleave unto his wife: and they shall be one flesh" (Gen. 2:24). So, the first mention of marriage in the Bible is clearly defined, and God blessed it (Gen. 1:26-28). Therefore, according to the Law of First Mention, God's intent for marriage has been established here.

The Bible also says, in Romans 1:26-27, that people are naturally born heterosexual. They simply exchange the normal with the abnormal. They deliberately choose to live in the realm of deception: "For this cause God gave them up unto vile affections: for even their women did change the natural use into that which is against nature: [27] And likewise also the men, leaving the natural use of the woman, burned in their lust one toward another; men with men working that which is unseemly, and receiving in themselves that recompense of their error which was meet." They exchanged the truth of God for a lie, and worshiped and served the creature rather than the Creator, who is forever worthy of praise! Amen.

Homosexuality is a vice character. According to the survey carried out in Denmark and Sweden, people belonging to the same sexual minority groups have higher levels of suicide than heterosexuals. Studies across several decades and many different countries have found sexual minority individuals, defined as people who identify as lesbian, gay, or bisexual, or engage in same-sex sexual relationships regardless of sexual identity, more frequently report serious suicidal ideation and suicide attempts compared with heterosexual individuals. There is a 40% suicide among transgender. It is because they have confused minds. The secular institutions use the same-sex union to promote birth control. They ignore the fact that Gay, bisexual, and other men who reported male-to-male sexual contact are the population most affected by HIV in the United States.

I want to say that homosexuality should be treated as one of many sins which can be forgiven once repented. Sin does not just make you look bad, it kills you. Jesus gives you power over that tormenting sin. There is no sin greater than grace. I suggest that homosexuals seek professional help from experienced counselors and members of the clergy. Remember that we were habitual offenders until we were saved. The Bible says that "And that is what some of you were. But you were washed, you were sanctified, you were justified, in the name of the Lord Jesus Christ and by the Spirit of our God." (1 Corinthians 6:11). Justification of the blood of Jesus alone restores the lost relationship with God. Sanctification is a joint process whereby God works with us by the power of the Holy through the Word to cleanse us. Sometimes it takes a while to completely abandon our bad habits. But we must repent, and turn around, and start walking in the right direction. A homosexual person who has admitted that he or she is in sin, who has repented, and who has seen the need to seek help from the church leadership should be rendered the same help as a heterosexual believer that is struggling with fornication and adultery. We are very forgiving when it comes to the things we have done. Let us use the same standard of judgment to judge others because God is going to use the same lens we use to judge others to judge us. "Do not judge, or you too will be judged. For in the same way you judge others, you will be judged, and with the measure you use, it will be measured to you." (Mathew 7:2). In this case, judging means condemning. We have the responsibility to help others to come out of their predicaments rather than judging them.

Leviticus 18:22 "Do not practice homosexuality, having sex with another man as with a woman. It is a detestable sin."

Leviticus 20:13 "If a man practices homosexuality, having sex with another man as with a woman, both men have committed a detestable act. They must both be put to death, for they are guilty of a capital offense."

1 Corinthians 6:9-11 "Don't you realize that those who do wrong will not inherit the Kingdom of God? Don't fool yourselves. Those who indulge in sexual sin, or who worship idols, or commit adultery, or are male prostitutes, or practice homosexuality, or are thieves, or greedy people, or drunkards, or are abusive or cheat people none of these will inherit the Kingdom of God. Some of you were once like that. But you were cleansed; you were made holy; you were made right with God by calling on the name of the Lord Jesus Christ and by the Spirit of our God."

1 Timothy 1:8-10 "Now we know that the law is good, if one uses it lawfully, understanding this, that the law is not laid down for the just but for the lawless and disobedient, for the ungodly and sinners, for the unholy and profane, for those who strike their fathers and mothers, for murderers, the sexually immoral, men who practice homosexuality, enslavers, liars, perjurers, and whatever else is contrary to sound doctrine".

Jude 7: "And don't forget Sodom and Gomorrah and their neighboring towns, which were filled with immorality and every kind of sexual perversion. Those cities were destroyed by fire and serve as a warning of the eternal fire of God's judgment."

What about rape?

Rape involves unwanted sexual intercourse. It is very painful because in the first place it is unwanted. Most of the victims of rape are women. Women are naturally different from men such that they have to prepare themselves in order to have sex. Rape violates their right to choose when to have sex. Unwanted sex is painful to them. The worst part of it is the unwanted pregnancy and the danger of venereal diseases.

Sexual violence is shockingly common in our society. According to the Centers for Disease Control and Prevention (CDC), nearly 1 in 5 women in the USA are raped or sexually assaulted at some point in their lives, often by someone they know and trust. In some Asian, African, and Middle Eastern countries, that figure is even higher. And sexual assault isn't limited to women; many men and boys suffer rape and sexual trauma each year. According to the government of Uganda, the Annual Police Crime and Traffic Safety Report 2020 states that a total of 14,230 victims were defiled in 2020, of whom, 140 were male juveniles. The number is much lower, compared to those reported of girls, and this is likely because many people do not report cases of boys who have been defiled. It is assumed that boys, especially those who are in their mid or late teenage, are willing partners and so people see no need to report the case. In addition, many boys are not willing to open and speak up about what they are facing and so keep quiet about what has been done to them.

Regardless of age or gender, the impact of sexual violence goes far beyond any physical injuries. The trauma of being raped or sexually assaulted can be shattering, leaving you feeling scared, ashamed, and alone or plagued by nightmares, flashbacks, and other unpleasant memories. The world doesn't feel like a safe place anymore. You no longer trust others. You don't even trust yourself. You may question your judgment, your self-worth, and even your sanity. You may blame yourself for what happened or believe that you're "dirty" or "damaged goods." Relationships feel dangerous, intimacy seems impossible. And on top of that, like many rape survivors, you may struggle with PTSD, anxiety, and depression. One of the rape victims wrote: "Today I wore a pair of faded old jeans and a plain grey baggy shirt. I hadn't even taken a shower, and I did not put on an ounce of makeup. I grabbed a worn-out black oversize jacket to cover myself with even though it is warm outside. I have made conscious decisions lately to look like less of what I felt a male would want to see. I want to disappear."

Rape happens when people lose their self-control. Women do not get raped because they weren't careful enough. Women get raped because someone raped them. Rape is one of the most terrible crimes on earth and it happens every few minutes. The problem with groups that deal with rape is that they try to educate women about how to defend themselves. In as much as it is good to teach women to take precautions like avoiding wearing revealing clothes, staying away from dangerous and isolated places, avoid getting drunk in public places, men should be educated to exercise self-control.

What do you say to the victim of rape? I am going to begin with what not to say. Never tell the rape victim that you know how they feel when you don't have a crew regarding being raped. The only person who has the legitimacy to say that "I know how you feel" is a person that has been raped before. That person can relate to the rape victim and her testimony can be timely and useful.

There are three go-to statements if you don't know what to say: "I believe you," "It's not your fault" and "You have options." Many survivors are questioned, and with disbelief, comes victim-blaming. The third (statement) speaks to the trauma of feeling that your options were taken away from you, like being able to say no, or advancing your career without enduring unwanted advances. Survivors should be re-empowered with the right to make their own decisions.

Disclosing trauma should be at the survivor's pace, so we tend to steer people away from asking questions; that can feel invasive, and we want survivors to feel in control of what they share. But, if they allow you to ask questions, make sure they are not phrased in a way that insinuates victim-blaming. Asking, "How did it happen?" feels a lot different than "Why did it happen," or, "What were you doing when it happened?"

Rape is intended to emotionally hurt your feelings. But there is the backlash of breaking your faith replacing it with anxiety. Turn to the Bible for spiritual insight; it is an anxiety reliever. In the Bible, there is neither bad news nor grievances for redressing. The Bible revokes and replaces the bad news of rape with the 'Good News'. Jesus never breaks hearts but He picks up the broken pieces of our lives and puts them together. There is an art to brokenness. The knack lies in humility, throwing yourself at the Rock (Jesus). "The Lord is close to the brokenhearted and saves those who are crushed in spirit" (Psalms 34:18).

Scriptures for the victims of rape: Psalm 9:9-10 – The Lord is a shelter for the oppressed, a refuge in times of trouble. Those who know your name trust in you, for you, O Lord, do not abandon those who search for you.

Isaiah 43:2-3a: When you go through deep waters, I will be with you. When you go through rivers of difficulty, you will not drown. When you walk through the fire of oppression, you will not be burned up; the flames will not consume you. For I am the Lord, your God.

Isaiah 61: 1-3: The Spirit of the Lord God is upon me, because the Lord has anointed me to bring good news to the suffering and afflicted. He has sent me to comfort the brokenhearted, to announce liberty to captives, and to open the eyes of the blind. He has sent me to tell those who mourn that the time of God's favor to them has come, and the day of his wrath to their enemies. To all who mourn in Israel he will give: beauty for ashes; joy instead of mourning; praise instead of heaviness.

What about the sin of suicide?

Suicide involves taking your life prematurely. Depression is the major cause of suicide. There are a number of people in the Bible who contemplated killing themselves and who actually killed themselves. According to Matthew 27:1–10, after learning that Jesus was to be crucified, Judas attempted to return the money he had been paid for his betrayal to the chief priests and committed suicide by hanging.

Moses was stressed with the burden of the people he was leading to the Promise Land. He asked God to take his life: "I cannot carry all these people by myself; it is too burdensome for me. If this is how You are going to treat me, please kill me right now—if I have found favor in Your eyes—and let me not see my own wretchedness." (Numbers 11:14-15).

Elijah the prophet wanted to die. He asked God to take his life because he had come to the conclusion that he was a failure. Elijah had just been victorious in the showdown with the 450 prophets of Baal on Mount

Carmel. God had sent fire down from heaven to consume Elijah's sacrifice (see I Kings 18:17-40). In addition, the prophet had predicted a terrible famine, and the Lord had not sent rain for three years. After that time, Elijah prayed for rain, and God produced a torrential downpour (see verse. 41-46). At Elijah's cry, God rained fire from heaven upon the altar, and the flames not only consumed the sacrifice but the wood, the altar, and the dust around it. After seeing this amazing display, the people fell on their knees and proclaimed, "The Lord, he is God! The Lord, he is God! (1 Kings 18:39). God was working mightily through His servant Elijah. This made him very unpopular with Ahab and Jezebel, the wicked king and queen of Israel. We read in I Kings 19:1-3: And Ahab told Jezebel all that Elijah had done, and withal how he had slain 850 prophets of Baal with the sword. Then Jezebel sent a messenger unto Elijah, saying, So let the gods do to me, and more also if I make not thy life as the life of one of them by tomorrow about this time. And when he saw that, he arose, and went for his life, and came to Beersheba, which belongs to Judah, and left his servant there. He traveled about 100 miles from Jezreel down to Beersheba, located along the outer border of Israel. Considering all the powerful works the Lord had just performed through Elijah, it is hard to understand why the prophet didn't stay and face Jezebel, trusting God to protect him. Instead, he fled into the wilderness and requested to die.

Depression is the major cause of suicide. Nobody is exempted from depression. "Christians are not altogether immune from depression. The fact is: the trend of events and the mounting tide of evil are enough to give one sobering thoughts, Christian or not. David, the sweet singer of Israel, was not always on top of his depression. Sometimes his glad song was turned to depressive mourning. "My tears have been my meat day and night, while continually they say unto me, Where is thy God? Why art thou cast down, O my soul, and why art thou disquieted in me?" I find that the cure for depression is praise. In other words: be so busy counting your blessings, that thoughts of gloom and despair will be crowded out." ~ Denis McDowell

Depressive symptoms, even in the absence of a depression diagnosis, are associated with significant health and social problems including psychosocial dysfunction, substance use disorders, functional impairments, and other anti-social natural events. According to the survey, there is a sharp spike regarding suicide among youth. The surging is not due to an epidemic of Covid since old people are most likely to suffer from the virus than young people. Part of the reason is the closing of churches and schools.

In the culture of materialism we live in, there is what we call ego competitive identity – Who has archived more? Who owns what? Who looks better? And etc. This causes anger, bitterness, envy, and pride. These very things are the recipe for suicide. Our hope is in Christ alone. A born-again believer is supposed to compete only against himself. "My goal is not to be better than anyone else but to be better than I used to be." These are the words of a prominent scholar. And it's heart-rending to learn this directly from a scholar.

People contemplate committing suicide after losing hope. "Just as man cannot live without dreams, he cannot live without hope. If dreams reflect the past, hope summons the future." The greatest deception of Satan is that you are the reason for your very existence and that beyond you there is nobody. Betrayed by yourself, you end up hopeless. "Your will to live can sustain you when you are sick but if you lose it, your last hope is gone (Proverbs,18:14)."

People commit suicide because they have no hope. A born-again believer has hope. Hope begins with Jesus. The moment you turn to God by repenting your sins to Jesus Christ, He gives to you the hope and peace that you need to navigate through life. There is hope no matter what you are going through. "My faith is in Jesus. Regardless of the situation, I am convinced that my tomorrow will be better than today." God gives hope when you learn to trust Jesus instead of your own capabilities. Hope begins with a new heart and a renewed mind. Faith is trusting in what Jesus can do in you and for you. There is nothing under the sun that is impossible. And if we trust in God, we must admit that there is nothing impossible with Him. At times, He takes time to intervene but His timing is the best timing. What defeats humans does not defeat Him. Hope is the last buttress of life. We should never lose it. "When you are hanging on by the thread, make sure it's the hem of His garment."

God addresses the cause of the problems instead of the symptoms. The problem of man is the human heart. The Bible says that the heart is deceitful above all things and beyond cure. Who can understand it?

(Jeremiah 17:9). The heart is deceitful. You cannot find the answer to change your life from the corrupt heart. God recalls all the hearts of men in exchange for a new and transformed heart. A transformed heart is equipped with the Divine virtues. There is power in perseverance and the transformed heart cannot be stopped or shaken. Faith is when you come to the end of yourself and allow God to fix you. Naturally, people give up prematurely. It makes me wonder how many times that I have given up on something or someone just when the tide was ready to turn.

Suicide is self-condemnation. It is judging yourself unworthy to live. Condemnation is from the devil. The Spirit of God does not condemn us but convicts us of the righteousness of God. I want to say that we are all guilty in one way or another. A natural man is rebranded by guilty because of the good he could have done but he did not do. The gravitation of sin is evident in guilt and shame. The Law proves that all people are guilty and all need to be redeemed. God alone can absolve a fallen man's conscience from guilt. God's grace restores our ultimate innocence undeservingly. Innocence is therefore man's only emblem of returning to God. Innocence means an intimate relationship with purity. God prescribed His holiness to mankind through a relationship with His Son that comes with knowing, trusting, and fellowshipping. It means there is a purifying concept for the soul while living this life. When your life expires before you are saved, you are lost eternally.

Get saved, baptized with Spirit, and filled with the Spirit. We are led by the Spirit when we are guided by the Word regularly. I like this posting: "The Bible says in Psalms 92:10" But you will increase my strength like those of the buffalo; I will be anointed with fresh oil. "Did you know that the Buffalo when it feels attacked by its predators, shifts its hump by distributing fatty oil all over its body at the skin level as a defense mechanism? When predators put their claws on it, they slip because of the oil distributed throughout their skin. Just likewise when the enemy comes with his claws upon us, he will slip because of the oil of the anointing of the Holy Spirit that God has deposited on us. This is the time to seek the infilling of the Holy Spirit and the fresh oil."

Many people ask me if a person who has committed suicide can go to heaven. Suicide is a mortal sin as the rest of the sins. When a person who is born again suffers from mental sickness and commits suicide, he or she goes to heaven. The reason is that all their sins (past, present, and future) were forgiven; They go to heaven on the merits of Christ – The same righteousness of Christ as we do. However, a person who is born again, and who is in sound minds will not contemplate committing suicide. If you are contemplating committing suicide, you need to fall on your knee and repent because chances are you are not truly yet born again. Chances are you are a church-goer religiously but not a committed believer that knows Jesus intimately. What does this mean? It means if you commit suicide, you are heading to hell. And you don't want your life to end in a most miserable way because hell is real and it is eternal torment. Hell is by far a million times hotter than the tragedies of life you are facing now.

Today's prayer: "Lord, some folks are about as happy as they make up their mind to be and they see no need of you, but they are not exempted from misery and fear. Others know that they need You but they ignore the liberating truth, yet they're scared of what they're ignorant of. Lord, you are ultimately involved with our lives regardless of our views because we are Your creations. You are not on the sideline watching us. You send rain to nourish the righteous and the unrighteous on the earth (Matthew 5:45). And Your heavenly blessings are bestowed to the redeemed undeservingly by Your grace. The best of us are capable of the worst and the worst of us are capable of the best. But there is no sorrow that heaven cannot heal. You turn the impossibility into possibility. No life is so hard that You can't simplify it. No life is so unmanageable that You can't restrain it. I decide to believe in nothing less than Your truth. "When peace like a river, attendeth my way, When sorrows like sea billows roll. Whatever my lot, thou hast taught me to say; It is well, it is well, with my soul". In Jesus' name, I pray.

"How long must I take counsel in my soul and have sorrow in my heart all the day? How long shall my enemy be exalted over me? Consider and answer me, O Lord my God; light up my eyes, lest I sleep the sleep of death, lest my enemy say, "I have prevailed over him," lest my foes rejoice because I am shaken." (Psalm 13:2-4).

"Do you not know that you are God's temple and that God's Spirit dwells in you? If anyone destroys God's temple, God will destroy him. For God's temple is holy, and you are that temple" (Corinthians 3:16-17).

"Be not overly wicked, neither be a fool. Why should you die before your time?" (Ecclesiastic 7:17).

"When the righteous cry for help, the Lord hears and delivers them out of all their troubles. The Lord is near to the brokenhearted and saves the crushed in spirit. Many are the afflictions of the righteous, but the Lord delivers him out of them all. He keeps all his bones; not one of them is broken." (Psalm 17:34-17-20). Trust in the Lord with all your heart, and do not lean on your own understanding. In all your ways acknowledge him, and he will make straight your paths (Proverbs 3:5-6).

"For you were bought with a price. So glorify God in your body." (1 Corinthians 6:20).

"You shall not murder." (Exodus 20:13).

"The thief comes only to steal and kill and destroy. I came that they may have life and have it abundantly" (John 10:10).

"I call heaven and earth to witness against you today, that I have set before you life and death, blessing and curse. Therefore choose life, that you and your offspring may live" (Deuteronomy 30:19).

"For "everyone who calls on the name of the Lord will be saved." (Romans 10:13).

"Live each day as if it is your last on Earth. Do something today that will outstay you".

Printed in the United States
by Baker & Taylor Publisher Services